As We Are Now

As We Are Now

MIXBLOOD ESSAYS ON RACE
AND IDENTITY

EDITED BY
WILLIAM S. PENN

UNIVERSITY OF CALIFORNIA PRESS
Berkeley   Los Angeles   London

University of California Press
Berkeley and Los Angeles, California

University of California Press, Ltd.
London, England

© 1997 by
The Regents of the University of California
Library of Congress Cataloging-in-Publication Data

 As we are now : mixblood essays on race and identity / edited by
William S. Penn.
        p.   cm.
    Includes bibliographic references.
    ISBN 0-520-21072-7 (cloth : alk. paper).—ISBN 0-520-21073-5
(pbk. : alk. paper)
        1. Indians of North and South America—Mixed descent.
2. Indians of North and South America—Ethnic identity.   3. Indians of
North and South America—Social conditions.   4. Chicanos—Mixed
descent.   5. Chicanos—Ethnic identity.   6. Chicanos—Social conditions.
7. African Americans—Ethnic identity.   I. Penn, W. S., 1949-   .
    E99.M693A7   1998
    305.897—dc 2197-12057
Printed in the United States of America
9 8 7 6 5 4 3 2 1

11786414

Contents

Introduction

William S. Penn

Robert Berkhofer, Jr., writes, "That Whites of earlier centuries should see the Indian as without history makes sense given their lack of knowledge about the past of Native American peoples and the shortness of their encounter. That later whites should harbor the same assumption seems surprising given the discoveries of archaeology and the changed condition of the tribes as a result of White contact and policy. Yet most Whites still conceive of the 'real' Indian as the aborigine he once was, rather than as he is now. White Europeans and Americans expect even at present to see an Indian out of the forest or Wild West show rather than on a farm or in a city" (29).

Currently, there is a broad and often romanticizing interest in and fascination with things Indian—literature, crafts and art, music, dance, and medicine. Conceiving of Indians as aboriginal also entails perceiving them as anthropological artifacts that are tragic, romantic, and vanishing or already vanished. Even the best of current ethnography tends

1

to articulate the traditions and presence of Native Americans who live on or near reservations, failing to account for the traditions and beliefs of the three to four million Indians who have been living and working in urban or suburban settings for two or three generations. In many cases, these Indians, who make up more than half the Indian population in the United States, have grown up with mixed blood—a result of intermarriages between tribes relocated to Indian Territory as well as between Indians and African- and Latino-Americans. Only a few can remake themselves as full-blood essentialists. The rest have grown up influenced by a mixture of Native traditions as a result of their participation in urban Indian centers such as those in Los Angeles or Chicago where Hopi children learned Apache ways, or Nez Perce children learned Osage dances. *As We Are Now* aims to begin correcting the perceptions that define contemporary Indians in terms of the tragic and outmoded vision of early anthropologists—in terms, in other words, of the false classifications of race. More than that, this collection aims to envision and articulate the outer limits and the complexity of Native American experience by expressing the autobiographical, historical, intellectual, cross-cultural, and artistic experiences of mixblood Americans who, in all cases but one, have grown up in cities and towns, away from reservations and tribal councils.

Umberto Eco suggests that the American imagination demands the authentic or real and that to attain it has to create the absolute fake. In relation to Native Americans, this creation of fakery is pervasive: Kachinas made in Taiwan, Sweat Lodge ceremonies at local health clubs, dreamcatcher key chains, authentic reproductions of Anasazi dwellings at "The Garden of the Gods" in Colorado Springs, or crystal skulls through which Laguna women teach people to channel. In literature, there are examples such as Forrest Carter, a one-time member of the Ku Klux Klan, who fakes an Indian child's narrative (*The Education of LittleTree*), or the most famous fake of all, *Black Elk Speaks*, in which John Neihardt freely augmented, embellished, and altered the notes his niece recorded in her own invented stenographic shorthand as Black Elk's nephew translated what his uncle was saying—without regard for the multiple difficulties of translation, recording, and transmission.

In the midst of all the fakery, much of it commercially produced and propagated by Native Americans themselves, there is a steadier renaissance in the descriptions of Native America and its relation to the umbrella of American culture—race and identity—and American history. These descriptions—which cross boundaries in the fields of storytelling, ethnography, history, psychology, dance, music, and art—are often narrative and nonlinear: rooted as they must be in the overwhelming respect for the power of words and the oral tradition of "telling" or "saying," the new generation of Native American writers is appropriating the genres and modes of the Western tradition to its own purposes. Ignoring some of the "Western" demarcations, they are writing prose that sometimes incorporates poetic language and even the line lengths of poetry, as well as playlike dialogues and stage directions, mixing genres and modes as well as chronology and tense on purpose, to better bridge the gap between themselves and the dominant culture around them, as well as the gap within themselves (for example, Indian and white, Chicano and Anglo). This narrative mixture of modes is often produced by the act of reclamation, an imaginative act of identity and selfhood that must be reenacted every time the mixblood writer sets out to write, an act that always involves recognizing the gap, entering the dialogue between disagreements (European or Native American, linear or circular, direct or indirect, historical image or historical actuality), and then finding a way to bridge that gap—or to express it. Behind *As We Are Now* is the belief that to lose that gap, to lose the tension, to lose the enhancements, transformations, and experimentations that result from the dialogue is—for urban mixbloods, at least—to lose whatever is American Indian.

Concurrently, *As We Are Now* aims to express the idea that the nonreservation or urban mixblood, besides being underrepresented in literature about Native America, is a person whose comfort with English combines with his or her desire to be, remain, or represent "Indian," to create possibilities, choices of technique as well as of relations, writer to story, writer to audience or other people, writer to world. If Karl Kroeber (quoted in *Narrative Chance*) is correct that the American idea of progress "destroys diverse modes of imagining," then a renewed diversity of imagination and thinking is something mixblood writers—whatever their backgrounds or disciplines—offer postmodern America and Western culture. *As We Are Now* intends to offer a new vision of race and identity, of Indians—at least that half of Indian America that has grown up in cities or towns—and to begin the integration of that vision into the vision of America's future.

This collection of essays is, as one critic already has noted, "trail-breaking." Nothing like it has been done before, although we hope that if it breaks a trail, many books like it will be done after. Its uniqueness is not simply in the broad, multidisciplinary way it begins a new dialogue about race and identity or that it offers new voices of Native American experience in place of the voices with which people of the Americas are all too familiar. It is also in the extension of the boundaries from Native American to urban mixbloods generally and its inclusion of Chicanos/as, Latinos/as, as well as one writer of black and German ancestry. It crosses the lines of essay writing along with the lines of race and begins to highlight the north-south axis which is so powerfully offered in novels such as *Almanac of the Dead* as a defense against the usual east-west axis of thought.

Opening with the more personal accounts of race and identity (essays by Erika Aigner-Varoz, Craig Womack, Alfonso Rodriguez, Carol Kalafatic, and Inez Petersen), the collection moves toward the combination of personal with public, the personal with the political or historical (essays by William S. Penn, Kimberly Blaeser, and Rainier Spencer), bridging into the final movement of essays, which are more analytical, historical, or political (essays by Arturo Aldama, Diane DuBose Brunner, Shari Huhndorf, and Rolando Romero), and capped by Patricia Hilden's essay, which brings back all the themes and ideas, as well as the orally-based aesthetics, of the other essays. It is the grounding of all the essays in varied but often similar oral traditions—the belief, as Leslie Silko puts it, "that stories are all we have" and that it is narrativity that in part admits to the survival of the cultures represented here—that makes these essays "narrative." Narrative essays try to tell the truth the way Nez Perce storytellers or historians tried to tell it: they may augment in detail or description, they may change the actual wording, they may tell who said what and how they said it; they use, in other words, the elements and techniques of fiction to give the truth context, to make the truth "truer" for the audience willing to listen and participate in the telling. Here the telling is written. Yet, in all of these tellings, there is the representation of different oralities, whether Chicano/a, African, or the varieties of Native American.

The classical Maya wrote their histories by recording and *giving context to* the events considered to be most important to the people. Narrative essays, I suggest, do the same. Thus, in contextualizing ideas, they may well seem loose, nonlinear, fractured, or digressive. But in reality they are carefully structured, and each structure may be both described and defended. They are not loose, but oral and even conversational—as though talking to a really imagined audience; they are nonlinear only in the sense that for most of us all things are connected, and thus to give the proper context dialogue rarely follows from A to B to Z; they are not digressive but, as I have begun to insist, "augmentative"—and augmentation (a term I borrowed from my father-in-law) adds connection and context, gives life to dull "facts," and celebrates the power of imagination, metaphor, and the cross-connections between the speaker and the listener, which is another way to claim that narrative essays work toward community, toward inclusion and not the exclusivity of colonization. The narrative essay is, in my opinion, where scholarly or academic writing is heading, or where it will head if it wants to revive its relation to an audience greater than seven. Yet it is not something we, the essayists, have chosen or decided to do; it is what we have always done, telling, even as grade school students, the story of ideas. Only lately is the rest of the world coming to narrativity, and sometimes out of the usual economic necessity—for example, publishers are asking academic writers to incorporate their footnotes into the text because footnotes scare off readers or increase the costs of publication. Given the language, ideas, methods, and structure of their essays, the participants in this collection agree, at least implicitly, about the need for narrative.

Here, then, are essays that cut and pin patterns of identity and survival. Here are essays that express what it may be like to be an Indian storyteller who, most usually asked to tell creation stories, stories of animal people and earth or sky figures that fit with the romanticized preconceptions of what Indians are, would rather tell about his Uncle Sonny Boy, "who got drunk and bit off my Uncle Gool Coachman's ear," or about what it is like to be a mixblood Indian man who is gay—an identity that most Americans seem to find fantastic. There are essays that involve us with the questions and considerations of the diversity of Chicanos and the need to confront "unpleasant truths about our individual and collective past." Some offer more questions than answers: questions about the meanings of "tradition" or "authenticity" and the delusions of "blood quantum," which seem to take in people who are insecure about who they are and thus become raving essentialists; about the current polemics regarding affirmative action and the movement to limit immigration in states like California, especially if those immigrants are from Middle or South America; about the importance of language; or about the contortions demanded by the search for an active and meaningful identity.

Ultimately, the collection is unique because of the way in which it presents diverse modes of imagining race and identity by mixbloods who are not yet well known. The essayists come from varied backgrounds and disciplines. Some are historians, some are trained in literature, and others are storytellers, writers, or people who have been struggling with the problems of race and identity and found they had something to say for this collection. The claim to newness or novelty, of course, invites irony: the Museum of the American Indian in New York, which offers up the same old, static repetitions of an artifactual and romanticized Native America, a "New" Museum of the American Indian housed in the "Old Customs House" in an irony that is so thorough that it achieves perfection. These essays, I hope, are not subject to that kind of irony, aiming as they do at creating dialogue about some serious questions about "race" and "identity."

To those of us classified to one extent or another by it, "race" is both a curse and an invention, a problem and a celebration. Most of us might agree with Kwame Anthony Appiah's saying that "there is nothing in the world that can do all we ask race to do for us"; personally, historically, and politically race has done a lot, both negative and, more recently, positive. Even though we may agree with Rainier Spencer, who finds a delicate irony in his need to use inaccurate terms like "black" and "white" if only to discredit them as terms, whenever we say that race does not matter, we are forced in the moment of saying to admit that yes it does—if only because it matters so much to other people. Other people invent it and use it and make it matter, sometimes unintentionally like a college department chair who claims only experts can teach his field but "anyone" can teach a course titled "The Oral Tradition and Native American

Literature and Ideas," especially if that "anyone" is also identifiable as "Indian." Sometimes the intention is obvious in legislative propositions like the one in California that is meant to discriminate and exclude the people on whose backs the Golden State was constructed. Its meaning continually shows in the faces of all those senators and journalists and pundits who assert that race doesn't matter, that the experience of a Native American novel or an African American novel is for the Native or the African, essentially, the same as the experience of a Finn or a Pole.

While I would never in my life deny the intensity or importance or sensitivity of the Finn or the Pole, the British or the German, there is a particular moment in which Indian or Chicano or black readers and listeners recognize the well-intentioned skewer of race. It comes when a reviewer of a grant proposal for a new collection of Indian legends and stories says that there are already enough of these around, as though there is no new work being done in the translation of stories and as though we have not heard endless collections of tales and stories from other, more dominant and dominating cultures. It comes hidden beneath the linear faces of clocks and the sour faces of those baptized in the faith called Progress and the assumption that anything other than their "progress" means regress. It comes, too, when academics assume that all Native American scholars are experts in Indian literature or Indian history (all Indian literature and history), categorizing the young Native American student as someone who has automatic interests and automatic associations. It comes back when Native people assert that only Native Americans can study, write about, or teach Native American literature and ideas, and yet once again when we notice the certain and continuous cultural assumptions at play in even very liberal-minded and sympathetic non-Native scholars. As a young black man of about my height put it, "Nobody ask *you* if you play basketball." True, but they may allow a hungry audience to equate the surprise of Sand Creek with the iconographic romance of Custer's "defensive" posture at the Battle of the Little Big Horn (a.k.a. "Custer's Last Stand").

The project that has resulted in this book was born two years ago when I was invited to participate on a university panel on "Ethnic Studies." I was asked by the associate dean to give a paper on my views of what a future "Ethnic Studies" program at Michigan State University should be. There was precious little else in the way of definition or description of what we'd be panelizing about, so I went prepared to speak or (preferably) not speak, hating, as I do, the sound of my own voice (an honest statement that my graduate and undergraduate students alike would find odd if not comic). But lately I had been finding support for some of my inclusive views in storytelling by Leslie Silko, Louis Owens, Tomás Rivera, Rolando Hinojosa, Manlio Argueta, Rosario Ferré, and Jack Forbes, or in essays like those included in Arnold Krupat and Brian Swann's anthologies. Inclusion had been with me since my early boyhood when my innocent first love affair had been with a Mexican girl whose mother fed me spicy lunches, and I had grown up with the visual and aural joy of Olvera Street, which is so nicely recalled in Patricia Hilden's "Richie Valens Is Dead: *E Pluribus Unum.*"

I found myself—the passivity is literal, like Dante's "I came to myself in the middle of the journey of my life"—up on a dais beside a local Asian and an imported Chicano "star" facing an audience of deans, directors, low-level administrators, and professors (possibly with the odd student thrown in like bell peppers for color and spice), wondering if the fever I felt (my forehead beaded with sweat) was due to being very sick or to being made sick with words. Or both.

"I am panelizing," I told myself, trying to keep old habits of truth and directness down like the flu. "You (I said, feverishly adopting yet a second person to get through the afternoon) asked for this by agreeing to be empaneled on the dais."

What was billed as a panel discussion of Ethnic Studies had turned into a skirmish over turf, a skirmish that I have turned into full-dress battle, an unpitched battle over who owns the past and present, with the "star" panelizer calling for a "domestic ethnic studies."

Domestic Ethnic Studies? I wondered. No cross-border influences? No studying Guatemalan or Quechua Indigenos? It's like a stockade fence, the U.S. border. Used to keep people out as well as to keep people in, to keep people on their familiar turf—turf they, minority or nonminority, can defend.

Out of that moment came a new course to teach, one that would side-step the question of what Ethnic Studies was or wasn't, and would cross the old borders to celebrate the mixture.

Out of that moment came this project. The project itself has sometimes made me feel sad with a comic abrasion. In the long run, however, the comic won out, and these are the results: of reading and talking with other people who identify themselves as mixbloods either from urban settings, living in them presently, or (in the case of one essayist) commuting to them to work; of waiting for the essayists to get their essays to me and for me to get their essays back to them; of finding friends—and when all is said and done, I hope that is what this is, a group of writers from a variety of backgrounds and experiences who may call themselves "friends."

"Mixbloods" and not "mixed bloods" because they express the unified and inseparable strands of their heritage and experience. Mixblood instead of crossblood, though in this instance mainly because crossblood has been so long confused with "mixedblood."

Their essays raise some questions about race and identity, and perhaps even suggest some answers. They are eclectic. I do not agree with everything they say, and they do not always agree with the things other essayists say; I tried to exercise great care in editing them, leaving the ideas and stylistic processes free, shaping only the structures slightly and not the ideas. In few cases did the heavy hand of the editor unmask itself, but I hope for a more coherent expression of the essayist's ideas and not for agreement with my own. New essays by new writers, some of whom will probably one day become the old, usual writers excluded by someone like me because everybody knows their names.

Some final notes and acknowledgments. An old good friend warned me years ago not to edit collections of anything, and I am here to say that wisdom drips slowly into the mind like a leaky faucet, for only now, twenty years later, do I understand at least in large part what he must have meant. This project took a year longer than I had imagined to complete and mail—some of that delay stemming from the slowness of some of the essayists to write and revise, but much of it my fault, as I was interrupted by other planned projects and deadlines, teaching, and travel. Though there have been times I have emerged weary from my study and times I have felt the centrifugal force of personal responsibility pushing me out of the circle, I would not have not done this. In the process, I have learned a great deal from the individual writers and I have been lucky enough to have made many of them my friends. Many have been the times I've needed their friendship, and often have been the moments when their words—by e-mail or phone—have shown me how little I know or understand, and for that I am very, very grateful.

The people who suffered most, perhaps, were Jennifer, my wife and closest pal, and Rachel and William, my daughter and son, who are per-fections, themselves. They are the ones who say, "Let's do *x*," and have me say defensively, "I have to do *y*." They are the ones who ask if they can go to the park and have daddy say he's too tired. It has come to seem strange, to me, by means of this process, that it is to the very people for whom one does the work that one is often saying no. For my work is *for them,* and I hope some of it is good. In the long run, I can say that with-out them, the care and time and joy they give beyond reason, nothing.

In addition, I need to thank A. C. Goodson, the director of compara-tive literature at Michigan State University, a real human being who stays true to his words. No one has been more supportive of my work at this university. I want to thank David Morris, who sicked the University of California Press on me. All the essayists have to be thanked, but it was Patricia Hilden who helped me find several of them and who sometimes helped them revise their essays. Other people have contributed in their ways, too: Arnold Krupat with his friendship and constant insight and care; my father, who has put up with much, and my grandfather, who put up with much in his turn; my father-in-law, Tony Siani, now deceased, but who provides still many of the arguments I often argue against or for; and last, but far from least, Jack Hicks for his encouragement, patience, unstinting help, sense of humor, and friendship.

WORKS CITED

Appiah, Kwame Anthony. *In My Father's House: Africa in the Philosophy of Culture*. Oxford: Oxford University Press, 1992.

Berkhofer, Robert F., Jr. *The White Man's Indian*. New York: Vintage Books, 1979.

Carter, Forrest. *The Education of LittleTree: A True Story*. New York: Delacorte Press, 1976.

Eco, Umberto. *Travels in Hyperreality*. San Diego: Harcourt Brace Jovanovich, 1986.

Narrative Chance: Postmodern Discourse on Native American Indian Literatures. Edited by Gerald Vizenor. Albuquerque: University of New Mexico Press, 1989.

Neihardt, John. *Black Elk Speaks: Being the Life Story of a Holy Man of the Oglala Sioux, as Told through John G. Neihardt (Flaming Rainbow)*. Lincoln: University of Nebraska Press, 1979.

Swann, Brian, and Arnold Krupat. *Everything Matters*. New York: Random House, 1997.

Swann, Brian, and Arnold Krupat. *I Tell You Now: Autobiographical Essays by Native American Writers*. Lincoln: University of Nebraska Press, 1987.

Silko, Leslie Marmon. *Almanac of the Dead*. New York: Simon & Schuster, 1991.

Cutting and Pinning Patterns

Erika Aigner-Varoz

My native El Paso, Texas, is a hot, dusty city in between the trickle known as the Rio Grande and the tail end of the Rockies, the Franklin Mountains. My alma mater, the University of Texas at El Paso, is confined and protected within the mountains. From the university library that looks like a Bhutanese palace, I can see the river and the *colonias* of Juarez, Mexico. Shacks of cardboard and mud, painted fluorescent greens, pinks, and blues litter the hill beyond the Rio. Known as "Hollywood on the Border" and "Wa-Zoo" to the university students, the *colonias* and the city of Juarez are holding tanks for the people waiting to cross the river to find a better life in the States, people waiting to get where I am—people like my maternal grandmother Juanita in the 1940s.

Most of what I know about Juanita I learned during an interview with my mother for my master's thesis on cultural and linguistic negotiations within Mexican-German marriages—phenomena common in El Paso because of the military installation. My mother and I seated ourselves across from one another at the kitchen table with the tape recorder and the microphone in the middle. I carefully pressed the play and record buttons and asked her the first question. Mom giggled, cleared her throat, and then whispered, "Turn it off. Turn it off!" I put the recorder on pause and asked her what was wrong. "What if I just write down my answers instead of you asking me and me having to answer on tape?" she asked. I told her that it wouldn't be the same and that the completion of my master's degree was dependent on her. I had learned to be good at guilt.

She finally agreed to talk to me, and what she told me was a story that I'd never heard before:

I'm not straight on the story, so I hate to even tell you because it's probably—it may not be right. I know that at one point my father was deported, but I don't know why. He was very politically active and that was part of the problem. . . . And he—he actually started out going—studying law. But he didn't really like it, or he quit two years before he was to finish. And then he began working as a writer in the newspaper. He liked that better.

And so that's what he was doing when my mother met him, and they didn't really marry. He, you know, took her with him. And against my grandma's wishes, you know, or permission. And so they went to Laredo . . . or Torreon. And that's where all my brothers and sisters were born. And then they lived there, I guess for a long time, since all the kids were born there. And—but he, because of the way he wrote—you know, he didn't care about the danger, and that was during the time of . . . some political turmoil in Mexico, so his life was threatened many times. And he even had a body guard when he went out publicly. And he was a very—he was a spendthrift—he never had any money because when he had money, he would spend it. . . . He would treat everybody in the office to lunch or whatever, so they never had any money; they never had any savings or anything. . . . He liked to live for the moment. . . . If things got really bad . . . my mother had to sell jewelry he had given her, which was good jewelry, and didn't get much for it. So they had a lot of hard times. . . .

He was an artist-type, and he liked women. I don't know that he ever cheated on my mother, but if . . . a good-looking woman passed by, he would follow her with his eyes. And yet he was extremely jealous of Mother. And I think that he probably thought she was so beautiful because he would say, "Even the women like you," because she would attract a lot of attention. . . .

So then one time . . . because his life had been threatened, I think that's when they moved to Monterrey. And he didn't want to pack anything, so that people would not suspect that he was leaving. I think they left everything behind, even his typewriter, you know. They took only clothes, I guess. And there he was the editor and publisher of a newspaper. The paper was not his; it belonged to someone else, but I guess he ran it. He really didn't earn all that much because most of the time; . . . we were living in one-room apartments . . . without any of the conveniences—the restrooms were outside and all that. And he would mainly work at home, reviewing the writing of others or writing his own stories, and then he would go and he'd come back. . . . And I remember that he would always bring candy to us, and he was a very nice father, according to what my mother used to say. . . . He would carry us around and sing to us, and if she would so much as pinch us or spank us or anything, he would make a big fuss about it. . . . She was the disciplinarian, and he pampered them—the kids.

He married my mother on his deathbed, and my mother never forgave him for it because he had promised that he would marry her, and yet he never made good on it [until the end]. And though many times she had wanted to leave him and she didn't do so because she said, "I'm going to hold him to that promise." So it was not a happy union. I think she was in awe of him. She admired and respected him because he was very intelligent, and maybe that was the attraction for her because she had not had the opportunity to have an education. Since her father died when she was twelve or so, she took his role in the family; she was the oldest child.

◆ ———— ◆

When I was a kid, I entered what was my mother's birth world, across the border, infrequently with my family to take advantage of the low prices. In the orange vinyl back seat of my dad's old Volkswagen Karmann-Ghia, I sat anxiously as he double-clutched over a huge hill—the bridge over the Rio Grande that led into Mexico—and what seemed like a dozen speed bumps before we approached the Mexican customs agent. My dad always declared *nada* in his German accent, and *el federale* would wave us through. Traffic always moved quickly in the southward direction. Dad popped the car into gear, and the engine buzzed shrilly. With the windows rolled down, the stifling air circulated even through the back seat, where my brother Karl and I sat. We zipped along the street, past a small replica of an Aztec village, and on to the section where the markets began. From both sides of the road and in the median, Mexican vendors selling *cigarros*, fresh flowers, purses, *dulces*, *helados*, and many other things called out to the Americans in their fancy cars and to us too. Cigarettes were the only thing we ever stopped for. Mexico was the place to go for cigarettes, liquor, coffee, haircuts, and government-subsidized bread, tortillas, and meats.

Before going *al mercado*, we would go to the barbershop. The door was always open, and the barbers were standing around laughing, drinking pop, and listening to mariachi music on the radio. I used to love to watch Karl have his hair cut. Our regular barber, a very distinguished gentleman with slicked back silver hair, would squeeze a stream of smelly tonic from a brown bottle onto my brother's head. The barber wore a stoic expression as he massaged the tonic in, pulling Karl's hair and scalp so hard that his eyebrows lifted. With each pull, Karl would grimace, forcing his eyebrows down. Both puppet and puppeteer made me laugh. "Stop that or I'm going to pinch you," Mom would whisper because my laughter would either embarrass Karl or make him laugh, causing him to squirm in both cases, resulting in a bad haircut. During his own haircut, Dad usually fell asleep and was snoring soundly by the middle of his Elvis-swoop cut.

We went on to the Del Rio Mercado afterwards. A marimba band usually kept me and my brother amused while my parents went inside to shop. I loved to watch and listen to the musicians plunk away at their untuned instruments—the guitars and the harp. The band that usually played at Del Rio had not one but two marimbas, and two trumpet players, making them extra good. We didn't really listen to the words of their songs, but the melodies spoke of lost love and defying death in the bullring. After we got bored, my brother and I would walk into the market. The first things we noticed were the brightly colored piñatas and huge paper sunflowers—the stuff that real parties were made of. Glassware and blown-glass figurines were in the section to the right. We always stopped to watch the man seated next to a little grindstone who stooped over to engrave champagne glasses with flowers, doves, or people's names. I thought they were beautiful and was often tempted to ask the man to teach me how to do it.

The next stop was at the leather-goods section. At home, we wore moccasins instead of slippers, so we were always on the lookout for sales on them. As soon as we got beyond the leather section, closer to groceries, flies swarmed and the stench of rotten meat permeated the aisles. Del Rio was known for its own meat cutting, which was one of the reasons my father liked it. My brother and I squeezed our noses shut and plotted to get our parents to buy us a Coke or an ice-cream cone.

Heading home was a dreaded event. The line to go back over the bridge to the U.S. side was always miles long, and we never knew if my Dad's Ghia was going to make it back in the heat. Sometimes it would stall, and the whole family would get out to push. On good days, when the car didn't stall, I would sit back, sweating and watching the dark Spanish-speaking vendors and beggars. The vendors walked slowly by, allowing the people in the cars enough time to look over their goods and stop them if they wanted to buy. The beggars were painful to look at. Old people with lines of despair etched in their faces, others with facial deformities or amputated arms or legs, women holding babies and leading several other children. It wasn't until much later that I realized that one of those women could have been me if my grandmother hadn't been as strong as she was. Mexico was a place of poverty and a place to be exploited for its prices. When we thankfully reached the booth with the U.S. customs officer, I proudly declared, "American," with the rest of my family and listened to my father declare all that we'd brought back, eager to get on I-10 and get the airflow going again in the un-air-conditioned Volkswagen.

◆ —————— ◆

Being half Mexican gave me a sense of uneasiness when I was growing up; kids in grade school had pejorative labels for the darker-skinned, especially those who didn't do well in their classes. Olive-skinned and hazel-eyed, I claimed my father's German heritage when asked, "So what are you?" by classmates who blinked in disbelief and regarded me with renewed respect afterwards. I always understood what it meant to be German because my father told stories of his family and childhood, outlining very clear definitions of German identity by asserting who he was, where he came from, and, in turn, where I came from. Being German meant working hard, being resourceful under difficult conditions, and telling people what you thought whether they wanted to hear it or not. Being Mexican was more intuitive. My mother rarely told stories about herself and family, and never outlined definitions or set boundaries around who she was or who my brother and I were supposed to grow up to be. Her reactions to people and situations provided me with the main clues about her identity and mine.

Mom served as an "interpreter" for me and my father. Dad, the engineer, was our household math expert. He was not, however, the most patient tutor in the world, nor was I the most patient learner. His tutorials usually ended with me crying and throwing my pencil across the room and him vowing never to help me again. Mom stepped in and saved us both. Whenever I needed help with algebra, she would sit through my father's explanations and then come over and describe the process to me. She was a whiz with fractions and geometry, so I didn't bother going to anyone but her for help. She also served as mediator during disagreements with my father. Whenever I asked him for anything—to buy a new pair of trendy running shoes, to go to the pizza joint after a football game, to go out on my first real date—and his response was "Not only no, but Hell No," Mom would say, "Let me work on him for a while," and she usually returned with a reversal of his original verdict, along with their terms for his agreement. From my mother and grandmother, I related being female and Mexican with speaking Spanish, discarding selfish ambition for family, and, most important, being able to deal effectively with stubborn people.

My mother wanted me to have the advantage of bilingualism in both the outside and family spheres by raising me to speak and read both English and Spanish. She wrote out flash cards with names of the body parts: arm—*brazo*, leg—*pierna*, and the hardest one was belly button—*ombligo*. Although I don't remember it very well, I must have been bilingual because when Grandma Juanita, my mother's mother, came to live with us when I was four, I didn't have any problems communicating with her.

Grandma was very round, had dark black hair and a face that was smooth and fair-skinned. I remember her hands—knobby and callused by a lifetime of work and washing dishes. She sang to me as she caressed my back with the palm of her hand, its roughness gently scratching my skin. I felt safe and loved. Her hands not only soothed—they created art. She was the most wonderful seamstress. My mother would take us to Walgreens or the Singer store, and Grandma and I spent hours going through the pattern catalogues. I picked out dresses and jumpsuits that I liked, and she sometimes would sketch my choices into a notepad and make her own patterns at home or would just buy the patterns at the store. We'd pick out the fabric we liked and head home to start on the outfits. Armed with pencil, notepad, and measuring tape, she measured and recorded every angle of me. If she was making her own pattern, she would glance at her sketches and draw the pattern on a disassembled grocery sack. After cutting out the pattern, she would pin it together and then pin it onto the clothes I was wearing to judge whether it had come out right. She sometimes whistled through her teeth as she overlaid the pattern onto the fabric and began to cut. She bent for hours over the whirring sewing machine. She fussed that her eyes were going because many of the straight pins got away from her, embedding themselves in the carpet where she could not find them. That was my job. While she sewed, I hunted for pins and stuck them in the little tomato-shaped pincushion. She praised me for my efforts and told me that she wished that she had my eyes of youth.

Her own youth had been spent working, trying to immigrate to the States with her five children and send them to private Catholic primary schools, since Mexican nationals were not allowed to attend American public schools. I had always been told that it had been my grandfather's dying wish that she bring the family to the United States, the land of opportunity. So she moved the family from Torreon, Mexico, to Juarez, where they remained for five years before she earned enough to go across to El Paso. Her strength, sewing, and strong Catholicism were what I imagined her secrets of success to be.

She taught me and my brother about God, Jesus, and faith. She took us to church and showed us how to make the sign of the cross, assuring us that "Jesu Cristo ama a todos los niños chiquitos." The last thing she did before she left us to go live with one of my aunts for a while was help my little brother learn to walk. It was a couple of years before I saw her again, and then I could no longer understand or speak Spanish. I angrily blamed her for our difficulties communicating; after all, she was the adult, and it was her job to learn English—just as my mother had—since we were all living in the United States.

She bought and played records of English lessons and learned to speak a few words and standard phrases but eventually gave up. All I remember hearing out of that record player afterwards were the Franciscan monks' renditions of "Cielito Lindo" and "De Colores." I was required to take a Spanish class in grade school, but it only made me more aware of my inability to conjugate verbs correctly in conversation. My grandmother's attempts to help me only made me angrier. I stopped wanting to see her because of the language barrier. As a labor of love, she made a beautiful lacy cotton dress for my favorite doll. I loved the dress, but I avoided calling her because I didn't want to sputter a thanks in Spanish. I grudgingly did so weeks later, only after my mother forced me to the phone, threatening to pinch me and telling me that I would remember and regret my behavior some day. She too was adept with guilt, and she was also right.

When I was eleven, my grandmother had a heart attack and was put in a hospital that didn't allow children into the cardiac wing. My cousins, Lucy and Susan, both drew pictures for her every day, and my aunt and uncle delivered them to her and posted them on the wall in her room. I couldn't make myself do that. I planned to spend every minute with her as soon as she got out instead of drawing silly pictures that couldn't re-place spending time together. Even if we couldn't speak very well, I could sit in her lap and everything would be okay; she would understand.

After two weeks, Grandma was finally released, and she came home with my family. In the car, I noticed that she was holding a stuffed animal, a little owl, in her lap and I wanted it. I asked her if I could have it, and she said no in a nice way. I imagine that she probably said something like I could have it one day, but not now. We got home and Mom and Dad slowly and carefully helped Grandma walk to the door. She carefully sat down on the brown and beige tweed couch in our den. I sat next to her the entire time as she and my mother talked. My brother came and sat beside her too. As Mom cooked dinner, Grandma drew pictures on a little pad—a stork at the top of one page and then a series of stick people playing soccer at the bottom of the pages. She told me to hold the edge of the pad and flip quickly through the pages. The stick people moved, kicking the ball along the bottom of the pages into a "goal!" that was printed on the last page; she had made a little animated cartoon. I laughed and hugged her.

The phone rang, and it was my uncle calling for Grandma. When she got up to talk to him from the kitchen phone, I went off to watch TV in the living room. After about a half hour, my mother called for me, "Edeecah! Get your father to the phone!" Her voice had the same urgency as when someone from Dad's family called. My Dad was sound asleep in his La-Z-Boy recliner, so I shook him and told him that he had a long distance call from Germany. He jumped up and ran to the bedroom phone. Just as he called out, "Hey, what's going on? There's nobody there," I went back to the kitchen to see my mother struggling to hold up my grandmother. My grandmother's face was completely white, her lips were blue, and her eyes were closed. "No. Get Daddy here. She's heavy; I can't hold her up. I need help."

My parents lowered her to the floor and seemed to move in slow motion. I called 911 but then panicked when I heard the voice on the other end, and I hung up. My parents were searching for her doctor's number and eventually called an ambulance. After what seemed like hours sirens, red lights, and people in uniforms descended on the scene. I remember a mask, tubes, the shiny silver railing and the horrible clacking of the wheels of the stretcher going over the threshold as they left.

I never saw her again. The following night I saw my father put his hand on my mother's shoulder as she sat on the bed. Karl and I were still hoping and praying, but Grandma had already passed on. My parents didn't tell us that she had died because they were waiting to tell all of my mother's siblings who were flying in first. So for one whole night, my mother had to pretend that her mother was alive and that there was still a chance. "The doctor tried very hard to save her," Mom told me later.

"They had all these tubes in her mouth, and she made the motion for them to take them away, like she wanted to say something. What could we do? We told her to relax quietly because we couldn't remove the tubes for her breathing. She just shrugged her shoulders and looked sad." Grandma didn't get to say good-bye, except maybe in the form of the stork and stick figures she drew and the little brown owl that I got to keep—birds of life and death and images of play.

◆ ———————— ◆

Language was always painful. I had lost my Spanish, straining my relationship with my grandmother. My father's native tongue, German, was never spoken in the home, except around Christmas time to keep secrets between my parents and aggravate us kids. My mother spoke German haltingly. She tried different endings on certain words (the verbs, I imagine) and received many corrections from my father. She would repeat the correct form that my father provided and speak smoothly until the next verb. Mom learned German by listening to lessons recorded on albums in preparation for going with my father to his native country. That was over thirty years ago, shortly after they were married and my father was still in the Luftwaffe. Dad never learned Spanish, except what to say to the Mexican customs officer as we drove across the bridge into Juarez and the names of his favorite foods.

Both of my parents spoke English with accents of their native languages, and they were determined that their children would speak "perfect English," so English was always the language of the home with our immediate family. Their accents distinguished them from other people— my friends and teachers, for example—and were part of what gave my home its warmth. The way they pronounced my name, for example, was a constant reminder of who they were and where they came from. My father's "E-ree-ka" rolled the *r* and clipped the final *a*. My mother's "Edeecah" was melodically pronounced with the soft Spanish *r* and a drawn-out final "ahh." I never realized how closely I identified with what they called me until I was nine and brought home an Anglo friend from school for the first time—a little blue-eyed blond named Barbie. My mother wanted to be the perfect hostess, so while we were playing in the hallway between the kitchen and the bedrooms, she said, "Erika," with a hard American *r*, "Would you girls like something to drink?" My name sounded strange, and I felt as though I didn't recognize the woman who had just asked the question. I stopped playing, forgetting that Barbie was there, and said angrily, "Don't you ever call me that again." A distance or a coldness invaded the space between me and the person with whom I had always felt safe.

"What's wrong with you? Isn't that your name?" bewildered Barbie asked, jolting me back as she stared at me.

"Well, it is to you but not to her. I'm Edeecah to her," was my response. In my nine-year-old mind, I thought that my mother had pushed me away by trying to sound like everybody else, by sounding American; she was renouncing our special relationship by mispronouncing my name. She laughed off my response, saying my name in her usual way, and asked again whether we wanted beverages. She later explained to me that she hadn't meant to hurt me; she only thought that I wouldn't want to be singled out as different so she said my name the American way. Years later, I realized that she had thought that I would be embarrassed by her accent—something that had never occurred to me. After she had explained everything, I told her that I didn't feel like me and she didn't seem like her when she did that and to, please, never call me that again.

My brother and I did learn to speak "perfect English," and both of us went on to college. I majored in English, and Mom continued helping me with my homework. Often, when I couldn't think of anything to write about, she would suggest a topic. In freshman English, I remember being assigned Horace Miner's "Body Ritual among the Nacirema," a parody of anthropological writing about the backwards American (and "American" spelled backwards). Assigned to write an essay in response in any genre of my choosing, my reaction was, "I like the essay, but I have nothing to say about it." Hours later, after several attempts to crank out the assignment, I gave up in total despair. Mom, who had excelled in several college English courses, borrowed my book, read the essay, and suggested that I write a story from the perspective of an alien reporting back to its spaceship about other "Nacirema" rituals not included in Miner's. Based on her suggestion, I constructed an eyewitness account of strange

American customs for my extraterrestrial Amazon sisters on our mothership. Mom read my paper, gave me additional suggestions, and even edited for me. We received an "A" on the assignment because my composition instructor appreciated the unique approach.

Mom continued helping me when I moved away to go to graduate school. We spent lots of money on long-distance calls so that I could read parts of my essays to her. For a required Spanish class in my doctoral program, I had to write many essays after years without reading, speaking, or hearing anything other than English. For the first essay, I remember calling Mom and telling her it would be a short call because I'd already written the essay but I wasn't sure about the grammar. After reading the piece in my tongue-twisted Spanish, I heard Mom sigh, and I could almost see her shaking her head. "Oh God," she said, "tell me again, but in English." My literal, word for word translation had resulted in something that wasn't quite Spanish. She translated, not line by line, but idea by idea into her native tongue until we had a complete essay. Afterwards, Mom lamented that she hadn't insisted that I speak Spanish while I was growing up and that she had given in to my hostility when she had tried to do so. I wrote subsequent essays for this class on my own after realizing that my Spanish instructor's expectations were lower than my mother's and that my first essay had established me as a good student.

It is only now that I realize that most of what I understood about being Mexican was based on experience, while my German identity came from my father's stories. What I looked and listened for was how the relationships between my parents and their parents worked, what kind of childhood they had, and how men and women treated each other. From both my experiences and my father's stories, I tried to figure out who my parents were and who I would be.

My father told stories of his childhood in Nazi Germany and the depression that followed. How the sirens went off during the bomb raids and he and his family would pile into the basement and he would sleep in the large, tin bathtub. How once he had not taken shelter below and watched an American bomber aim for cows grazing in the fields, often the only source of sustenance for German families. How he and his brother stole tobacco from his father, my grandfather—my Opa—so that they could trade it for chocolate through a chain-link fence with East European war prisoners who were being held in a POW camp about a block away from his father's lab.

The punishment for going to the camp and for stealing the tobacco would have been a severe beating. "Ja, your Opa used to beat the hell out of us kids," Dad would tell me and my brother as he laughed. Then he sobered and went on, "You don't know how good you kids got it." Opa was a well-respected chemist, a dodger of Nazi party membership, and a gregarious, generous eccentric. Around the local taverns, he was known for his jokes and for buying rounds of drinks for everyone. As he walked along the street into town, many people recognized him and waved. At home, he was very different. Opa liked his household run just so—all of his meals cooked from scratch and on the table at the appropriate times, his laundry perfectly starched and ironed, his house cleaned by the time he came home. If things were not just so, he got angry.

My father would often say that he really didn't like people all that much; he preferred animals because they were never intentionally cruel. When he wasn't doing chores or homework, he often escaped to the woods and the brook. He grew up watching does with their fawns and described how their eyes mesmerized him: "I could never shoot a deer. Their eyes were so beautiful, so innocent." In a time when hunting was necessary for survival, this was not a laudable principle to live by. He often watched the swans build their enormous nests in the brook that fed into the Lech River. The swans were graceful and fierce, attacking dogs, small children, or anyone who approached their nests when they had their young. I believe that it was from the woods that Dad learned his role in the family. I always knew that he would be ready to assume the role of swan for my mother, brother, or me. Whenever he heard news reports of violent criminals on television, usually when the whole family was seated to dinner, he would clench his fists and say, "I blast 'em one if they ever come near you all—just that you know."

Aside from stories of survival during the war, growing up in the woods, and encounters with wild animals, one of my father's favorite topics was his sister Frida, whom he brought up whenever I made him mad. "You are insolent and crazy like your Aunt Frida," he would tell me. Of course, I probably remember only the details that were convenient for my cause. From his descriptions, I envisioned Frida as the ultimate nonconformist, an independent woman with a loose screw, probably the result of some genetic fluke. She was "less than five foot tall," weighed less than ninety pounds, and rode a big motorcycle back in the 1940s. She lived in her own apartment in Munich—Germany's equivalent to New York City at the time. He said that she had been engaged to be married twice but eventually discarded her fiancés because they got on her nerves and cramped her style. "The minute they tried to tell her what to do, she threw them out, ja?" Dad said, throwing his head back and laughing. "She was nuts!" What she was, was my heroine. "Insolent" and "crazy" became positive labels in my mind, signifiers of independence and strength.

A few years ago, my father went to visit his sister Frida after twenty years. She was in her late seventies and living in a retirement home in Munich. She was battling cancer without painkillers. Part of her stomach had been removed years before and had been replaced with part of a goat's stomach. She had recently had a leg amputated, but she was still able to zip around in her wheelchair and raise hell. She nearly drove my father crazy. She instructed him where and how fast he was to push her wheelchair, and when he did not respond quickly enough, she would ask him, "Are you stupid?" She treated him to lunch at a place she had frequented before she became a resident at the old-age home. The restaurant had good beer and a traditional oompah polka band—two of her favorite things in the world. The problem began when the waiter delivered their meal. Frida scrutinized the pork chops they had been served and threw a fit. She shouted for the manager to complain about the inferior size of the pork chops and the lack of value for money. She threatened to report the establishment to a connection she had with a national restaurant association, city hall, or some other higher authority. She must have thrown in the right names because the manager replaced their meals with enormous chops about an inch and a half thick. Frida enjoyed her food without remorse. I imagine that my father was not quite as comfortable. He probably chewed his food, trying to concentrate on not looking like he was related to the woman who had caused the scene. After he told me the story, I pointed out to him that Frida's behavior was the embodiment of his philosophy of honesty, and he replied "There is a difference between honesty and being downright obnoxious, ja?"

On that trip, my father told Frida that I was just like her. She liked that very much. My father explained that I had postponed my wedding twice and had then canceled. "Tell her not to do it if she doesn't want to!" Frida had shouted. My Dad was pretty sure that Aunt Frida put me in her will after his story. When she passed away, she left behind many different versions of her will, and I was excluded from the last one. I figured she had deleted me after I went through with the wedding.

Compromise and tact were not part of Frida's philosophy, an approach to life that was very different from that of my mother. My mother believed that happiness and financial security were based upon the ability to compromise. The didactic Mexican *dichos* that she used in responding to my stubbornness and back talk illustrated that. She always began, "You know, we have a saying in Spanish," and ended with, "Do you know what that means?" I could pick out words of the *dichos,* but their meanings escaped me and her tone annoyed me. She provided a literal translation of the saying, followed by the interpretation and the application to the present situation. Two of her favorites were "En boca cerrada, no entra mosca" (In a closed mouth, no flies enter) and "Mas vale malo por conocido que buena por conocer" (A familiar difficulty is preferable to an unknown comfort). They were sayings about timely silence and satisfaction with the present situation, both refusals to risk losing what one had for something better.

Financial stability was what my mother valued because she had experienced poverty. The few stories that she did tell were about how she and her family happened to immigrate to the United States and the hardships they endured in the process. Her father, Luis, had been a newspaperman, putting out a Spanish-language newspaper based in El Paso. Her mother, Juanita, and her Aunt Magda worked for him—distributing the papers to the delivery people. When he received death threats because of his editorials and was forced to leave El Paso, Juanita went with him. They had five children together and remained fairly mobile in Mexico—ready to pick up and leave whenever necessary. At some point, Luis developed a hernia. Because he refused to see doctors, Juanita did what she could for him—administered hot compresses to his bulging abdomen and tried to make him more comfortable. Once he did agree to see a doctor, he was beyond help. On his deathbed, he asked my grandmother to take the family back to the United States for a better life. Until the interview with my mother four years ago, that was all that I knew of the story.

The Grandma that I had known was completely selfless. She was the one who had sacrificed everything for her children—working as a seamstress from dawn until dusk to immigrate with her family to the United States and put all five of her children through Catholic primary schools. I grew up feeling that I could never be like her and that my thoughts, feelings, and actions could never get me into the heaven where she would go. The story of Juanita's passion for my grandfather and her opting to stay with him even though he did not provide her with a stable life or financial security made her real and infinitely complex—a whole other person before becoming my grandmother.

Who and where my mother came from and who she came to be made sense to me for the first time. She wanted to have for herself and for her children a stable, comfortable lifestyle that came with education, financial security, and the ability to compromise and negotiate. Through the personal sacrifices made by both my parents, their generosity in telling me my families' stories, and my mother's pains to give me enough freedom to form my own opinions, I have been allowed to place myself within and between all their stories of confinement, of protection, and ultimately of strength.

While I like going back to El Paso to visit, I don't think I'll ever live there again. Juanita had the strength to cross the border and arrive at that destination, forging opportunities for her children and the generations beyond. My mother and father used their determination, tenacity, and intelligence to cross geographical, cultural, and emotional boundaries; they negotiated the spaces in which my brother and I were raised and provided us with what they believed were the necessary implements not just for survival but for success. The challenges I face are *en otras fronteras, mas internas,* and I am grateful.

Howling at the Moon

THE QUEER BUT TRUE STORY OF

MY LIFE AS A HANK WILLIAMS SONG

Craig Womack

In the summer the hills around Martinez, California, are dry and barren, covered with short, dead yellow grass. We used to slide down these hills on pieces of cardboard, and one time—only once, mind you—I tried rolling down in a fifty-five-gallon barrel. You see cattle grazing on the steep slopes, looking like they might tip over if somebody gave them a good push. From a distance these hills look almost treeless, although if you've ever been up in them you know this isn't the case. The oaks that from the highway seem only to dot the steep slopes here and there grow much thicker in places not easily seen from a car. This is the land that I see now, but another place exists a little behind this one, alive in my memory; this landscape is the one my grandparents painted with stories about sharecropping and picking cotton for white people in eastern Oklahoma. My grandparents' stories created two Oklahomas for me, the one we visited when me and my mom took that long bus ride through the orchards and alfalfa fields of the San Joaquin Valley, then through Needles and out across I-40, and the other Oklahoma of my grandparents' stories, the place that occupies so much space in my imagination.

The landscape comes alive in Oklahoma when everything in California is so dry during the rainless summer. The air hangs as heavy as a wet sheet on a wash line during these months. There is a point, when driving Highway 9 toward Eufaula, Oklahoma, when you enter a new country; there the cross timbers, a vast and densely wooded expanse that stretches between the north and south forks of the Canadian River, form the frontier where two landscapes meet. Called the cross timbers because these woods run between the two forks of the *Oktahutche*, Creek for the Canadian. Here the flat pastures and fields of wheat and alfalfa, dotted with various jigsaw-shaped farm ponds, rise up into rolling hills, densely covered with post oaks and blackjacks. This ain't the musical where the wind comes whistling down the plains; this is eastern Oklahoma, and I feel something different here. Red-tailed hawks, perched on the telephone lines, or hidden in the trees, more visible in winter when the branches are so bare, occasionally lift off and hie over the road, silhouetted against the sun as if it meant to touch fire to their wing tips. The cricket choruses incessantly hum in a minor key, the voices of old settlers camped in the trees.

Eastern Oklahoma roadsides are a charnel house. You can't help seeing the armadillos, run over and lying in the ditches, as little cartoon characters since they always seem to die with all four feet sticking straight up in the air, pointing—this is the Bible Belt—toward Jesus. Even the roadkill is born again in Oklahoma. Like most everybody else in Indian Territory, they are intruders, come up from Texas, in pipes brought up with oil workers, my uncle tells me. Of course this is the same uncle who says coyotes run relays, so I don't know if I should believe anything he says, but I like the story. However they got there, the next thing anybody knew the armadillos had taken over the whole goddamn state. The latest onslaught of Sooners and Booners. Their forerunners, groups of crooks and murderers, the state still holds in high esteem and celebrates on official holidays, getting school kids to reenact their genocide during pageants. I suppose, realistically, this comparison isn't fair to armadillos. And, worse, the truth is I'm related to some of these guys, Sooners that is, no armadillos that I can name.

Other road deaths are more grotesque. Some days you might see, for instance, like I did once, the sight of a decapitated red fox, its head in the middle of the road, its body in a ditch. Smashed turtles are everywhere, and their surviving kin plod across the shimmering pavement, oblivious to the destruction of automobiles.

Loca. Turtles. Women shaking shells. Night dances under the arbors. Fireflies flitting over the willow boughs that roof them. *Shuguta Shuguta Shuguta,* women stepping toe to heel, the sound of shells shaking, the turtle voices. Fire embers slithering up the night sky.

When I recall my Creek and Cherokee and Irish and German kinfolk—Whisenhunts and Blues, Coachmans and Sessions, Selfs and Bracketts, Madewells and Womacks, and Joneses and Ausmuses, and the ones before them I don't even know about—then think about what all these people have been through, it is a humbling and formidable task to scratch out these chicken tracks I'm calling my own life. I hope they don't think me too pretentious for the effort, and I ask their pardon if they do. I'm conscious as I write, even now, of babbling on in the first person like Rush Limbaugh with his stack of I-told-you-so books behind him. There is something about the task that ends up being grotesque, no matter how you look at it.

My grandfather Lester Womack's great-grandparents, James and Lucinda Sessions, were in Indian removal. They were Georgia Cherokees, and at first they ran off and hid with Creeks in Georgia, then Seminoles in Florida—hanging out with, hiding out with, and marrying out with Creeks has a long history in my family. They got "removed" like everybody else when the army caught up with them, and, in Sallisaw, Oklahoma, at Dwight Presbyterian mission, James Sessions met Lucinda, another Cherokee, whom he married, and he worked there, at first as an interpreter for Cherokees, Creeks, and Choctaws, and, later, as a teacher. I begin with this little bit of history in order to underscore the way in which my family has always been somewhere between Creekness and Cherokeeness, Creekified Cherokees or Cherokeefied Creeks, depending on how you wanna look at it.

I'm always being asked by, well, for lack of a better term, white people, to come to various gatherings and tell stories. I get the feeling that they already have a certain type of story in mind, and the feeling is confirmed whenever I begin to tell what I perceive to be some kind of real story about Indian people. It ends up they want a creation story, or a trickster story; a story, in short, that mirrors their own culture back at them and makes them feel good, unimplicated. It's not that these traditional stories are inherently bland and apolitical—quite the opposite, they originated in a genre that was strongly nationalistic in their tribal contexts—but they often get presented as kiddie stories. I used to go about telling these stories, but now I'm wondering who am I to tell them and about the ways I get used doing this, as well as the possible abuse to the Indian community.

Almost every week someone calls me up at home or in my office at the University of Nebraska about speaking at the high school or local colleges or some event in Omaha. If this was a matter of speaking to Indian kids about going to college, for instance, I'd go in a heartbeat, but, instead, they want me to come and give 'em some of that old-time religion, old-time oral tradition, and I don't feel qualified.

When we present the oral tradition in a highly palatable pan-tribal stew for a non-Indian audience, my concern has to do with the way we play into colonial discourse with these stories, the way we depoliticize our own literatures in an oral-tradition genre that was once strongly nationalistic, and the way significant tribal differences are blurred and a sense of specific sovereignty diminished. I am concerned about what happens to the political intent of the stories when they are separated from their tribal contexts, removed from a total existential situation. For example, in Creek stories, a pan-tribal context might cause a divorce from a sense of "Creekness," knowledge of what it means to be from a clan, a town, a nation where these narratives are contextualized with other stories, songs, and ceremonies from within the Creek Nation rather than performed as isolated fragments alongside a confusing array of tellings from other tribal traditions. Would these stories better serve our own folks in the context of the passed-on, tribally specific traditions, histories, religious practices, and political thought that create their meanings?

Carrying forward something of a corollary problem, I have to fess up that in the writing of this essay I'm somewhat ambivalent about the whole notion of celebrating mixedblood identity for some of the same reasons—emphasizing a generic identity over tribal specificity. It's not the issue of mixedblood identity that bothers me since, for better or worse or a combination of the two, this is a contemporary reality for many Indian people, including myself. What bothers me is making mixedblood identity the primary focus of one's identification or one's writing. I'm wondering if identifying as mixedblood, rather than as part of a tribal nation, diminishes sovereignty? Perhaps the two need not be mutually exclusive; maybe one can face the reality of a mixed existence while still asserting the primacy of nationalism, the latter not being exclusively defined by degree of blood but by an interplay of biological, cultural, and political factors. What might be called for is a view of identity in terms of the larger picture—the tribal nation—rather than in terms of the fragmented mixedblood individual, just as it may help to place traditional stories in the tribally specific contexts of the nations they originate from.

Maybe teachers and students should hear some other kind of story. What about this story, for instance? Here in Omaha, 50 percent of the Indian kids drop out of high school, 80 percent in Lincoln, more on the rez. Or what about the fact that the average life expectancy is around forty-seven on the three rezzes in Nebraska or that the average income is under $6,000 a year for an entire family?

But then again they also need to hear the ways in which these tribes are surviving, healthy, culturally intact, spiritually in tune, politically sophisticated, and evolving, bringing Indian realities into the twentieth century.

Rather than coyote stories, I'd just as soon tell about my Uncle Sonny Boy who got drunk and bit off my Uncle Gool Coachman's ear during a poker game; or the time in seventh grade my mom took me aside and told me not to hang out with the school fag because people might say the same thing about me that they said about him; or another time when a tornado came in Haskell, Oklahoma, and my grandma was plumb wore out after chopping cotton, and my granddad told her, "You can sit on your goddamned ass and get blowed away, but I'm taking my kids to the cellar";

or about my dad, who's an identical twin and his name is Coy Floyd and his twin brother's name is Foy Boyd and the fact that they play on a baseball team for guys over fifty and have won the World Series for over-fifties two years running now and I'm proud as can be for the two of them and that they are insane and practice fielding imaginary grounders inside shopping malls; or my Aunt Barbara Coachman's story about the guy who stood up at the Creek Baptist church in Weleetka, Oklahoma, where my dad's from, and said the forbidden fruit must have been a persimmon; or the first time I saw a storm cellar at age four while I was visiting my great-grandma Wilma Self in Haskell, Oklahoma, and that big red rooster they killed (I thought just on account of me) and the tree swing my Uncle Pete built; or about my high school friend Dave out in California, the Assembly of God preacher's son who died of AIDS a few years ago; or the unnamable shadow of sexual abuse that has hung over some of the women in my family; or the army tanks that run right through the middle of the Wichita mountains in Oklahoma, sacred Kiowa and Comanche country, making you wanna duck behind the neck of your Ford Taurus every time they sneak up behind you; or about my grandpa's siblings, one who got stabbed to death by his best friend, a Creek guy from Weleetka, another who died lighting a cigarette after spraying arsenic on white people's cotton fields, and yet another, the aforementioned ear mauler; or the contemporary legacies of these men like my little brother, who smoked too much PCP and boarded up all the windows of our house and stood on top of the roof with a shotgun; or some of my equally insane acts of self-hatred; or my grandpa, who took me out to chop wood when I was thirteen and told me I swung the ax like a little four-year-old girl; or just a whole shitload of other things that I could tell these people if they really wanted to hear Indian stories.

And then I'm ambivalent about all of that too because what if I leave my audience with a predominant impression of the dysfunctionalism wrought by colonialism rather than the incredibly sane, healthy, and spiritual ways some of my kin have survived? Storytelling, it now seems to me, is a vast terrain with many possibilities for getting lost, as well as for finding one's way, and not enough folks talking about better maps that represent the real territory in question.

APPARITIONS

like ghosts we appear on the streets of America,
    me waiting in line,
Chrystos standing in front of the Roxie Theater,
San Francisco, end of the trail but

not vanishing like a good ghost should,
I sneak up and hug her,
feel good solid flesh beneath my arms,
thank grandmother spirits we're still alive and
floating through our old haunts, and Chrystos
yells for the whole street to hear,
"Hey, girlfriend!"

a queer situation, indeed,
a Creek and Menominee skin skulking up and down
city streets once hunted by Pomo and Miwok

ghosts
yet what can we expect here in America?
certainly not citizenship,
even after 1924 and 1978 they can still
imprison us as sodomites in almost half of their United States,
(whose rules are these anyway? We have our own nations)
beat us up or kill us in all of them,
deny us housing and employment,
ban us from their military, though,
you'd think they'd have grown tired of hunting us down after the
    19th century,
sit smirking from BIA offices while we die of AIDS
disproportionate to other populations,
a queer smallpox
spread like blankets among the unsuspecting,
every day some friend dead and another
giveaway
furniture, clothes, remains but
no naming ceremony and

"Oh," the ghosts of their Calvinists forefathers sigh,
"can *we* help it you have no immunity?"

I was talking to Rabbit the other day, and I say, "*Choffee,* them white
people's wanting me to tell them some stories."
"So what?" he says. "That's what they're always wanting you to do,
aieeeeee . . . "
"Yeah," I say, "but I don't know where to start."
He scratched his ear with his hind paw. "What say you begin at the
beginning, how bout it?"
"Which one?" I ask.

When my mom was young, and pregnant with me, at age sixteen, in
Richmond, California, she watched the Peter Gunn detective show on TV.
This would be 1959 since I was born on February 29th in 1960. Leap year
only comes once every four years, making me 8.75 years of age at the time
of this essay. I may not seem like much, but for an eight-year-old, I reckon,
I'm prodigious. The star of that show was a handsome young actor
named Craig Stevens. I suspect that Mom had a crush on him, but the
way she tells it she waddn't the least bit interested. When, at age seventeen, she gave birth to me, she named me Craig Steven. That is how I got
my traditional Ind'n name.

It could have been worse. My dad is an identical twin, and he and his
brother were born premature out there by the curve in the road next to
the black cemetery in Weleetka, Oklahoma. Weleetka, in Creek, means
running water. Dad and his brother weren't born on that curve exactly;
there used to be a house there. He barely survived, says he, and his
brother had to be heated up on the wood stove to get revived. Am I to believe this? My grandma named my dad Coy Floyd and his twin brother
Foy Boyd. I wish this were fiction. When I tell people my dad's named
Coy and his twin brother's named Foy, they ask me if they are Chinese.
As far as I know they are not, unless one of my great-great grandmothers
is a Chinese princess, a fullblood. Someday, I'm going to visit that castle
in Oklahoma where all those princesses are housed.

Mark Twain said that children should be taught to lie at as young an
age as possible. As a child I'd never heard of Mark Twain, but I learned
about lying with my first breath.

Every day after classes let out at Martinez Junior High School, I would
rush out, having arranged my books and pocketed my pencils in perfect

synchronization with the long hand of the clock striking 2:30 and the bell sounding. I ran down the playground ramp, shot full of dread, not looking back, wanting to get home before Gary caught up with me. Ah, but why didn't I mention Gary earlier, you ask? He exists in my memory as a suffering servant, a locust's castoff shell, a tall, skinny, transparent no one. My classmates and I, behind the eyes of our hard little bodies, saw him as our punching bag, and since I was no good at punching, I avoided him altogether. I tried to push ahead on the crest of the wave of junior highers spilling from hallways, Gary just at my heels, dodging bodies and skirting the crowd, about to catch up. Gary was from Oklahoma too, but a skinny little white boy. He was my only friend, and I was ashamed to be seen with him. One day my mom had noticed me walking home with Gary, and she sat me down on the living room sofa. She looked worried.

"Now honey," she said while fidgeting with her curlers and dropping down to sotto voce, "you know if you hang around that boy, people will start to say the same thing about you that they say about him."

Gary was extremely girlish, a real fem. I knew what my mom said was right, and I was just as eager to avoid him, because of what my classmates would think, as she was to have me not seen in his presence. What everyone knew about Gary, no one had guessed about me. By the way, I don't hold this against my mother; how can I when she was just a kid herself when I was growing up, seventeen the year of my birth. So I learned to lie.

QUEER INDIANS

Here in America where
we're a dirty joke,
a punch line,
a wink and an elbow in
some good ole boy's ribs,
rumors and whispers,
the name of a team
on their caps and t-shirts,
a prop in a movie for
their beautiful white heroes,

let us give thanks like the Pequots
who fed the Pilgrims and sat down with them
that first cold winter at Plymouth.
We know what happened
to the Pequots, some of us
do anyway.
Seventeen short years
later the gratitude
of limbs hacked to pieces,
and what's nonexistence
compared to what happens
when we're real?

I got saved at age four; the deacon of the white Southern Baptist church we went to out in California led me through the sinner's prayer one night when he'd come over to our house visiting. The same evening he told a nigger joke. Salvation only grew thornier for me in the years to come.

My dad taught me to play the guitar, which I took up at age sixteen. My dad loves Hank Williams songs, and his dad used to tell me stories about the hobos and the freight trains, having hopped boxcars himself from Eufaula out to the San Joaquin Valley, starting at age fourteen, to work in the fields and orchards, then going back and forth to Oklahoma. We are a coming and going bunch. So grandpa, Lester Womack, liked all those Jimmie Rogers songs. Hobo Bill's Last Ride. All around the water tower, waiting for a train. I'm going to California, where they sleep out every night. An Oklahoma Indian friend of mine, one night when we were sitting smoking and drinking coffee in Norman, told me "In high school I used to go with my friends in Lawton to get somebody to buy beer for us. We'd get six packs of Little Kings and listen to Hank Williams, parked at the cemetery north of town." This was a small miracle; I had been listening to Hank Williams all my life. I told my friend how my dad sang Hank's songs incessantly; I may have been the only kid my age in Martinez, California, who knew that Hank started out doing talking blues and calling himself Luke the Drifter, singing sad songs, one that I particularly remembered about the town slut who gets killed saving a little boy from a car wreck, the community realizing only too late that they had misjudged her. The name of the song is "Be Careful of Stones that you Throw."

I said to my buddy, "Yeah, I remember really clearly the day I first heard 'I'm So Lonesome I Could Cry.' That was the purest, rawest, most emotional thing I'd ever listened to. I thought, good God, this isn't an expression of pain, this *is* pain, the stuff of which pain is made."

Sometime later, one beautiful Oklahoma summer evening, he and I and a couple of friends were driving back from the movies in Oklahoma City. I had stuck "Hank Williams' Greatest Hits" in my coat pocket and surreptitiously slipped it in the tape player when our two white compatriots weren't looking (one of them referred to my Hank Williams collection as incestuous hillbilly warbling). My friend and I rolled down the windows and let in the humid summer air while we belted out "Howling at the Moon" in true coyote abandon, and this was minus the Little Kings. After the chorus, "You got me chasing rabbits, scratching fleas, and howling at the moon," we turned our faces up toward the black sky and wailed. Our friends looked aghast, and there was something about those Hank Williams songs that he and I shared that the other people in the car did not. I don't know quite how to put my finger on it, but it has to do with alienation, loneliness, a shitload of pain, and not being able to speak to the one you love, remaining hidden and silent in the shadows for a lifetime. The songs have everything to do with being queer; the songs have everything to do with being Indian, and me and my buddy were the only two people that night who knew the beauty and terror of both identities.

I hear a lot of Hank Williams in BR5-49, all that stuff about your snag running off with some redneck . . .

There are two Craig Womacks, and I'm not sure which one to tell you about. One of them—silent and afraid, full of shame and hatred—I no longer know, though I recognize him like a blur on a faraway shore. Upon graduating from high school, early and at the age of seventeen, I chose to send myself to the very worst place a young Indian gay man could subject himself to. I enrolled in an Assembly of God Bible College. Looking back on that experience, I see this as analogous to all those freaked-out Flannery O'Connor characters who strap barbed wire around their chests and put glass shards in their shoes. I couldn't have chosen a better place to be beat up, a better place to have my spirit bludgeoned to death with a bloody cudgel. I pretty much signed up and paid tuition for gay bashing and Indian hating. I still do not have the words for this experience, and I have only recently even begun telling people about it. I guess I thought attending Bible College was an act of faith that would take care of my "problem." I saw my sexual orientation as a kind of twenty-four-hour flu; if I only did the right combination of things, surely, I would get over this disease. Find the right woman, just have more faith, more commitment, more time standing in healing lines asking Jesus to take away this burden. The Assemblies of God, an inherently racist institution, certainly worked to drive out any sense of a tribal identity from me; their missionary stories alone created a whole corpus of didactic narratives that associated any nonwhite culture with that which is fleshly, that which is carnal, that which is to be mortified, that which is to be put to death.

I don't know how well all this worked on me back then because I'm not sure if you can go from dead to deader. I come up against a wall here, like the concept of a limit in calculus, when trying to describe this experience in abstract language, so I just wanna tell a couple of stories.

There was a woman with a healing ministry by the name of Roxanne Brant who would always come through the Bible College. God bless her, she's dead now of cancer, so I guess the physician-heal-thyself dictum applies here. Ms. Brant's story was that she was a former commie-pinko-humanist-leftist-feminist, card-carrying-ACLU-member and fag-sympathizer-medical-student when Jesus struck her down on the Yale Medical School quad like Paul on the road to Damascus. As a result of her experience studying medicine, she had a tremendous medical vocabulary, which she drew upon during her healing meetings, which were replete with very concrete descriptions of human anatomy. She would begin to sway back and forth—she was tall and rather wraithlike, garbed in loose-fitting, long sheer gowns with lots of layers and colors, a bit of a female Ichabod Crane with a Saks charge card—and she would say, eyes shut, brows furrowed in deep communication with Jesus, "There's a woman in the third row," her long bony finger pointing now, "who has a contusion under her left armpit, swollen to about the size of a musk melon, and from the left side of the swelling is leaking brown necrotic material." But that was only the beginning. She would go on to name "feminine problems" in glorious detail, and the faithful got to come to church to talk dirty. She was entranced with the female body, and I have suspicions looking back; she was single all her life, a real oddity in Christian fundamentalism.

The only one who came close to competing with Roxanne was a German guy by the name of the Reverend Paul Shoch. He quoted the verse from the Pauline epistles, the book of Romans to be more precise, that says that when believers don't know what to pray the Holy Spirit makes intercession for them with "groanings which cannot be uttered." Reverend Shoch would get huge gatherings of people to simultaneously "groan in the spirit" (he evidently hadn't thought through the "cannot be uttered" part), and it was like one thousand or more mutual orgasms. Surely he went back to his hotel room at night with a smirk and a hard-on.

Another one of the circus sideshows that came through with their "ministry" was a "converted" gay man married to a "converted" lesbian preaching deliverance from the demonic forces of homosexuality. A person doesn't need a Ph.D. in astrophysics to understand what was going on (or not going on) in that relationship, but I never even considered the possibility that this wasn't a ministry but the perfect cover-up, and I don't know that any of the rest of the faithful did either. Our very lives, temporally and eternally, depended on it all being true.

The Assemblies of God was the most pervasively sexual experience I have ever had except they didn't allow actually getting laid, strictly off-limits, only for marriage between man and wife, and, even then, a necessary evil though they didn't exactly say that. I did get hit on by really closeted older guys who masked their sexual interest behind spiritual mentorship and took me on camping trips and outings, the usual perversities, though nothing ever really happened besides this incredibly pervasive unspoken tension like a wire stretched taut, all of us ready to snap. Every song we sang: "He touched me, he touched me, and oh, the joy that floods my soul," all that yearning for Jesus, falling on the floor, being slain in the spirit, speaking in tongues. I cannot think of a time in my life where I have been more sick or disturbed or dead or storyless or afraid or nonexistent. Like I said, "I'm So Lonesome I Could Cry." Never did give up those Hank songs, even for "He Touched Me."

I'm gonna stop here because I really have to guard myself since I have so much anger over those years. I have to be careful about planes, airports, public places because if anybody comes up and starts telling me about Jesus I wanna kill them, and it almost seems like just retaliation. Yet I also have to own up to the fact that I did this to myself, a painful and embarrassing admission. By way of contrast and in hope of healing, I offer the following poem:

TWO MEN LAUGHING AT THE DAWN

face taut as a drumhead
stretched out over pebbles
bones
washed in riverbeds
beneath your skin
eyes coiled
ready to strike

fingers, my fingers
trace light spreading over your chest
passing this ground of yours
a drop of blood falls from my fingertips
to the dust of your belly
the first songs of laughter well up
between us

pulling light in our teeth
feet braced
sky in our mouths
a holy tug-of-war for light, for love
in the very middle of the morning red we stand

I want to talk about a series of events that happened at the University of Oklahoma. I recognize there is a shift here in the tone of my story, a change in voice, and perhaps some of that awkwardness reflects my ongoing struggle with connecting private and public concerns, linking personal history with a committed political activism, a necessity no less important for its difficulty.

On a Sunday evening in the spring of 1994, the Sunday that would end Spring Break and resume classes the following Monday morning, Native American students were gathered inside a ceremonial tipi that was to be blessed the following morning, kicking off a celebration of Native American Heritage Week at the University of Oklahoma. At around one o'clock in the morning, twelve to fifteen drunk and naked fraternity members joined ranks on a grassy knoll across from Bizell Library and proceeded to charge the tipi, knocking over one of the poles in the process, and urinating on it. Two male Native American students followed the drunken frat members to their fraternity house and called the police, who arrived but refused to take down any names. The same fraternity had a history of racist attacks on Indians; they had thrown rocks and beer bottles at the Jim Thorpe Multi-cultural Center, and in that incident as well the police had refused to charge anyone. In the tipi attack, seven of the twelve individuals were identified, and the university promised the Indian community that appropriate action would be taken against them. A hearing was scheduled in which both the individuals involved and the fraternity would be investigated. The day before the hearing was to take place, the university announced that the fraternity had been exonerated, and whatever disciplinary actions were taken against the individuals would not be disclosed because the matter was between the offenders and the university and had nothing to do with the Indian community. The community was enraged and, at times, also deeply divided over the issue, largely because of contradictory information in the press. Since the fraternity members were protected by a complete veil of silence which the university had arranged, they had no opportunities to implicate themselves in the press; whereas Indian people were being questioned and quoted in the paper every day, some of them disagreeing over trivial details of the attack (one person in the tipi, for instance, said he wasn't sure it had been urinated on). In spite of these minor disagreements, however, over time a powerful coalition took form, and Native American students came together at OU in a way they never had before. Francis Wise, a graduate student at OU and longtime committed activist, led a courageous battle that lasted for months, trying to get the university to conduct a proper investigation of the hate crime.

While many administrators dismissed the incident as insignificant, people like Francis Wise argued that if you let a group of racists get away with knocking over a tipi, you will have more incidents of racism in the future. Later events proved that inattention to the racist attack had life and death consequences. That December, the same fraternity, drunk again, was messing around in front of their frat house. They were shaking their flagpole, all puns intended considering their earlier difficulties with toilet training, and, in an incident that is so bizarre it is almost unfathomable, the pole broke off, hit one of the members in the head, and killed him. A pole had been knocked over in the attack on the tipi and its occupants, too.

This is not a revenge story; this is a story about responsibility, and, in my estimation, the University of Oklahoma shares in the responsibility for this young man's death. The frat was closed down temporarily by President David Boren but has been allowed to reopen. One can't help but wonder how many people are going to have to be hurt or killed before this fraternity is shut down forever.

A week before the racist attack on the Indian community (referred to as "the tipi incident" at the University of Oklahoma), I was teaching class, and my students were giving presentations. The police came, one OU cop and one Norman cop, to arrest a woman they had a warrant for. This person, a Native American student, was literally in the middle of giving a presentation in my class. I asked the officers if they could at least wait until the end of class, so as to minimize the disruption. The police refused. I then asked if they could wait until her presentation was over. Again, they refused. They asked me to identify the woman for them because they didn't know who she was, and I said no. The cops said that they were going to arrest me for harboring a felon, and I still said that I would not cooperate. They said that if I refused to tell them who the woman was, they were going into the class to call her out in front of everybody. Not wanting my student to suffer such humiliation, I felt compelled to comply but experienced a thousand different stabs of guilt and shame at having to hand over one of my own to the police. They handcuffed her in front of all of us and led her away. My students, who had heard me contending with the officers outside the classroom, thought that I was being arrested and were very frightened. Many of them called their parents when they got home.

I do not know of any time before or since that I have been so angry, and when class was over, I headed over to the OU police department to kick some ass, either literally or verbally, whichever came first. My department chair intercepted me and told me that there was no sense going over there because as soon as I got inside I would be arrested, which surely would have been the case as distraught as I was and as racist an institution as OU is. I staggered home livid and catatonic, and my roommate took one look at me and said, "Oh, my god, what has happened to you?" I couldn't speak on the phone because I was too pissed, so she started calling people, and we found out that both OU police policy and Norman City Police policy had been violated. OU police are not supposed to pull people from classes, and Norman police are supposed to submit to OU's jurisdiction when they're on campus.

I went down to the city jail to make sure my student was OK; unlike the white frat boys, she was named, booked, arrested, jailed. She was given a uniform to wear, and it wasn't Ralph Lauren or Polo or Calvin Klein. (One can't help but wonder what would have happened in the aforementioned case, the tipi "incident" referred to earlier, if some of us had pissed on the Norman Southern Baptist Church. I suspect we'd still be in jail or prison, probably with multiple fractures.) Fortunately, my student, pulled in on a felony car-theft charge, got out that same day, which made me suspect further whether or not she needed to be arrested during class time. If the allegations were all that serious, they would have held her instead of releasing her. I had to speak with my class about the event because they were so frightened, and to not say anything would have been like the family who gets beat up by the husband and nobody talks about it the next day. I found out that my students, like me, felt violated, that the sanctity of a space where I had been trying for an entire semester to create a safe environment to explore differing viewpoints had been destroyed. I felt awkward, at first, dealing with this since the student who had been arrested was back in class, but it might have been the best class session of the entire semester. White students who, before the police assault, couldn't always relate to the viewpoint of minority writers expressing experiences with racism, had just witnessed a dramatic example before their very eyes. In addition to filing a complaint against the police department, I wrote an article for the school paper's editorial page entitled "Nowhere Is Safe in Occupied Territory," and everyone in the class, including some very conservative class members, signed a letter to accompany the article. The college newspaper refused to print the article because they called OU police, who told them that no policies had been broken. I reminded them, to no avail, of the dangers of asking the police for permission to run editorials. Finally, after weeks of effort, culminating in Amnesty International pressuring the paper to relent, they ran the editorial.

These two events taught me a great deal about teaching literature, probably more than I learned in any class or reading or study of criticism and theory before or since. My students would come to class asking me about the "tipi incident" and what the university was doing about it. I learned that semester that the teaching of Native American literature *must* be linked with the spirit of resistance that has been a part of Native American survival. As Joy Harjo says, "The Indian wars never ended in this country" (*The Woman Who Fell from the Sky*, 43). The way events at OU relate to my larger story is that they were a beginning point for me, and they have everything to do with a personal struggle for identity. They were a beginning in the sense that I could finally turn loose some of that pent-up internalization, struggling with who I am as an Indian person, as a gay man, wanting to speak but feeling constrained and inarticulate. In joining the rally that started to build for some kind of justice at OU, I think I began to focus on something outside myself—the political struggle of a community of people against racism—and the whole issue of who *I* am was subsumed by the more important question of who *we* are. I began to see that every angle of vision from which I saw myself was refracted through the larger lens of being Indian and fighting for survival. It was no longer a matter of reconciling being gay with being Indian but of being Indian, period, and understanding being gay in Indian terms.

It may sound funny, but sometimes my life makes the most sense to me when I think of it as a narrative, kind of like a creation story, where you start with chaos, confusion, as in the Creek story where everyone is stumbling about in a thick fog, bumping into each other and getting hurt.

But then, by the end of the story, the fog lifts, individuals have banded to-gether with the animals they ran into and discovered their clans and their place among the people. My experience in Oklahoma seems to me to be like the last part of that story. The OU fight helped me to realize that there are still important ways to be a warrior and that I had a place in this strug-gle; some of the identity search was laid to rest. I think the story is like a circle; periodically, you end up back in the fog and chaos, but as you get further along, the darkness becomes more manageable, and you know eventually you will emerge out into the light of the broader landscape. Most of our stories involve a movement toward healing, and, through the outcry against events at OU, I began to see myself with more humor, more laughter, more irony, more distance. As a trickster rather than as a victim. Creek trickster is Rabbit, *choffee,* and I began to learn to speak for myself and to define myself in terms that were appropriate to my own sense of self as well as to an Indian community rather than being defined by dominant-culture definitions of what is normal.

QUILTING

A missing student,
gone a week, nothing unusual—
another Indian kid on the extended weekend plan.
Most likely homesick or partying or just laying out.
An officious memo came through intercampus mail.
"Please be understanding," it said.
The student's cousin and
the cousin's baby daughter,
shot to death in Tulsa.
Father taken into custody.
The aunt died of a heart attack
when she heard the news.

We don't have a dance for this,
the terror of turning on each other
no cedar to burn
or shells to shake

or smoke to blow
or stomp dance songs to sing.

The old witches never came from within
our own houses.
Three generations gone in a day,
skin against skin,
wiped out in the Indian wars.

She'd written an essay
before her disappearance—
a story her aunt had told her:
how to piece a quilt together for
extra winter covers.
She got an A that semester
for surviving

pieces of patchwork everywhere.

I want to be as honest as I can be about the issue of Indian identity, a complicated one in my view. At this point I don't have a roll number, a fact that sometimes pains me and, at other times, means little at all. Of my four grandparents, three of them are mixedblood Oklahoma Indians. Their parents were in northwestern Arkansas during the Dawes Commission enrollment, and you will find split families where one sibling enrolled, while another, with the same blood quantum, did not cross over into Oklahoma and get on the rolls. This is a commonplace historical reality for many families. So my direct ancestors have blood relatives on the Dawes Commission rolls—brothers, sisters, and all kinds of other kinfolk, but they did not get enrolled themselves. I suspect that eventually I will get all this straightened out (in terms of enrollment), but that is where it stands now.

The issue gets even more complicated for me because my family is made up largely of Cherokees who moved from northwestern Arkansas to the Eufaula and Weleetka areas, where they grew up actually speaking Creek. As a youngster I always believed I was Creek and didn't know too much about the Cherokee background because my relatives spoke the language and married Creek men and my kin didn't tell me any different.

As an adult, looking at tribal records, I found out that my family had more Cherokee blood than Creek blood. I have always written more about Creek issues because these are the people I grew up around. I don't speak Cherokee, but I do know some Creek language, and my granddad, Lester Womack, and his brother, Elijah Ernest Womack, spoke Creek. Some of their female siblings married fullblood Creek men, including my Aunt Barbara Coachman, who married principal chief Ward Coachman's grandson. Coachman was chief in the late 1870s and instrumental in building the council house at Okmulgee, where Creek constitutional government was established.

So what do you do? I could do like some of my mixedblood relatives and pretend not to be Indian, but they ended up drunk and crazy and often dead at a young age. Further, Indian people have always recognized me as being Indian, so that's not been an option, even if I wanted it, which I don't. If I were to take a position in my writing, as a non-Indian author, I would be lying. Or, as some folks would argue I should, I could simply not write about Indians at all. The problem is I'm not simply writing *about* Indians; I'm telling my family's story, and my story, which is at once Indian and poor and southern and white and a combination of all these things.

I got pulled over by the police the other night for still having Oklahoma plates on my car, which I haven't changed over yet since moving to Nebraska, and noticed on the ticket that the cop had marked "Indian" in the race category. This happens every time I go to get a driver's license or have any other dealings with the "authorities." So the police, anyway, don't have any doubts.

I used to think I had answers for all this, knew what constituted Indian identity, but now I no longer do. The only thing I know to say at this point is that if Creek people themselves, or even Creek writers, were to say that they didn't know who I was or that I should not be claiming Creek identity and writing about Creeks, that I would have to concede to that opinion because I believe in the right of tribes to determine who their own are. I know that at the stomp grounds I am welcomed and invited to participate, but I don't want to assume some kind of "right" because of that in the larger political sense of what constitutes a Creek. So I don't have the answers anymore, and I'm simply trying to do the best I know how at behaving responsibly.

So, who am I finally? An Indian man? Yes. A gay man? Yes. But who I am really isn't the question, is it? What matters is the people, survival, continuance, protection of our Nations, and sovereignty. We must find ways to write about such issues in our stories and poems in a way that makes our people themselves want to read what we have to say. There aren't easy answers, but we have to keep posing the questions, searching, realizing we all have a long ways to go.

Crossing Borders from the Beginning

Alfonso Rodriguez

Some years ago, at the annual meeting of the National Association for Chicano Studies (NACS) in Albuquerque, a general session was devoted to the discussion of Aztlán, the ancient homeland of the pre-Colombian inhabitants who migrated to Anáhuac, the central valley of Mexico, centuries before the coming of the Spaniards. The panel of presenters included anthropologists, historians, literary critics and creative writers. Since the advent of the Chicano Movement in the sixties, many Chicanos have been referring to the Southwest as Aztlán, even though some historians claim that Aztlán was located in an island off the coast of Nayarit, a state in western Mexico. The Chicano Movement manifested a profound sentiment on behalf of the pre-Colombian cultural legacy, and Chicanos appropriated a myth, which served as a symbol of unity and cultural identity. This was of utmost import during those days of militant activism. Chicanos viewed indigenous peoples of the Americas as the underdogs in a historical process that divided peoples into two groups:

50

colonizers and colonized. For the most part, they also viewed their own condition as mestizos within contemporary American society as very similar to that of indigenous people. Thus, the strong identification with Native American reality and with Aztlán as the Chicano homeland.

After the formal presentations a member of the audience posed the issue: "Why is it that our discussions always revolve around our indigenous past? I think that, for once, we should explore our Hispanic roots. Isn't there much to be proud of on that side of our heritage?" His questions were met by a thunderous chorus of boos. There were murmurings all across the huge auditorium. After a while, the moderator managed to restore order, and one of the panelists offered a clarification with respect to the purpose and focus of the session, indicating that certain comments were not pertinent there. Suddenly, from the other side of the floor, another intrepid voice offered this assessment: "The Spaniard is our father and the Indian is our mother, and it is wrong for us to disdain any part of our blood." The discussion grew more intense, and from that moment on there was little consensus on anything. But not all was in vain. In some ways it was an enlightening experience for me. Up to that point I had assumed, naively perhaps, that if not all Chicanos, at least all Chicano professionals or would-be professionals, like everyone in the audience, had dealt with the question of identity in the same way I had.

As I looked back, I felt at peace with myself because I realized that my journey had been a fruitful one up to that point. For me, attaining a sense of balance had been an arduous but exciting process, in part because the search for identity always entails the confrontation of unpleasant truths about our individual and collective past. It implies the willingness to struggle to divest ourselves of regressive notions and the courage to seek that which is more transcendent; that which promotes human dignity. It means leaving one's comfort zone in order to change and mature because change is part of the reality of our existence. The expression of ethnic or existential identity is not static but highly dynamic. I see ethnic and spiritual harmony as the natural consequence of a strong sense of identity. It is true that membership in a given ethnic community will give us part of our identity, and, on occasion, we can turn to our own people for emotional support and replenishment. But in a very real sense the search for identity is an individual conquest because it involves inner realities.

In spite of our common heritage, Chicanos are a diverse group, even in small numbers. I noticed that, in that general session at the NACS conference, Chicanos who identified more strongly with indigenous culture were in the majority. That was to be expected. Those mestizos in blood as well as feelings were rather scarce. However, represented in the assembly were also those New Mexican and southern Colorado Hispanos who claim direct descent from the original Spanish explorers who colonized the Southwest—an identity that they affirm with remarkable zeal and which impels them to repudiate the terms "Chicano" or "Mexican-American" as ethnic identifiers. As one of them from San Luis, Colorado, told me, "To us, words like 'Chicano,' 'Mexican-American,' or 'Mexicano' are cuss words. We are Hispanos, and we have a long tradition to prove it." Many Hispanos believe that they have "pure Spanish blood," as awkward as that may sound, considering that racial blending in Spain has occurred throughout the centuries, in spite of the Spaniard's eternal obsession with racial purity. Still, the Hispanos are rooted to certain traditions that are an important part of the Hispanic/Mexican culture of the Southwest.

That general session at the conference made me realize how enormously complex the question of identity really is. Anyone who decides to take it seriously knows that conflict is unavoidable. It is a thorny issue that some people of color prefer to ignore because, in the long run, it can become an onerous load on one's soul. One can grow weary grappling with the question of identity in a society that does not value diversity. Identity is intimately related to the quest for meaning. It is not a one-time application of a wonder balm but an ongoing process. One may lament having to endure the conflict of identity typical of the mestizo in American society. Why should one have to be concerned with it? Monocultural people in the mainstream are not; or at least, on the surface, they seem to be very comfortable. The questions of ethnicity that are so vexing to some members of minority groups are not a concern to monocultural mainstream people. Perhaps, as a defense mechanism, mestizos may even choose to remain anchored in one single facet of their identity while other facets are ignored.

For instance, there was a time during my high school years when I thought that to be truly Mexicano you had to speak fluent Spanish. However, I did not realize this was only a rationalization on my part because my English was deficient and I spoke it with an accent. So I tended to look down upon those who were English-dominant, thinking that their lack of Spanish made them too Anglicized and, therefore, *vendidos*—that is, sellouts. But as I developed my proficiency in English, my views began to change. Also, at one time, I felt strongly that true Chicanismo could be found only close to the U.S.-Mexico border, where one's cultural and linguistic roots were strong and could be preserved. Then, after I moved from Texas and spent seven years in the Midwest, I found that Chicanos there, although different from us *Tejanos* in some ways, could be just as genuine as those from the Rio Grande Valley or the Winter Garden district.

For about three decades I had been struggling with these issues, endeavoring to make sense out of this thing we call identity, going at times from bewilderment and discouragement to enlightenment and exhilaration. After so much reflection and growth I had made peace with both sides of my past, and I felt an unusual sense of harmony. I have noticed that for some people identity is not much more than a label. They refer to it as if it were some kind of cosmetic that one can either wear or do without. But identity is central to our human condition, and whether we realize it or not it cuts deeply into our psyche. For me, cultural identity is inextricably fused to the quest for meaning or existential identity. The manifestations of significant human experiences are always connected to specific historical and cultural contexts, and, invariably, myth is at the center of it all. When Moses felt called to lead the Israelites out of Egypt, he did so in a given moment in history, and the ethos of the Israelites during the Exodus was expressed through their unique culture. In the same way, when the ancient inhabitants of Aztlán migrated to Anáhuac, they did so during a particular period in their history, and their experience was expressed in accordance with the tenets of their culture. But the exodus experience was essentially similar in both cases. There are a limited number of human emotions and actions, but they are expressed in different ways depending on one's culture, historical circumstances, and peculiar vision of the world. The experience of internal exile and return for a Navajo citizen of the United States may be different on the surface from the experience of a Salvadoran peasant who is uprooted from his homeland for whatever reason and, after a period of painful exile, returns. But the feeling of alienation, then the subsequent restoration of emotional health, is essentially the same in both cases.

Several centuries before the existentialist philosophers came onto the scene, Nezahualcoyotl, the poet-prince of Texcoco was dealing with the question of existential identity. He said that we appear on this earth only for a brief moment, during which we must find the meaning of our pain. In the twentieth century, José Ortega y Gasset, the Spanish philosopher, echoes those words when he affirms that the quest for meaning is arduous but necessary. We did not ask to be brought into this world, he says, but since we are already here, we must assume the responsibility of knowing who we are and defining our purpose on earth. Ortega y Gasset was referring to the most essential life project, which every human person needs, regardless of ethnic background, in order to make sense of his or her earthly existence. Existential identity and ethnic identity are two sides of the same thing.

For many years I carried in my wallet a picture of my parents. In the midst of my struggle to define myself I would often look at the picture, and I would think of them with immense gratitude and affection. It was my way of communing with them when I could not be at their side or hear their voices on the phone. One time, I noticed something I had not noticed before. My mother's facial features were clearly indigenous, and my father's were those of a Spaniard. Then, I re-created a mental picture of my relatives on both sides of the family. And, sure enough, those on my mother's side were more indigenous, and those on my father's side were more European, although both were mestizos. That discovery helped me later on to make other discoveries about my indigenous past and my Spanish past. When I visited Spain for the first time many years ago, in the different towns and villages of Castilla, Extremadura, and Andalucía I could see images of my relatives on my father's side: my grandparents, my uncles, my aunt Aurora. And although Spaniards were strangers to me, and I was a stranger to them, I saw part of me in their eyes and in their smiles. Their spirit of hospitality moved me very deeply. Our common language made it easier for us to identify with one another, but there was something beyond language that impressed me, perhaps a certain way of being that was part of my own experience.

In Mexico, oftentimes one cannot distinguish an Indian from a mestizo by their physical features, although one notices at once that indigenous people are at the bottom of the social pyramid. They have a strong sense of identity, but they do not consider themselves Mexicans. It is a dilemma. On the one hand, they look to the government for support. On the other, they resist integration into what the government calls "national development" because this would mean the erosion of their culture. Thus, feelings of Mexican nationalism are rather foreign to them. They are Huicholes, Yaquis, Mixes, Tarascos, Mazatecs, Tarahumaras, but not Mexicans. Their experience with the federal government has been a bitter one. They have endured so much encroachment into their communities that they have become naturally suspicious of outsiders.

I shall never forget the time an anthropologist friend of mine and I traveled to Mexico City in the early eighties to visit the Office of Indigenous Education. We were attempting to initiate an agreement between that agency and the University of Northern Colorado. Our plan was to send some of our students to study the native cultures of Mexico and to have indigenous students come and earn degrees in education at our institution. The Office of Indigenous Education asked one of its employees, a native from the state of Oaxaca, to be our guide on a tour of two "centers for social integration" (as the Mexican government calls them), located in the states of Querétaro and Hidalgo. These centers were designed to train young men and women from different indigenous communities in Mexico to become primary school teachers. Then they would send them back to their communities equipped with the tools to teach children in transitional bilingual programs. The visit to those two sites gave me a deeper insight into the other side of my heritage. Again, some of the people I came in contact with bore an amazing physical resemblance to certain members on my mother's side of the family, especially my uncle Carlos, dark, lean, and serious, with a wry sense of humor, and my aunts Irene and Carmela, strong in body and character, who always wore their long, black hair in braids. In them I found expressions of patience, resignation, and quiet suffering that I had seen so many times in my family, especially in my mother.

At one of the sites, I felt like an intruder when our guide interrupted a meeting of superintendents from different indigenous communities. He introduced my colleague and me to the group and added that we were there to try to establish an exchange program which would benefit their young people. One of the superintendents, an elderly person, stood up and said, in a gentle but firm manner, "If we negotiate such a program we must do it in the spirit of mutual respect, because we do not appreciate anthropologists coming into our communities, showing little or no respect for our people, and then leaving to publish their dissertations about our way of life." I explained that we were well acquainted with the history of their struggle to preserve their way of life in the midst of callousness and injustice. I told them that I had gone through a similar struggle within my community in the United States and that I was very sensitive to their needs because of my own experience. I assured them that we would instruct our students on the right type of conduct within their communities, that they would be there to learn under the instruction and supervision of indigenous teachers.

A substantial part of my identity has been conditioned by my experience crossing borders from the very beginning of my life, physical, social, cultural and spiritual borders. I was born in a rural community just a few miles from the border on the Mexican side in the state of Coahuila. This is a community with a strong sense of tradition. I spent part of my childhood there, then my parents moved about twenty-five miles from my place of birth to the border city of Piedras Negras, across from Eagle Pass, Texas. There, I attended school through the fourth grade. The teachers instilled in me a strong pride in being Mexicano, meaning mestizo. As children, we studied history at a very superficial level, of course. It was enough to forge a feeling of patriotism as we learned about our forefathers: Cuauhtémoc, Hidalgo, Morelos, Juárez, and Zapata, among others. Through skits we reenacted the Spanish conquest of the Aztec empire, and we performed pre-Colombian ritual dances; but I never saw a real Spaniard or an Indian until some years later.

In 1953, my parents obtained residence in the United States. So we entered this country through Eagle Pass and established our permanent home in Crystal City, only about forty-three miles from the Rio Grande, right in the heart of the Winter Garden district. Our new home was less than seventy-five miles from my birthplace. The landscape was almost identical on both sides of the border; the Mexicanos looked no different on either side. Yet it was an entirely different world because of the presence of the Texas Anglo culture. Since my parents had not had an education beyond the third grade, we had to join the migrant stream, but our home base was Crystal City, a small town of about 10,000 inhabitants, whose population in the fifties and sixties was about 85 percent Mexicano and almost 15 percent Anglo. The rest, less than 1 percent, was black. Today, the town's population is about 98 percent Mexicano. In those days, the only other person of a different background was an Arab who lived by himself in an old shack behind a packing shed, next to one of the barrios. This man became everyone's neighbor because he spent his life walking up and down the streets of every barrio praying in a strange tongue and reciting the Lord's Prayer in Spanish. Anytime someone met him in the street, he would offer a blessing. With his long graying beard, shepherd's staff, and worn-out sandals he had the aura of an Old Testament prophet. Everyone was friendly to *el Arabe,* but one day he disappeared, and no one heard from him again.

Since childhood an important part of my identity has always been associated with language, both standard Spanish and Tex-Mex. Tex-Mex is a hybrid form of Spanish that contains multiple Anglicisms, typical Mexican idioms, archaisms from sixteenth-century Spain which remained in the Southwest and are still very much in use, neologisms born in the barrios of the Southwest, and other modalities that are peculiar to our regional variety of Spanish. Language, especially the language of the people, not the language of academicians, adds spice and flavor to one's culture. It is a particular flavor that cannot be obtained through any other cultural element. Well, in school, speaking Spanish was against the rules, except in Spanish classes. It was all right to discuss Spanish literature and other topics of interest in our native tongue, as long as it was done in class. If such discussions continued in the hallway or out in the playground we were in violation of the rules, and if we were caught, the physical punishment was very severe. These rules did not make any sense to us, and we rebelled against them through the affirmation of our language identity, occasionally getting caught and suffering the consequences.

But language prejudice on the part of Anglo teachers and administrators was not all we had to endure. They denigrated almost anything that was Mexican, except food. At first, I was tormented with inner conflicts because, back in Mexico, I had been instilled with so much pride in being Mexicano that I was convinced, without doubt, of the greatness and beauty of my heritage. But the problem was that, in Crystal City, I did not have a voice; I couldn't articulate any kind of defense of my culture. I did not have the words to explain about Mexico's great artistic traditions, its music and literature, the diversity of its people. My mute pride was expressed at times through blind rage and, on rare occasions, fist fights when Anglo kids made disparaging remarks about my background. Many other Mexicanos went through the same experience. Publicly in school, we were Mexican-Americans, although behind closed doors we were referred to as *Meskins* or *greasers*. Outside of school we thought of ourselves as Mexicanos. That was our identity. The word Chicano had not been reintroduced yet into the Spanish vocabulary of the Southwest. It had been in use back in the early part of the century to refer to Mexican *campesinos* who came to the United States to work on the railroad or in agricultural industries.

In Crystal City, most of us understood that we could not be anything other than Mexicanos, so, instead of trying to conform and assimilate, we affirmed our identity with greater passion. True, the pressure was too strong, and there were moments of doubt, transitory feelings of inferiority, and even attitudes of self-denigration. But we were able to overcome all of that because of family and community support. There were a few Mexicanos, mostly members of the middle class, who could not identify with Mexican culture because it was offensive to the Anglo minority in town. They felt ashamed of their background. Since they could not endure the stigma of being Mexicanos, they became "Latin Americans" and chose the path of assimilation, a high price to pay for the sake of acceptance by the Anglo community. The identification with Latin Americans implied, in a very subtle way, that their immediate ancestors were perhaps from Argentina, Chile, Uruguay, or Costa Rica, those Latin American countries that had a large white population, although, God forbid, not from Ecuador, Bolivia, Peru, or Haiti. The "Latin Americans" amongst us did all they could to please the Anglo by displaying ostentatiously the "proper behavior." They never spoke Spanish. They only went to see American movies at the Guild Theater, never did they set foot in the Teatro Luna or Teatro Alameda, the barrio theaters which showed Mexican movies, exclusively. They ate more white bread with peanut butter and jelly than rice, pinto beans, and tortillas. If, at times, their families found themselves in the dire necessity of traveling to the midwestern states as migrant workers, they returned home saying that they had been on vacation in Michigan, Wisconsin, or Minnesota. Interesting irony: all their zeal was to no avail. Still, they were not accepted as equals by the Anglo community. There was a certain mold into which they could not fit; although one could understand discrimination in the case of those with bronze skins and indigenous features, what about those with light complexions? As far as the Anglo community was concerned, no matter how they looked or what they did to earn respect, they were still "dirty Meskins." Years later, with the consciousness engendered by the Chicano Movement, the Mexicano majority in town took control of the city government and the school board. Painful changes began to take place, but from the beginning the "Latin Americans" were opposed to the Mexicano assumption of power. That's when the Mexicanos started calling them "Cocos" (coconuts), because they were "brown on the outside and white in the inside."

During all these years in Crystal City the word "identity" was not part of our vocabulary; yet there was no confusion in terms of who we were. All we knew was that the boundaries were drawn very clearly by the Anglo power brokers and that we were not a part of their world. Also, we were certain that our culture was too firmly rooted in a common historical experience to be eradicated by prejudice, and we felt a certain amount of pride in being able to affirm who we were without fear of reprisals. Mexicano culture was alive and well in a person's life from the cradle to the grave, and it was evidenced in the externals: baptisms, first communions, confirmations, *quinceañeras,* weddings, funerals, celebrations of Mexican holidays, Tex-Mex food and music. But also, there was a deeper stratum of culture somewhat difficult to grasp or define. It was manifested in a system of signs and symbols, in the intricacies of a vibrant dialect, in our expressions of pain and joy, in an ancestral resiliency in the face of suffering, in our conception of time and death, in the way we dealt with hopes and fears. In sum, it was seen in our collective vision of the world. This type of community experience is what Spanish writer Miguel de Unamuno referred to as *intrahistory.*

If culturally we were full participants in the life of our community, politically we were on the sidelines observing the action and being affected by it. We lacked two very important qualities: collective awareness and savvy. We were too complacent. Although we did not want to admit it, deep down we felt that it was perhaps inevitable for the Anglos to rule even though they constituted the numerical minority. The truth of the matter was that we did not have our act together. Finally, in 1963, in a propitious moment, an awareness began to grow in the people and it spread like wildfire. Mexicano political activism eventually led to a power shift, but the community went through an unutterable ordeal for several years. The Anglo community tolerated our culture the way one tolerates pesky mosquitos. You can resist them up to a certain point, but you know you can never get rid of them. However, what they could never tolerate was our becoming politically active in order to gain power. Savvy came after many trials and errors and, with it, some political maturity. But if there is one lesson to be learned from the experience, it is that democracy does not come by fantasizing about it. People have to pay a price to make it happen. And for Chicanos and other minority groups within the United States, political empowerment has a marvelous effect on the development of a strong sense of identity because the community's goals are easier to reach.

For some Chicanos, the higher they move up the educational ladder, the more alienated they feel from the ways of their parents and their community. For me, the opposite was true. As I gained more formal knowledge, and as I acquired more college degrees, I drew closer to my parents and my community. At times, during my childhood and teenage years I lamented selfishly my parents' lack of formal education because they were not able to represent me at certain functions where I needed their support, especially those in which fluency in English was needed. I wanted them to have a voice that others outside our community would respect, but they didn't have one. However, years later, I understood so clearly the unspeakable sacrifice they had to endure so that I could enjoy the opportunities that they didn't have. I also understood the basic difference between *education* and *educación*—that is, the Anglo and the Mexicano conceptions of what it means to be educated. For the Anglo, *education* means, above all, formal training in an academic institution. For the Mexicano, *educación* is primarily moral, and the other dimension, the academic, comes later. Thus, a person may have earned a Ph.D. from a reputable institution, but if that person's moral behavior is deleterious to others, then that person is *mal educado,* not well educated. During my college years, as I analyzed the moral teachings my parents provided for my two sisters and me, I no longer saw them as uneducated farmworkers but as persons of profound wisdom and sanity.

During my college years I began to look at the question of ethnic identity in a more logical and dispassionate manner. It was then that I made a disturbing discovery, which at first I refused to face: within certain social contexts, away from my community, where I was one of very few Chicanos, I was beginning to think and act like an Anglo. My first reaction was one of horror. Then guilt. Then denial. I didn't relish the thought of viewing myself as a traitor, but it was inevitable. I have to say, however, that, in my travels outside the state as a migrant worker, I rejoiced upon discovering that Anglos in the Midwest were very different from Texas Anglos. After I wrestled with the problem of my Anglo-like behavior for a while, I came to the conclusion that adopting Anglo ways was merely the natural outcome of a process of acculturation which I had been undergoing for years. That in itself, I thought, was not a disadvantage but an advantage because now I was able to understand so many things about the Anglo world and the mainstream culture that I had ignored before. Moreover, I began to realize that there is beauty and greatness in the Anglo-Saxon culture, and I wanted to partake of it. Besides, success within the mainstream culture implies a high degree of acculturation.

The danger resided in drifting too far to the other side, to the point of no return, becoming assimilated—that is, absorbed completely by mainstream society. When that happens, the first thing to go is one's native language, then one's sensitivity to certain cultural patterns. At that point, a type of cultural inertia sets in, and by the time one realizes it, the loss is irreparable. I had seen that happen to many Chicanos, and I made one of the most important commitments in my life: it was not going to happen to me. So I decided that acculturation into American society was not only necessary but desirable; but I was going to do it on my own terms.

So I set as one of my goals in life to work hard to attain the highest levels of bilinguality and biculturality. I saw that as the best of the four options. The other three: remaining partially bilingual with Spanish dominance, remaining partially bilingual with English dominance, or eventually becoming monolingual in English. Bilinguality became an important facet of the identity that I was now constantly working out. Some time ago, during a poetry reading, I heard Czeslaw Milosz, the great Polish Nobel laureate who had spent about thirty years in the United States, give an interesting testimony. He said that to express himself in his native language was to speak with the voice of the soul, and that part of himself he could never surrender. This is precisely the way I've always felt.

For me, a vital facet of human identity also involves a real experience with the realm of the sacred, which is linked to the existential search for meaning mentioned earlier. The fundamental assumption is that part of our reality lies beyond the material and the sensory, and that our final destiny belongs in that other realm, where life originates. That other realm is inscrutable because science and reason are not the right tools to explain it. To comprehend the supernatural we need to operate in faith. For the sake of clarity let's simply call that other realm God. To this day what St. Augustine said many centuries ago still makes a lot of sense to those who take this dimension of identity seriously: "We were created by God, and our souls are restless until they rest in God." What that suggests is that the way we relate to the sacred realm will determine to an extent how we express our identity during our earthly existence. And identity always involves "the other." Thus, the vertical dimension and the horizontal dimension of faith are inseparable. Jesus explained it in terms of a relationship to God and an obligation to neighbor based on love. The ancient Mayans had a similar belief: "You are my other self, I see myself in you." This leads to the inescapable conclusion that my conduct requires respect and consideration for "the other." It is a question of empathy. And who is "the other"? Any human being on the face of the earth regardless of gender, race, color, creed, place of origin, or social condition. For me, does "the other" include the Anglo? Yes, but I must find a way to let him know (if he is not already aware) that we are equal in the sight of God and that neither one of us is going to disappear suddenly from the face of the earth. Therefore, we must seek to identify those things, tangible and intangible, that unite us as human beings. At the same time we must look at our differences and learn to live with them.

Not until my early twenties was I able to understand the significance of these principles, although my parents taught them to my sisters and me in a very rudimentary manner as we were growing up: sometimes by example, but mostly by drilling them daily into our conscious and subconscious to the point of fatigue and irritation. My parents never had the sophistication of educated folks in matters of the faith. They only knew that the Judeo-Christian heritage into which they were born was good. They went to church only on special days during the year because my father always harbored a suspicion toward institutionalized religion, but their devotion to the faith was genuine, and they made sure we got the basic teachings.

It was in my early twenties that I had what I would call a conversion experience, a spiritual transformation that changed my life and embarked me on an adventure that continues to this day. Socially and intellectually, I thought I had not done too badly up to that point; but spiritually I was an infant. This conversion happened in the mid-sixties, during a time of social turmoil. I was beginning to develop my critical-thinking skills, trying very hard to assess issues relative to the impact of the Vietnam war on our society. As both an observer and a participant, I was trying to assess the meaning of the Civil Rights Movement and the importance of ethnic identity in my life and the life of my community. I was searching for my role as a citizen. I was trying to figure out what aspects of the Chicano Movement I could identify with and what was merely superficial glorification of regressive elements within our culture. (Since cultures are forged by humans, they all contain regressive elements, which we must try to outgrow). I had to filter a lot of the information in order to try to determine for myself what demands for meaningful social change were legitimate and what messages were based merely on hatred and bitterness toward the Anglo but couched in the rhetoric of social progress. In those days it was easy to blame the Anglo for all our misfortunes, perhaps because there was so much resistance to change and we had acquired an audacity that we did not have before. Yet, at times, it was not easy to see that much of the anger was misdirected. Fairly and unfairly, Chicanos and other minorities were blaming Anglos, and the white, middle-class hippies and other youths on the radical left were directing their attacks against "the establishment." There were the legitimate demands for social justice, and there was the rhetoric of hate and anarchy, but, in spite of all the social confusion, certain important truths about ourselves were revealed, and we are better off for it today.

In retrospect, I realize how vital a role faith played in my search for identity. It helped me to put things in their proper perspective; although at certain moments I felt conflicts between faith and reason, in the end, things worked out well. Faith taught me to peer beyond the multiple mirages to gain a deeper understanding of reality. I struggled to develop self-discipline in the things of the spirit; and I feel I gained a modicum of clarity in seeing how, in times of social dissolution, certain human ideals are betrayed because of our stubbornness and prejudice, and how we are always in danger of regressing to a more primitive stage of human behavior if we lose sight of our commitment to and consideration for one another. I noticed with disappointment how we allowed seemingly progressive ideologies to become dogmas, or how we held on to philosophies of liberation even after these had lost their momentary relevance and turned into oppressive myths. Through the exercise of faith coupled with reason I gained a sense of balance. I developed the desire to work with people of other backgrounds to gain more knowledge about them and learn how they struggle to construct their identities. I began to believe very strongly that relative harmony can be achieved within a diverse society if we are willing to respect differences and work toward common goals. Of course, it is easy to verbalize that vision, but it takes a great deal of pain to make it a reality. Still, we should not view it as a quixotic adventure but as a necessary endeavor.

The question of ethnic identity today is at the center of the controversy over cultural pluralism in this country. No matter what side we take in this polemics there is an indisputable truth: the United States is a culturally diverse society, and it isn't going to change soon. The old notion of the melting pot was valid only for certain groups, especially those that came from Northern Europe. It was easy for Swedes, Norwegians, Germans, and others to blend into the mainstream; and that was good. They worked out their own identity here in accordance with their own collective experience. However, for people of color the reality was segregation. Even if they tried to assimilate, they were not allowed to. Now, these groups feel just as American as everyone else, and they are, but they refuse to abandon the other identity, regardless of the price they have to pay. To them, the affirmation of ethnic identity is an inalienable right, and they are certain they can make a contribution to American society.

In spite of our differences, we must look for that essential similarity in all of us, that which makes us human. Today, the mainstream culture and all the ethnic cultures within our country are being afflicted by what Aleksandr Solzhenitsyn called "the crisis of the spirit." We are facing enormous challenges. Individuals are suffering from alienation and despair, families are fragmented, children's minds are being polluted with a daily dose of violence and pornography through the media, countless women are being scarred by abuse and mutilation at the hands of violent men, racial tension continues unabated. There is general moral decadence in our society. In his commencement address at Harvard University in 1995, Václav Havel, president of the Czech Republic and one of the most important writers in Europe, alluded to the thin veneer of our civilization, pointing to the lack of spirituality as the root of our dilemma. His vision is one which calls for a spiritual politics and personal responsibility. He says: "We must recollect our original spiritual and moral substance, which grew out of the same essential experience of humanity. I believe that this is the only way to achieve a genuine renewal of our sense of responsibility for ourselves and for the world. And at the same time, it is the only way to achieve a deeper understanding among cultures that will enable them to work together in a truly ecumenical way to create a new order for the world" (*Harvard Magazine*, July-August 1995).

To paraphrase Charles Dickens: we are living in the worst of times and in the best of times. Although the challenges that confront us are discouraging at times, it is good to remind ourselves that everywhere people of all colors, in all walks of life, are putting aside differences and working hard to forge a better society. The task of human civilization continues. Perhaps we will never be able to explain why our blood blended the way it did or why our particular culture developed the way it did, but there is a part of us that will always be identified with our origins. At the same time, there's an intuition that tells us that we are all one on this planet and that we must transcend our particular circumstances to join others in a common cause. The forces of sickness and destruction are powerful. The discordant voices of extremism are distracting. But if we are to overcome, the voices of reason and sanity will have to multiply day by day and sound loud and clear throughout the land.

Knots

Carol Kalafatic

Soon after attending the opening of the National Museum of the American Indian, two friends and I returned to walk through it and look more carefully. I couldn't sleep that night, so I wrote to one of them:

11/28/94 and the museum

DEAR PAT,

I rarely get headaches. The one that began when the three of us split up after lunch today is probably the fourth I've had all year, but it's gotten strong enough that after buying a can of ground tomatoes, I went back into Sloan's to buy a six-pack.

I rarely drink, . . . [b]ut after today, the temptation to make my brain float is almost as strong as my urge to write this letter. Almost.

I would always write letters—especially when I was in college. After years as a teenager who stuttered the pronouns "I" and "you," geekdom and writing (of all kinds) were my refuge and recovery. I'd write to people who lived on campus with me or, later, lived in the same town. After grad school, I left upstate New York for the last place I wanted to live: here. Work, getting married and unmarried, and (most draining of all) finding my place within a community interrupted the letters.

Do you remember talking about that elusive "community" today on the bus . . . ? When identity curls in on itself, challenging, reaffirming, and negating us sometimes all in the same day, it seems hard to imagine we'd have the heart left to *be* a community. My sister challenged me *and* my parents once after reading "(Quechua/Spanish/Yugoslavian)" next to my name in an exhibition catalogue. "Why did you say that? How do you know we're Quechua? . . ." It went on for a couple of days, until I realized that I had to resort to the last thing I wanted to use to "prove" the *only* part of our identity that my sister felt needed proving: "The next time you chew gum, press it against the back of your front teeth. . . ."

Your essay and certain things we talked about . . . reminded me of the internal and external contortions we perform in defense against the serial, if not multiple, displacements. All the friends I've started writing to again are seasoned and talented contortionists. Our letters have been a refuge and a way to recover community. . . . The friends I've made over the past year, and the trips I took back home in January and September, have shown me that, as you say, this "peculiar, fraught tie, this mixed blood tie . . . is also a hiding place—a place where we belong . . . with each other." The things that give us headaches (and worse) *could* cut us off from each other, but the talking circle and other times we get together as a group—or in any combination—make the knife duller each time. And that's no red-road romanticism; if it were, I'd be finishing a six-pack instead of a letter.

Tu hermana.

This is not an autobiography. At thirty-four, I'm just now approaching the ability to look back at things and know what I'm seeing. Besides, my family hasn't told all the stories that would make my autobiography possible. But I'll offer my reading of the mestizo threads I juggle and of the resulting tangles and knots, the *quipus* that signify the displacements I'm learning to accept as legacy.[1] They mark the ironies and ambiguities of qualified inclusion that I share with most mixed bloods. When we decode these experiences by reading them with a sincere eye, we can rename them and, in turn, name ourselves, emerging—as complex as we need to be—from behind the masks of projected identities. We can keep Disney, the merchandisers, and the mythmongers at bay and, maybe more important, keep our own princess/warrior delusions in check.

I watched her make her way toward me through the noise of my weed-whacker. I didn't turn it off because an entire summer of groundskeeping in the Hamptons had made the pull-starter really grouchy.

She leaned on her cane every two or three steps while her driver sat in the long, black car on the shoulder, idling for the air conditioning. I didn't understand why *he* wasn't getting out to ask for directions.

My overall bib and straps were hanging down, and I had a muscle shirt on. My hair was braided so that I could work. I don't remember what she wore, but her face was covered with downy, platinum hairs, and she gave off that powdered lavender smell. "May I touch your arm? It looks like copper!" was all she said. Sixteen years ago, "I guess so" was all I could answer.

Thousands of centuries later the geological volcano became a social volcano when, like a great magnet, tin pulled men to the mountain.[2]

Grandpa George was one of several hundred thousand job-hungry Croatians to emigrate overseas in the years before World War I; under Austria-Hungary's thumb few in Croatia but educated Germans and Hungarians could find work. It was 1904 and he was eighteen when he and an uncle left Rijeka, on the Adriatic Sea, for the high desert of "alto Peru"—another name for Bolivia. They worked at the Catavi mine and for the railroads, laying tracks between Oruro and Cochabamba to connect the mining region in the southwest with the central farming valley.

Five years earlier Bolivia's Liberals had armed the Indian masses to help overthrow a Conservative government, only to disarm the Indians and execute their leaders after the coup. The Liberal government then subsidized mining and railroads, and destroyed Indian communities to expand the non-Indian hacienda system. The white oligarchy, still rigging presidential elections, created what's known as the *rosca:* government by university-trained politicians who catered to the needs of the wealthiest tin barons. In 1900, the boom in tin mining began as the elite continued its embrace of social Darwinism to defend Bolivia's social-caste system (as most do today).

The mainly Indian mine workers and their families—during massive strikes for reasonable wages and union recognition—would be massacred throughout the century. At the Catavi mine in 1967, hundreds were shot around the time of their most important annual ceremony, honoring the sun.

No one seems to have a photo of Grandma Isabel. She was from Tacopaya, in northern Potosí between the desert and the central Andean valley. She and Grandpa George spoke Spanish because he didn't know Quechua. They started a family in Catavi and then settled in Uyuni. She left the family soon after giving birth to Dad, the last child of five boys and three girls. I've only mentioned her name once in front of my father. And everyone back home either doesn't like to talk about her (and won't) or doesn't remember. But everyone remembers Grandpa George's temper. My cousin Giancarla and I visited our *abuelitos* at the crypt they now share and wondered how they were getting along.

My fair-skinned aunts look like my grandfather; I see them in the *New York Times* photos of Bosnians who mourn entire families, entire legacies. Blue eyes, green eyes. Grandma Isabel gave her sons different shades of brown and shiny black.

I'd never pass for white by physical markers. In the winter the guesses are "Polynesian," "Japanese," "Chinese," and sometimes "Korean." (Filipino nurses have expected my father to answer in their native language.) In the summer the "American Indian" guesses outnumber the "Hawaiian" or "Greenland Native" ones. But my birth certificate says *"raza: blanca ."* The clinic where I was born filled in the blank, and my mother agreed. In Bolivia it's how you live that determines your race label, your place within the national culture. Since the seventeenth century, when many rural full bloods moving to the cities adopted Spanish cultural norms and were labeled "cholos," race labels came to signify social-caste slots rather than blood. When combined with nineteenth-century Liberalism, the system became a means by which mixed bloods could "ascend" to whiteness, and Bolivia—while reveling in its independence from Spain—could "fulfill" its European aspirations. Your distance from indigenous culture determines how you live. And, in general, any amount of European blood can provide that desired distance.

A (visibly) Lakota friend and I once sat on my front stoop in this mostly white New York neighborhood. We asked a woman hanging a block-party flyer if there would be space for another art booth at the party. "Oh, but you have to *live* here to participate," she sniffed.

My dad's grade school friends teased him because he had light brown hair; they called him "gringo *mata wasa*" after the fair-colored horses who, lacking pigment, developed sun scabs on their backs (he had light brown hair, but no scabs). He and his high school friends belonged to "the Cemetery Gang." They'd meet among the headstones in Quillacollo and run around, pretending to be on secret missions. Dad's alias was "Pushkin." A friend filming her documentary on mixed-blood Afro-Russian life in Moscow taught me what most Russians (and others) consider a minor detail: Pushkin's great-grandfather was African.

The cold war inspired dad and his friends to play out imaginary Soviet intrigues, but it was nationally ingrained denial that veered me toward the history of struggle in Northern Ireland and South Africa rather than in Bolivia. As an undergraduate I devoured books about the IRA, recited Seamus Heaney, and played the flute along with my favorite Chieftains songs. I did day care at a women's shelter, was active in the nuclear-freeze movement, and co-founded an anti-apartheid/pro-divestment group. When I joined the push to get the United States out of El Salvador, at least I was getting warmer. The earlier years of activism seem scattered, but they were contortions that I understand now; I know the forces that created the knots.

When Grandpa George left his job with the railroad, he moved his family from Uyuni to Quillacollo in the central valley. He sold candy and dry goods from a little stand attached to the house. Bubblegum, *refrescos*, rice, flour, matches. He was kind to me and used to give me bubblegum even when I didn't want it. The more I'd resist, the louder he'd say, *"Toma!"* His house was tidy and felt shady and cool after running around the sunflowers and the *chirimuya* trees outside. Dad's oldest sister, Elena, kept chickens. Mom remembers visiting when Aunt Elena baked bread in the adobe oven out by the well. She's seventy-eight now and still single, but the bitterness left her over the years and let her sweet side in.

Dad came to New York just before I was born. He remembers trying to order breakfast from a hospital cafeteria worker who refused to overlook his accent. "I said 'PINE-a-pull juice'!" He told me that he'd wanted to yell, "I'm more American than you'll *ever* be!"—calling on his roots in this continent. Three years later, Mom and I left Quillacollo to be with him. We watched TV while he practiced tying sutures on a footrest we had in the apartment.

Aunt Elena came later to live with us and help look after my younger sister and brother. She was always praying. That was the year after I ran away from home for twenty-four hours because I didn't want to leave public school for St. Dominic's.

The racial mix of our first New York neighborhood and my first public school was just enough for me to sense ties with certain people: Nancy Lopez, Sui-Ling Ho, Yuki, and Yasu. But I was shy and withdrawn and could neither articulate my alternating alienation and belonging nor resist the race reality/white fantasy. I looked to the white kids for behavioral cues—how to act, speak, and what to want. The year Mom took me to the World's Fair in Flushing, New York, I asked her for a black little brother or sister. "It's a small world after all," sang the multihued, mechanical dolls in their native languages as we snapped photos of them from our tour boats.

Race issues intensified when we moved from the apartment building in Queens to a house in a small town where tennis-and-boating replaced ring-and-run. My father worked hard, and we lived a privileged life, in the material sense. Most of the town's kids were white, and some welcomed us by yelling, "You spic, go home!" or "You chink, go home!" or—in creative response to my sister's full lips—"Nigger-chink!" Not to be outdone by the nuns when it came to sadism, my sister's classmates threw her in a Dumpster in the school parking lot (the nuns blamed *her*). "Kids are like that," we'd tell each other, looking back. Then we remembered what their parents were like.

My brother was spared Catholic school and had it easier by the late 1970s; in first grade he was respected as the teacher-designated translator for his Latino classmates. My sister grew up to have mostly nonwhite, non-American friends.

Grandpa George farmed a little *terreno*, less than one acre, in Vinto. Peach trees and apple trees. Mom says Dad used to go there sometimes just to sleep outdoors, *bajo las estrellas*, because he missed the Uyuni stars. "There were so many and they were so big, it felt like they were *right there*." He said Uyuni made him feel like he was on the moon. It's small and isolated, at the edge of a huge salt flat (when I stood at the center of the flat, everything from my feet to the horizon was salt). It's in the southwest, in a desert 12,000 feet above sea level and bitter cold in the winter, windy all the time. He loves the moon. He almost drives right off the road watching it when it's big and orange. He was ten years old when they left Uyuni. Butch Cassidy and the Sundance Kid are supposed to be buried somewhere nearby.

Mom doesn't remember there being many westerns at the movie theater in Quillacollo. It was the gangster films and the romances that were popular. Her favorites were Gregory Peck and Esther Williams (Mom was a national swimming champion). She has powerful hands from heavy gardening and ceramics, and wields them in bulky furniture repair projects or delicate sewing projects.

Grandma Candelaria grew up playing the piano in the mestizo enclave of Totora. I miss her and remember her as a strong, tiny woman pulling runaway bulls back into the corral and letting me watch her kill chickens. She smelled like sweet tea and steamed feathers. Last year was the last time I walked with her. She slightly loosened her arthritic grip on my hand and stopped to examine my fingers, still entwined in hers. "*Wa!* I didn't know your fingers were so long! Good for punching!" she said, throwing our joined fists straight out in front of us. Aunt Carmen told me

Grandma Cande used to sew bras for the girls from their recycled clothes and once kept Grandpa's admirers at bay with a hammer. Aunt Carmen kept a magazine photo of Sammy Davis, Jr., and his pompadour tacked up over her bed. He was the first black man she'd seen, even in print. She loved his singing and couldn't get over his glass eye.

Until I was almost two years old Mom would bind me from the waist down in a *chumpi*, or winding cloth; around the 1950s Quechuas modified the whole-body wrapping custom that keeps infants warm at night and starts their legs growing straight. I walk with straight legs, mostly back and forth between contradictory understandings of who I am, sometimes inhabiting them simultaneously. Being conscious of the disparate worlds and their respective histories lets me oppose the race denial and understand the years of awkwardness in a belligerently racist society.

In Bolivia—where racism is an even more belligerent social institution (recent bilingual education programs notwithstanding)—the blood subtleties of *mestizaje* define the parameters of my family's place, but they are subtleties we didn't discuss until recently. As a child, I asked about our place in the United States and needed to have our "difference" explained. "We're Bolivian"—a name that negates the indigenous peoples, who are about 70 percent of Bolivia's population, and denies complex ancestries more often than it pays homage to them. As an adult I asked about these ancestries; writing is a way for me to name *all* I carry as a hybrid of opposing bloods, living the junctures within and between genotype and archetype.

In the Andes the meeting place or union of two opposing but complementary forces is a *tinku:* the ritual hand-to-hand rumbles between clan groups of northern Potosí, a cowlick, the confluence of rivers . . .

TD:Grandpa Cecilio became partially deaf in 1932, when something exploded near him during the Chaco War with Paraguay. Before being sent to the front line, he had been posted as a Morse code interpreter.

He called Mom *mi negrita-bola-botón* (she was dark and cute as a child). He called Aunt Carmen *china mat'iñawi*, teasing her about her tight little almond eyes. Calling Aunt Anita *princesa del dólar* is self-explanatory. I'm not sure what he called the rest of the eight kids. He'd get furious when people called him *ex-combatiente,* and, like many other vets, he refused to accept his war pension.

After he got sick, we were careful not to "get him started on the War." Like most people of his generation, he'd rail against the waste of so many lives (over 65,000 out of a population of only two million) in a conflict created by a blatantly corrupt, self-serving Bolivian president. I had to dig to learn that the war's human losses combined with the army's playing out of the national caste system—white officers, mestizo subofficers, and Indian peasant troops as cannon fodder—inspired the first broad-based challenge to the white oligarchy of Bolivia. Twenty years later, an all-out revolution replaced the pockets of stifled resentment ("Those mining barons live like *kings,* with their imported food and whiskey! Cookies in *tins!*" he'd say). But today's Indian vice-presidents can come and go; Bolivia's race-bound class distinctions still limit significant changes in attitude and access to political power.

When I last saw him alive in early 1994, I brought him boxes and boxes of peppermint gum. He had three teeth left, but he loved his Chicklets. "He'll be so happy," Mom said when I showed her the little white squares I was pushing into the soil at his grave that September.

He farmed about thirty hectares of land bought with the money he'd made as a livestock merchant. His parents were landless mestizos and were poor, so as a young boy he ran errands for a wealthy *hacendado* who taught him about the horses he raised. Grandpa Cecilio started his business as a teenager when he borrowed money from the guy to buy a horse he'd seen at another hacienda. He also made money selling wood to the railroad companies in the 1920s.

Mom remembers that on Sunday mornings he'd pay the Quechuas who worked and lived on the farm, and give them sacks of fruit, potatoes, corn, and other vegetables at harvest. Rather than killing him and his family or retaking the land during the Revolution in 1952, most of the workers just left the farm to become active in their communities or in the emerging communal landowner *sindicatos.* Bolivia had just clashed with the United States over low tin prices and had frozen production to force the negotiating terms, throwing itself into an economic depression. Urban whites and mestizos joined rural Indians in an armed, mass uprising to reinstate the legitimately elected MNR (Nationalist Revolutionary Movement). They also retook the once-communal lands which, since the sixteenth century, had been seized to make the 1,000-hectare haciendas. Grandpa Cecilio kept some fruit trees and replaced the work- intensive crops with alfalfa for livestock feed, while the middle-class MNR, forced by the revolt, decreed land redistribution.

I pushed myself to "prove them wrong" and so, as an adult, was able to study at two of "their" elite schools. I was always encouraged to do my best, but at the same time the alienation motivated me to beat "them" in the only contest open to me within the white canon. And it was middle-class privilege borne of *mestizaje* that helped me choose to fight them with my head rather than fight *myself* with a death wish (my struggles are laughable next to those of most Indians and, possibly, most mixed bloods).

Practicing medicine seemed the most direct way to be active in a community. It was also an homage to Dad, and art school was not a popular idea in my family. I wasn't brave enough to be a teacher, lawyer, or advocate of any kind. But I wound up teaching Spanish as a pre-med undergraduate, taking a few law classes, "organizing" on and off campus and—eventually—switching my focus to literature. After a couple of years of freelance writing and journalism I went back to medicine, but as an illustrator. Now I do all three, with detours to teach English to Mexican immigrants and to do my own artwork: mixed-media paintings . . . reading and translating the knots.

In grade school I was awarded, of all things, a Knights of Columbus/ Theodore Roosevelt Citizenship Award (I still don't know why). The more I learned about this country and its politics, the more I hated it. I decided against becoming a citizen in high school and put off naturalization until I was twenty-five—not long after I realized Bolivia is as depraved (if not as powerful) as the United States and that to defuse the assaults of a dominant society it helps to stick around and learn how that society works.

I got annoyed recently at a party, watching a documentary filmed by the European hostesses and listening to their feminist critique of a religious ceremony they'd filmed in Chiapas, Mexico. Who were they to decide what's good for Mayan women? "It's not worth it to get mad," a Cheyenne/Arapaho friend said as we left. "Just do your art." But both are important.

Dad, just out of medical school in the late 1950s, heard that the Bolivian government was looking for doctors to work in La Paz. Thinking it would be a great chance to learn more and to do some good work, he traveled there for an interview. He was about to hand in his application when he was told he'd have to join the MNR party. "What?! I came here to be a doctor, not a politician!" he said, and walked out.

During those years Maryknoll priests set up free health clinics and schools in a few Quechua communities. Despite atheist inclinations (he'd been a reluctant altar boy and was pushed by Aunt Elena to be a priest), Dad was still a volunteer at the clinics. Father Remitz asked him what his dreams were. "I want to leave Bolivia to learn more about medicine. If it could be to the United States, that would be great," he said. At twenty-seven he'd seen almost as many presidential coups as birthdays and was frustrated by the university strikes that sometimes lasted months. Land-locked. The first time he saw the ocean off the coast of Peru, he jumped in with all his clothes on.

"You know, rednecks are really friendly," the (white) CD-ROM entrepreneur assured us. My friend and I had planned to eat alone, as she had just come back from visiting home in Italy and had stories to tell. But we wound up having to share a table with the restaurant owner's friend and his travel stories/theories. "I stopped to take photos of this incredible art-deco, abandoned gas station in Texas, and this guy with a gun rack in his truck stopped to stare at me. Then he said, 'Hi there!'" A voracious talker, eater, and world traveler in search of the ultimate ethno-drug experience, our dinner companion was one among millions who look to indigenous peoples for some kind of New Age validation. To him, Bolivia meant cocaine, psychedelic *ayahuasca* trips, and Dennis Hopper films.[3] And Mexico meant peyote: "My cousin visits the Yaqui all the time! He does peyote with them and wears their traditional clothing. They totally accept him!" he beamed. Do I congratulate him? Teach him the "secret handshake"? Minutes earlier he'd commented on the restaurant's seventy-four-year-old (Latino) photographer. "Ya gotta see his shoes, he's wearing these lace-ups. . . . He's a *character,* he's *great!*" But ours was an interaction mediated by class. Would he have spoken to me without assuming I could relate to pop-cultural appropriations of indianness? Would I understand these appropriations without the escape from peasant class that my *mestizaje* provides? Would I even be eating at this "hip" New York restaurant with the owner's friend?

Business trips introduced me to the *pukakunka*—the rednecks—of the Southwest. A hyperactive cab driver in Reno, Nevada, sought camaraderie from me and my white coworker. He bragged about dumping Paiutes in the middle of the desert still miles from the reservation or refusing to pick them up, "the dirty, lazy, good-for-nothin' drunks!" He looked back at us in the rearview mirror a few times, maybe to see why we weren't chuckling along with him. When he handed me my luggage from the trunk, he took a closer look, cowered a little when he asked, "You Indian?" and stammered an apology. It was a case of mistaken identity. Race and class collided momentarily, one visible and the other inferred. Was it initially unimaginable to him that an Indian could be on a business trip? ("An Indian in a suit? Sitting at a conference table? Nah . . .") Or did he assume that all Indians trade their responsibilities for suits and, in assimilationist complicity, think nothing of laughing at their Paiute cousins?

Trips home introduced me to the *pukakunka* in my family and, by extension, in most mestizo Bolivians. "Ten points for every Indian we hit," my cousin joked as he floored the gas pedal down an unpaved road busy with pedestrians. He was taking me to see the lush beauty of the Chapare in the Amazon foothills that provide most of the country's coca leaf for traditional chewing, teas, and the nontraditional—but economically necessary—cocaine industry. Few in my family *don't* chew. I asked him to please slow down.

My mother and aunts take pride in cooking traditional meals. And they still speak some Quechua. At the table they sometimes talk about Andean herbal remedies, remember stories about old friends and their Quechua nicknames, and tease each other that the soup is too *q'ayma* or the potatoes, too *j'aku.* I know only a few words and phrases; they get jumbled with the Spanish and English I grew up with, the French I studied, and the Swedish I taught myself.

My parents had big parties in the 1970s with new friends who had come north like us. After everyone had eaten, I'd help move furniture and watch the adults dance to *cuecas* and *huayñus*. The next day I'd go to ballet class or piano lessons, sensing but not reading the clash of worlds. Later I became critical of the big parties and what seemed like superficial gestures toward cultural expression. Eventually I understood the weight of colonial history and how self-mangled and self-negating we mixed bloods could be.

Icons offered me escape through simplicity. I hopped from the ballerina icon to Marcia Brady and then to *Mod Squad*'s Peggy Lipton or even to my fourth-grade classmate Laura McCloskey. All blondes. All seeming to take up real space, solid in the world and comfortable in their skin. Peroxide was never an option because I knew that the truest way "in" was through the blood. I aspired without the faintest hope of success; it was pure fantasy.

MISSING MARILYN

damn E train doors
closed on my elbow
this morning
the jerk
coughed his way uptown
leaning
leaning
drunken locomotive
blowing a greasy wind
across the platform
and up the skirts of
women walking above

I wrote "Missing Marilyn" when I was twenty-three and beginning to sort white fantasies from red, learning the necessary roles and dangers of both. White romantic notions of indianness are toxic enough, as I found out from short-lived relationships with an otherwise intelligent myth-monger and a man who was an Indian . . . in another life. The discourse would get stuck between these men and their exotic projections. I was more animal Other to them, a supposed path back to the primitive dark-ness their hearts had lost along the way.

My ex-husband once romanticized my affinity for sunshine as a sign of my Inca ancestry, then added that I loved climbing trees, "just like [my] cousins, the monkeys." Perhaps he was paying homage—Swedish scien-tist that he is—to his predecessor Linnaeus and his taxonomic classifica-tions. On my first visit to Sweden, his neighbor rushed out all excited to shake my hand because he'd heard my blood type is O-positive; he'd only known people with A-type blood. Someone in my ex-husband's family eventually traveled to Bolivia to adopt the Aymara Indian infant they're now raising in Sweden.

Today the "open house" hours at my apartment were 3:30 to 5:00 P.M. This essay was hard enough to write without having to answer questions about closet space at the same time, so I cut the hours down. All of the dozen or so visitors this week have been polite and almost apologetic about having to disrupt my day. Except the one who barked into my intercom. While she climbed the stairs, I prepared myself for an encounter with a quintes-sentially Ugly American WASP. I turned to a blank page in my mind's gringology notebook and scribbled a heading: "Turf Assessment."

I heard the assertive heel-pounding of strictly-business pumps in the hallway, opened my door to a business suit, and looked into the face of an Andean woman whose blue-black hair, hooked nose, and short bowlegs made me almost homesick.

She asked about direct sunlight, air conditioning, and the landlord. She started to open my bedroom closet, then closed it. "Go ahead," I said, shaking my head; she was the only one who hadn't waited for my invitation.

When she came back from checking the bathroom and kitchen, she spat out a perfunctory "thank you." She looked at me and then noticed a small painting of the Andes I keep near my desk. "What nationality are you?" she asked. "I was born in Bolivia," I answered. "Oh," she lit up,

"I'm Peruvian!" "I know," I said to her. "I know," I said to cousins driving too fast or standing in business suits, trembling at closet doors.

NOTES

1. The Inca system of recording stories and historical events, and keeping accounts of all kinds, was based on the *quipu*—knotted strings of different colors hung from a heavy cord.
2. Translated from Roberto Querejazu Calvo, *Llallagua* (Editorial Los Amigos del Libro, La Paz, 1978).
3. A hallucenogenic drink made from various parts of a plant, *ayahuasca* is used by Amazonian shamans to attain visions for the sake of ritual healings.

What Part Moon

Inez Petersen

"What part Indian are you?" asked a woman whose face told me that she should know better than to ask such an ignorant question. It was a going-away party, summertime in a town which prides itself on the progressive, liberal nature of its political stances, and I was saying good-bye to a gathering of coworkers and their attendant family/significant others. We chatted in groups of twos and threes, milling about a backyard luxuriant with grass, trees, and shrubs. We nibbled at hummus, baby-back ribs, *tzatziki;* drank mineral water, deep Barolos, chilled bottles of long-neck beer; saved ourselves for the indulgent chocolate cake, *la maxine,* this woman's husband had baked for the occasion.

Not long before, at my brother's house, another group had gathered and eaten together: crabs and mussels gathered from the bay, assorted potato salads (some from Safeway), chips, and whatever-was-on-sale sodas. Not exactly your most traditional of Native foods. But then, we ourselves were a mixture of nationalities, of tribes and peoples, some urban, some reservation, others just plain rural. Our tribes included Siletz, Warm Spring, Quinault, and Klamath with sprinklings of French, Irish, Scot, Filipino, and mongrel white. That day we celebrated, not my going away, but our being together. No one in this gathering questions me on blood quantum; here I am always "Auntie Nez," hugged, welcomed, teased for the latest dousing of red to my hair.

"You hear 'bout that big rumor going 'round?"

Bristow, my brother's best friend and next-door neighbor, loves to stir up trouble, and he threw the question out, pure bait. His brown eyes crinkle into ready laughter. He measures the next words, spoken by his wife, as if sighting down the barrel of a rifle.

"You mean about Frank?" Christy asks, innocent enough.

My brother loves the attention, but feigns disbelief.

"I got a rumor?"

"Yeah. Seems that you and this woman . . . " Bristow strings innuendo out better than a fly-fisherman's line.

"Hey! This is great! Me and 'this woman?'" Frank lifts his eyebrows, grabs his chest in mock agony.

I nudge my sister-in-law Bonnie, sitting at the kitchen table beading yet another project for an upcoming powwow. Bonnie smiles down at her beadwork, says "Quit it, Frank," waits for the punch line.

Not until too late do I realize the direction of this elaborate setup. My brother turns to me and says, "I was so happy; here I was about to be the center of some hot gossip."

"Turns out, someone saw him kissing a woman at the last powwow," Bristow turns his broad smile on me. "Some redhead."

"Hot gossip all for nothing—it's my sister," Frank mournfully bows over his bowl of steaming mussels.

We laugh and keep eating.

Coloring my hair red is one of a series of mini-defiances I have made in my determination to deflate expectations of what a Native American woman should look like. It is hard-won, this minimal acceptance I have of my own appearance. Amidst the variant color tones of my immediate family, I am light-skinned and hazel-eyed. Of the privileges I experience in my life, "passing" ranks high, but for backward reasons: I am invisible to the dominant culture because they do not wish to see "other." It is supremely convenient for some to see me as white, but this "white-only" filter distorts any true picture.

Of course, I am white too; I would just as soon be dead as to think myself the lie of being only of one or the other. My life experience though comes from being a part of a community of Native American peoples. It is here I draw my truest sense of self. Identification is not so simple as the one-letter signifiers on an old application for school: A for Asian, B for Black, C for Caucasian, H for Hispanic, I for Indian. Where is the "M" for mixed-blood?

What would my own brothers and sisters mark on such a questionnaire? We are from multinational bloodlines: Filipino, Dane, African American, and good ole 'Merican white. Perhaps it is from loving my siblings that I can now rest easy amongst a pan-tribal gathering—especially amongst other Native mixed-bloods.

We are told stories live in the blood, yet my blood is not pure. Does that make the story of my life impure? Does that give full-bloods say-so about if I am Indian enough? They would not question my darker mother or elder brother. How can my mama be Quinault, my brother be Quinault, and I not be Indian enough? Who is the arbiter of my existence, telling where I do and do not belong?

I see my silly sallies at defying expectations. I know my fierce determination may be misinterpreted when reddening my brown hair; for me it is the metaphorical hiss between clenched teeth, "I am no Wannabe." Sometimes a person just does not want to play along with the subtle hints of beaded earrings and chiming in with a well-timed, "A-a-a-y."

Who would wish on themselves the curse of not appearing to belong? I rage at colorists and find myself in their midst. Recently, I hear about a well-known Native American author who questioned the blood-quantum of a woman whose book he had been asked to review; knowing this, I find it difficult to praise his very good writing, perhaps out of fear that he would not find me "Indian enough."

What I do know is that if we divide ourselves, we are doing the work of the dominant culture; there is no need for them to keep us down, for we do it to ourselves. What is true too: if I had no need of this generosity of spirit, to include all of us, the mixed-bloods, the traditionals, the urbans, the full-bloods, I might be just as exclusive as my author-colleague.

I do not enjoy the privileged status of only one race, nor can I claim a traditional upbringing. My grandmother died believing it best not to pass on her Salish tongue. My white father abandoned his children and their mother, leaving nothing but his blood in my veins and a twisted belief in the ongoing nature of absented love. I do not know my own traditions.

However, if I do not allow myself the right to dance intertribals, or sit in on non-Quinault sweat house ceremonies, or participate in rituals not specific to the Northwest, is not this the expected acquiescence of assimilation? Because my untaught mother taught me no tradition whatsoever, am I to refuse when a loving older Kiowa woman wants to teach me about fringing shawls? If I should exclude myself from belonging on the basis of my nontraditional upbringing and on the color of my skin, it would bring about unbearable loneliness.

At the same time, I find myself careful when about to meet other Native Americans, especially when addressing a crowd. Asked to read a poem for the opening of Joy Harjo's band one year at a "Columbus Day" celebration (the organizers determined to put the day on its head and celebrate ethnicity at the University of New Mexico), I nervously prepared at home for the event. I chose carefully: black dhoti pants, a sweater, black beads on black cotton would give just the right signifiers: classy, urban, nothing to prove (yeah, right). I hated the discomfort of my light skin once again and decided to address the crowd from that ambivalence.

Walking the few blocks from my cramped apartment to campus, I looked skyward, beyond the city lights of Albuquerque, and saw the tiniest crescent of moon in a bruised purple sky. Cupped within the sliver of bright light rested the dimmed round fullness of the moon, and I wondered if people questioned what part moon they could see or doubted the moon's wholeness when it was not full.

"What part Indian are you?" I intoned into the mike, my voice pleasingly amplified, rounder than real life. And I went on to tell the reactions of different mixed-blood Indian men, friends of mine. When asked this question, these men have, at one time or another, stood up and pretended to unzip their pants. A defiant gesture that delights me, even if somewhat vulgar and rude. At the mike, in front of 200 or so, I mimic my male friends' response, "unzippering," and get the laugh that puts me at ease. It is the laughter of Native people that makes me belong again.

As if speaking to Frank and Bonnie and Bristow and Christy, I tell them of the woman at that going-away party; I tell them of her dark skin, brown eyes, round face—maybe Chicana, maybe Asian. I say what I saw: a woman who did not recognize her own self anymore, who maybe thought herself white. I said how I wanted to slap her, shake her up; but more important I wanted her to know the ridiculousness of her question. And so when she asked me, "What part Indian are you?"

I said, "I think it is my heart."

Tradition and the Individual Imitation

William S. Penn

Cinco de Mayo, three hundred and fifteen years after the Pueblo Revolt. I'm on my way to Santa Fe, although it's my first trip there and so I have no idea how Santa Fe it is. My head and heart are filled with questions about tradition and celebration, answers both wrong and right, brought to mind by the anticipation of seeing my good friend Dave, an elder member of the Santa Clara Pueblo. Things to talk about. Wondering how complacent in my questions and answers I have become, knowing from weeks of dinners with Dave when we both allowed our diverse selves to be exploited by Colorado College as visiting lecturers that complacency is not something Dave allows—not in himself, not in his friends, among whom I hope I'm privileged to count myself, not in anyone who is willing to enter the dialogue about culture and tradition which—the dialogue— is like food for Dave.

Since last we saw each other, I have read the books he bought me, or convinced me to buy, a suitcase of heavy books like Michael Kammen's

Mystic Chords of Memory that made the airline's baggage checker shoot me a herniated frown as I watched my luggage trail off behind the rubber *shawala* hiding the brute handlers of baggage just waiting to test their mettle against the construction of my imitation brand-name, soft-side suitcases patched with silver duct tape.

Cinco de Mayo, the day after hearing an Indian man read an essentialist poem bad with guilt and New Age prospects to a mixblood crowd in which the Crossblood Indios remained silent but the non-Indios were staggered in their essentials by what one young groupie (essentially) afterward called "the power of his poem."

It makes you wonder.

It makes me wonder, at least, as I drive up the "Turquoise Trail" in my Rent-a-Camry.

I pass through Golden, which is neither golden in wealth nor spirit given the barefooted babies with drooping diapers, the school-bus cabins blocked up and yellowed by use, the hodgepodge of treadless tires and rusting children, and the plywood windows of houses scraped and peeled by weather that line the road with their porches out—once the homes of immigrants, shopkeepers who came from England and Germany, Holland, Belgium, Scotland, and Luxembourg to lay claim to land. They renamed the place Golden the way they renamed themselves and invented the tradition of "settlers," their movements and manners made manifest by the derivations of these words and names. They opened mines and then, using the tricks of advertising, they seduced other immigrants into remaking their destinies along with their identities, transforming themselves from eastern farmers into western miners, day laborers, drunks, lawmen, and bartenders. The new immigrants to Golden, who would buy from and vote for the indigenous shopkeepers, and who would labor and remain generations after the minerals were mined and shipped and the rich spare land stripped of all but mesquite and cholla, but only after making the shopkeepers and mine owners wealthy enough to leave Golden behind, abandon these houses and move on—farther west in search of a more satisfied avarice or back east in search of a consolidated transformation into the heads of estab-. lished families, less often north along the Makah coast, and less and less often south into the land they cut from Aztlán and *de donde* they made Mexicans *están*.

After Golden comes Madrid (pronounced *Mad*—rid in one of those ritualized divorces from reality accepted and propagated by the obscure mental processes of the unemployed miners), another mining town. A century after Golden's shopkeepers boarded up their windows, Mad-rid was invaded by hippies looking to get away from anger and truth. Get away they did, inventing a Mining Museum, rebuilding a general store and calling it a Trading Post, adding Art Galleries that sell not art but craft and often not even craft but guile, and installing coffee bars in the living rooms of anorectic houses. In Mad-rid they discovered that though in flight they still could have it all—have the money to send their free-form children to private colleges hidden beneath the veneer of uncon- and unre-stricted liberation, wearing the best of the beads themselves and selling the worst mounted on thin silver etched with only the hint of designs appropriated from those very *indigenos* the shopkeepers of Golden had tried to extinguish.

Finally, I cross beneath the interstate and edge into the outskirts of Santa Fe, past AutoWorld, a sea of autos so large it seems to wave. I pull over behind a Texaco station to use toilets which, like those in *Mad*—rid, are for customers ONLY, and to use the pay telephone, perched like a winnowing fan out beside the highway where it's hard to hear. Dave directs me on to the landmark mall with a Red Lobster restaurant where I park and wait, sniffing at the hint of truth about Santa Fe yet unable to see right in front of me the Red Lobster's disguise of Southwestern adobe because I'm watching for him—who will take me downtown to La Posada for brunch.

◆ ——————— ◆

At La Posada, we're early for brunch. While we wait for the help to set up, Dave draws circles of identities and arrows of in flux and fluence on the heavy white butcher paper used to protect the restaurant's linen from people like him as we talk about bones.

Not too long ago, the pueblo to which Dave belongs won the right to repatriate the bones of its ancestors that had been mined, numbered, shipped, tagged, and stored in the basement of the Smithsonian. Some of the bones were older than grandparents or great-grandparents, bones hundreds of years old that had undergone preparation, ceremony, and burial specific in their traditions, in their process, and in the meaning of the processes which may be called the same as belief. The belief in the meaning of the process was a part of the sacred and secular outlook and world-view of the tribe burying the bones. But where, perhaps, the sense of meaning and sacredness had not been lost or altered over hundreds of years, the processes themselves had—as the Santa Clara elders recognized. And now they were faced with a dilemma. Whereas they wished the bones to be reburied in their sacred or rightful place—the place from which they came and from which they departed on their journeys into the afterworld—would it be right and proper to rebury these bones using ceremonies that, in the time the bones were fleshed, would not have been appropriate, would perhaps not even resemble the ceremonies that were proper and appropriate? If the process and ceremony for burying bones creates and then prepares the way for the spirit's journey, wouldn't the wrong process conflict with the spirit of the bones and perhaps even block the spirit from the path it needed to take? Do the Santa Clara Pueblo people go ahead and risk this, and risk as well showing disrespect and dishonor to the bones of their ancestors by reburying them with rituals that may not even resemble the originals?

Where could the elders turn to find out how the ceremonies were performed?

For bones that were two hundred years old, nowhere. For bones that were one or two generations old, possibly to elders, to the narrative historians and keepers of the kiva. For bones a hundred years old, they could turn to the anthropological cousins of the archaeologists who dug and stole the bones, looking to their records and writings to find descriptions of sacred and private ceremonies where they were allowed to see and hear them. But even given the knowledge that anthropologists, as outsiders, would not have been allowed to know all of the details—that aside—depending on people from outside the kiva to describe what happened inside the kiva was very risky. The pueblo would run the risk of copying or reproducing, imitating, if you will, the representation or imitation "seen" and recorded by people who had little or no idea of what they were seeing but believed they knew what they should be seeing. In the extreme, the pueblo people might end up burying the bones with ceremonies that imitated the imitation of what a Pueblo ceremony should or ought to be.

What the Santa Clara Pueblo—or the Zuni or any other tribe—decides is, of course, up to them and not me and not even Dave, individually—as he knows—turning from the problem of bones to dance, to the idea of tradition in dance, a subject not as ossified as the repatriation of bones.

Anyone who has ever seen a ceremony and celebration that uses the Matachina Dance recognizes Pueblo costumes in a dance completely pervaded by Christian, specifically Catholic, images, right down to the Virgin Mary. Indeed, without the masks, the colors, the feathers, and the laugh of movement, one would simply take the Matachina for another Catholic procession.

Slowly taking up this subject, Dave draws a large circle on the butcher paper, the circle of the Pueblo people, their culture and traditions, their beliefs and processes, or ceremonies, their way of looking in and out at the world, and their way of behaving in the context of that world. Beside it, intersecting it to create the shape of a football, he draws a second, equally largish circle, which is the circle of culture, of what may be called the ways of being, of the Pueblo's Mexican cousins, with whom they intermarried, traded, fought, and modified their stories—the football shape, which Dave shades with angling lines, the third traditional culture created by the interreflexivity of the two cultures interacting on and with each other. Gradually, if Dave is right, and I think he knows a lot about which he has thought slowly and very carefully, the football enlarges and the unshaded, partly eclipsed circles tend to wither, if for no other reason than to maintain them the Pueblo (or the Mexican) people would have to rigidly fix the definition of "tradition" and adhere to it without the change that occurs simply by ceremonies being performed by different dancers, different singers, different elders or storytellers or leaders. Without change, things die. That is Dave's thesis for these circles and for the way he shades the butcher paper. It is not Dave's thesis, however, or even a part of it, that change means that things become less—less meaningful, less "traditional," less powerful; in other words, he is not judging the change as reductive or vitiatory, but only as necessary or perhaps inevitable, or even desirable.

As our football enlarges, there comes a curving double line with one large arrow point. A double curve, because it has to be large enough to be seen to influence and modify the right circle of the Pueblos and the left circle of the Mexicans, as well as the already existent intersection of the two. This is the arrow of Coronado, Oñate, the Castilian *conquistadores*, the encomienda system, the slavery, brutality, death, the Catholicism and its inquisitional agents, the friars. No one, Dave seems to believe, can deny the power of their influence, negative or not; in some way, the way the Matachina has survived is a hymn to the power of "tradition." But— and I'm getting ahead of Dave here—it is a tradition that has changed so much that possibly a traditional Pueblo person of 1680 would not even recognize it, let alone recognize it as "traditional."

After the double arrow from above, which becomes a part of that enlarging football, Dave draws two other arrows, both double, though (perhaps he's just running out of room) smaller. One is the arrow of invaders calling themselves "settlers," who bring with them their own attitudes and excuses they call their tradition, whether that tradition is the tradition of the farmer/shopkeeper or the tradition of the scout/soldier backed by armed Protestant mythologies. The other is the double arrow of anthropology and archaeology, the folks who come to study and dig, and record, whether or not they speak a word of the Pueblo's language. Like it or not, as the anthropologists spent an entire week or month getting to know the objects of their studies, becoming familiar with their daily lives, their traditions, and the ways in which they perceive the process and meaning of them before recording them, transcribing them, and then rewriting them with easy interpo- and extrapo-lation, the additions and modifications and corrections they make because like the fabulous John Neihardt they imagine themselves almost to "be" Indian (though Neihardt's worked it out so there's no "almost" in the absolute of his fakery), calling themselves "friends" in the way the people who stole Golden called themselves "settlers," renaming and recasting their words to trick themselves and their readers—during their week (or month, even) they brought with them influence, seeds, for good or ill, of change.

In a way, given Dave's circles, you could imagine the anthros taking a bite out of the hoop to take home with them, leaving behind filler to complete the circle. Even without imagining that, you have to be able to understand that the very experience of being studied and studied as objects must have been a force for change, if only to have Navaho people make up stories to tell because the real ones the anthros wanted to hear were out of season and thus could not be told, not even by one Navaho to another. And if you insist that no Navaho (or Laguna or Pueblo) would have done this, we can only offer the strange feeling of compliment—"We're important enough to study"—combining with the yeast of wanting things to be whole—"We have this opportunity to let people know about us in some possibly 'real' way"—combining with the dough of hospitality and graciousness, the almost Homeric treatment of strangers who were willing to talk and who seemed (at first, anyway, before people realized that a belief out of context was not the same as a belief in context, especially where context—like process—was equal to or greater than the belief itself, which suggests how so many Indians did and do manage to be Christians within the context of their tribal ways) to want to understand. Just as the Nez Perce greeted and cared for Meriwether Lewis and his horses, I suspect the Navaho—or most any other band or tribe—were gracious to these strangers.

Anthro, "settler," and missionary all brought influence and change—and who can predict exactly which change is bad? The strength of whatever may be called a "tradition" does not live in a leaden fixity and adamant resistance to change but in survival and continuation, in being handed down grandfather or grandmother to grandson or granddaughter and in their "using" it in the context of their processes, their ways of looking and believing, their ways of behaving.

◆ ———————— ◆

Traditional. *Tradition* is a word like *civilization*, and words, as Tom Joseph in *Wolfsong* tells us, are something "they" are always using to trick themselves. The word *tradition* for Indians, however, involves the debate over bones, as well as over art and artifacts and the images or words that are infinitely reproducible, even if Black Elk never said anything like them. Arnold Krupat writes,

> It is also possible, as Karen Warren has written, to conceive "the debate over 'cultural properties' as a debate over the ownership of the past," where "the past" is "understood not only as the physical remains of the past (e.g., artifacts, places, monuments, archaeological sites) but also the 'perceptions of the past itself' (e.g., information, myths, and stories used in transmitting the past)." (Krupat, p. 20)

When the forces of nature decide to reveal Makah villages 500 years old, eroding the mud that buried and preserved the artifacts and tools and lodges of an ancient Makah tribe,[1] there seems to be no question that if they value and are inspired by them, the artifacts and tools and images belong to the Makah people, to be used, preserved, or displayed or not as the Makah people wish.

What happens, though, when a young Makah goes off to the city, carrying with him his images, his name, his traditions, has children with a woman who is not Makah but who allows our Makah youth-become-man to raise his children with as much of the tradition and meaning and wisdom as he can in the cities? Do his children by right of a certain blood quantum inherit the "rights" to Makah images? If the eldest son chooses to become a woodcarver and in his artifice uses what are designated as "traditional" Makah images and symbols, is it okay for him to make a living by carving and selling in his artifice in Golden shops that get reinvented as "galleries"? Does the gallery have the right to photograph and reproduce the images of his carvings—even if only for flyers and show announcements or openings? Do they have the right to reproduce the images as postcards or posters? And when our Makah artist is no longer "with" that gallery, has the gallery purchased the copyrights, or do they revert to the artist, his family, or even as far away in time and space as the tribe?

Sad as it makes me, it seems that the argument may be made that once money or goods change hands in a capitalist world, so do the reproductive rights. Argue and fume about capitalism and the Western notions of "progress," no matter what arguments we might present, it—that mass of Jell-O that absorbs pieces of fruit into one big jiggling tasteless goopy mold, IT—does not give a shit. It buys, uses what it has bought by mechanical reproduction ad infinitum or at least ad profitum asymptotum, and then—having approached the infinitely regressive end, the last dot of reduction, having squeezed out the last drop of blood and meaning— trucks it off to a landfill of purchased things to take its place beside newspapers, loaded diapers, and plastic bottles stamped on the bottom with"1." It buys, uses, and discards. Or, like the trivializing plots of television, it buys, uses, stores, and recycles when it seems as though more commerce may be fueled by its use.

The value of a recycled image bought and used can be increased by authenticating it, and the way commercial capitalism authenticates its endlessly reproduced images and ideas is to certify, to give artifactualities the Good Housekeeping Seal of Approval. In the case of "Indian" art and artifact, that certification is an act of the descendants of "settlers," those very people who returned to the East after mining the West to consolidate their gains and use them to be elected to the federal government, one of whose branches is the Bureau of Indians Affairs, which, after taking down names of Indians (for relocation, extermination, or slow attrition to the thinning formulae of blood quantum), presume to "tell" them who they are and who they can be, even though identity, real identity, is something that can exist even in disguise, unrecognized by bureaucrats and statisticians who count the heads hanging around the fort. Coyote or Frog does not require traveling papers any more than Moses needs to wear a Star of David.

The individual Makah artist, however, is not the representative of the consensual tribe. So is it in the consensus that the ownership of the past belongs?

What about the other "Indian" artist, a girl of Nez Perce and Osage descent who grew up in Los Angeles with Apache, Laguna, Hopi, Miwok, Costanoan, Quechua, Mexicano (or Mestizaje), Cherokee, Choctaw, and other mixbloods or crossbloods? If her first art images are from all of these people, then, when she makes a drawing or painting forty years later and uses some of those images, is she appropriating cultural images? Are the images "hers"? Or is she expressing the growth of cross-cultural influence? If she is appropriating, then do we say that there are images that belong to an identifiable culture or cultural group and that only members of that group may use those images—and for what—for ceremony?

But also for sale?

Thomas Gilcrease, who made his money in Oklahoma oil. . . . began to buy rare books and documents, then Indian art and artifacts of the region. The outbreak of World War II in 1939 made him even more cognizant that objects outlast people, and that the surviving remains of past cultures must be cherished. (Kammen, p. 348)

At the grand opening in November 1924 [of the Metropolitan's American Wing] [R.T.H.] Halsey waxed eloquent about the Americanizing role of traditions ingrained in material culture. Somehow, all of that wonderfully glistening mahogany and all of those ball-and-claw feet would make new immigrants into more sober citizens.

—Said Halsey: "Traditions are one of the integral aspects of a country. . . . Many of our people are not cognizant of our traditions and the principles for which our fathers struggled and died."

—Said [Robert Weeks] de Forest: "We are honoring our fathers and our mothers, our grandfathers and our grandmothers, that their art may live long in the land which the Lord hath given us."

—Said Elihu Root (first vice-president of the Museum): Halsey, de Forest, Kent, and all the rest who made the Wing a reality "formed an old-fashioned American community, and in their spirit was born again that atmosphere that produced whatever was fine and warming and delightful in old American life." (Kammen, p. 349)

Says the literature of dominance: We must form a new old-fashion, that our artifice may last long in the tooth.

Said their Lord who gave them Indian land: If you build your house on a foundation of sand, then everything depends from illusion.

Said the anthropologists: If you paint, paint brightly, and twirl the Virgin Mary with your Matachina Dance.

But Lewis Mumford asked of the American Wing, "What is to keep us from harnessing machine production to a sickly desire to counterfeit the past?" (Kammen, p. 350).

What, in other words, is to keep and defend us from Disney?

How do we identify those privileged Indian artists, by blood, by community recognition, or do we let the federal government decide and do
it by identity cards, trump cards you can throw on the table to disguise
your lack of character and to hide the fact that even you suspect that you
are acting in accord with the literature of dominance and not survivance?[2] It is then okay for a woman or man carrying a card or a certain
quantum of blood to knock off jewelry with designs appropriate to her or
to his people and sell it to the descendants of Golden's and Mad-rid's
shopkeepers in search of turquoise or general weight?

The problem with Indian art is that while some is joyful and celebra-
tory, a statement of color and shape or a joke on Jesus, whose face is outlined in gunpowder and ignited, some of the painters (certified by the
Heard Museum or by the front men and women for corporate appropriation to the National Museum of the American Indian in the Old Customs
House)[3] seem to have bought the fast-drying acrylic and gaudy colors of
so-called Indian art as a bold excuse for a lack of training or vision, creating paintings that shout at the viewer that you can have modern traditions
in which the modern informs the tradition and not the other way around.

But an Ojibway basket, if it even has colors, is subtle in them; Comanche
beaders did not bead for brightness and easy visibility and targeting by
enemies on the plains; a Navaho blanket may have striking contrasts, but
the tradition is formal, even staid; and using earth and clay, berry and bug,
the traditions of image on rock or in sand seems less bold, more subtle and
delicate, less influenced by the bald acrylic cry of modernity.

But—as well as So—like powwows, perhaps, what people take to be
Indian painting may be a myth of modernity creating and inventing
"traditions." Like most dances, perhaps many of the images are, at best,
reinventions, if not pure invention, which is not to say bad or inauthen-
tic or wrong.

It may be, then, that because of perplexing and perhaps unanswerable
questions, some Indians have decided that the real question is not "tradition" but an authenticity of "blood"—the way an artist may let art dealers certify their work as "art," which often seems to mean commercial-
ized trivia—letting the dealers in blood quantum (a.k.a. the Feds or their
corporate and collegiate fronts) certify them as authentically bloody

enough to be called Indian, a certification which makes one neither more nor less Indian and trivializes the issues as well as makes Indians into limited-edition prints that can be bought and sold for a sum that increases the more the Feds can limit the numbers in a finitely regressive process of defining Indians down to a sum of zero.

The Declaration of Independence is a hymn to Manifest Manners. All men are created equal and have the right to life, liberty, and the pursuit of happiness. Those are the parts we quote, the bones we dig out of the Declaration's grave worldview that, in the parts we are not taught to quote, indicate that it is not all men—real men, who eat no quiche—but all white men who are created equal.[4] We cannot blame Thomas Jefferson any more than we should blame Andy Jackson for a world-view that made their sworn and life-pursuing duty the obligation to subdue the *bárbaros* who spoke no Greek or English, the Greek-less "primitive" people who became barbarians because they did not speak British Law any better than they spoke the Latin Columbus had his notaries read to the Indios, giving them the chance to submit to Spain, before Columbus had his men attack and slaughter. We cannot blame Thomas Jefferson because that is what he not only thought but believed in a belief that did not include the systems of other peoples, other cultures, and definitely did not include the barbarians as "men" who had any rights whatsoever.

What we can blame, however, is the memorization of the created-equal passages in the Declaration and the inability of memorializers to read farther. What we can blame are the descendants of Chief Joseph allowing the descendants of Tom Jefferson and his manifestly destined world view to "recognize" them or not in a way that makes the "recognition" downright Rousseauian: these recognitions are not understanding, they are the romantic nostalgias that invent the "noble" savage. To let Jefferson or Rousseau "recognize" who is "Indian" is a simulation of dominance created through Manifest Manners.

Gerald Vizenor *used* to say this.

Gerald Vizenor liked to quote Standing Bear, who saw Sitting Bull, invented as the man who killed Custer, appear in a theatrical simulation in Philadelphia:

Sitting Bull "addressed the audience in the Sioux tongue" and then the white man, the interpreter, misconstrued his speech in translation. "My friends, white people, we Indians are on our way to Washington to see the Grandfather, or President of the United States," and more was translated as the story of the massacre of General Custer at Little Big Horn. "He told so many lies I had to smile." (Vizenor, p. 5)

Faced with imperialism performed as benevolence, as the kindness of strangers towards childish old men after the inevitable events of Destiny are manifestly concluded, Standing Bear can do nothing else but smile. It is time we learned from Standing Bear "to hover at last over the ruins of tribal representations and surmount the scriptures of manifest manners with new stories, . . . counter the surveillance and literature of dominance with . . . simulations of survivance" (Vizenor, p. 5).

Videotapes and images are artifacts. And artifacts—what one card-carrying, supposed "Indian" bureau-crat proudly claims as a lot of "stuff" with the kind of ludicrous and absurd pride that goes not with ownership but with working for the owners—are the bones of old stories no longer heard in the heart which we don't have the ceremonies to tell.

In "Postindian Warriors," Vizenor's terminologies became their own definitions reflexively, the way a poem becomes its meaning in the dialogue between images and lines. Every time you were denied an absolute certainty, you were rewarded with a possibility, and it is in the mirrored images of certainty and uncertainty that the possibilities survived like the strobes of theatrical performance. The possibilities are stories that survive in dialogue, simulations of themselves. The "theater of tribal consciousness is the re-creation of the real, not the absence of the real in the simulations of dominance" (Vizenor, p. 5). These simulations of dominance include the acceptance of future events as though they are inevitable, true, but they also include the acceptance of un-re-created past events as though they are not only inevitable but some way good or necessary: without European encroachment and conquest and annihilation we would not have had the smallpox vaccine. Possibly, but perhaps we would not have had smallpox either. Without the superior minds of the Europeans, we would not have had the weapons to defend our nation against the Soviet Union when it was soviet and union. Besides their attitude, the superior weaponry of the invading Europeans was, without question, disease—as they, themselves, recognized when they infested blankets with the small-pox virus and gave them out to starving and cold Indian women, children, and men. With the return of millennialism—which might have been expected, given the Yeatsian arguments over when the millennium occurs, 1899-1901 or 1999-2001, as well as the psychological concept of Endspurt, a renewed energy and creativity countered by a doomsday death-wishfulness at the close of centuries, especially millennial ones—fertilizer and disease remain the weapons of dangerous choice, and you don't have to introduce a disease to a colony to act in accord with the literature of dominance; you may just let it go to run its course.

The simulations of dominance are complicated, and the theater in which they are performed seems absurd. One thing we can be certain of is that remains are not survivance. To cherish them too much defines their pastability. Civilization becomes a spaghetti with simmering sauce to be consumed. By whom is a factionalism.

In the spring of 1995, Dave gave me a copy of a column by George F. Will. Faced with the continuing immigration and survival of Latinos and Chicanos and the changes coming about in Norte Americano society that from his perspective are "nontraditional," Will called for the forsaking of factionalism and a return to "traditional" American civilization. Tradition and Civilization: these are the catchwords for historical revisionism, revising the truth back into the beloved falsity of invented historical consciousness in which Betsy Ross is not the self-promoting agent of icon, but a sweet colonial lady who sewed together stars with stripes.

"For all its faults, X is better than Y" is not an argument but a consolidation, and, to the people who built the Alamo, the changes that have occurred and will continue to occur are not acceptable unless the "factionalists" act like those Indians who propose New Age solutions to impossible problems—become an Eco-Injun, for example, or a channeler who haunts the "new" artifactuality of the National Museum of the American Indian, which is housed so appropriately in the *old* Customs House in New York. Only then can he or she become acceptable. Only then will she or he seem consistent with the values of a traditional "civilized" society, which are commercial fabrications and not good.

The fabrications of Will's argument take protean shapes:

After Woman Killer lost at Big Horn, the banner headlines called it a "massacre," as if it were the Indians and not the cavalry that had surprised the encampment. In the literature of dominance the image of the battle is linear, whites ranged defensively against mounted Indian attackers, while in the literature of survivance the Lakota image is confused, soldiers mingled among soldiers, their allegiances distinguished only by their uniforms in a running dogfight.

The continued use of "settler" (as Senator Bill Bradley used it just before he left office) to describe people who broke their word and the rule of their laws to do all the things that have been done in the name of Our Lord Civilization, who gave his only begotten Progress that we should be free from History.

The words they use every time they fear losing what they may not well deserve to have or use, or what they may never have had at all but for a trick of the light.

What George Will means by *civilization* is not what I mean by *civilized*.

And even a simpleminded and cursory glance at American history makes you wonder when the United States ever comprised more or less than factions. When, since the immigrants first arrived on the shores of what became the United States, have those in power not pitted one faction against the other in order to maintain their power? World War Two? Americans of Japanese descent might quibble there. The Civil War? Even limited by a degree in Domestic American Studies you can think of at least a couple of largish factions. Vietnam? The maudlin sentimentalism and thoughtless patriotism of our late century may fool some into believing the modes of change are all acceptable. Or now? Pitting Indian against Indio?

George Will is not a fool, and he is not being fooled. In the post-Vietnam Age of Homogenization every curd looks like a faction to those like him who own(ed) the process.

George Will is an object.

Two scholars collect and edit an anthology of women poets. Regretfully, these scholars are forced, because of the number of women poets, to leave out Joy Harjo, not to mention Roberta Hill Whiteman, Linda Hogan, and a bunch of other Native American women, and it is in this regretfulness that they reveal how the literature of dominance continues to repeat itself.

Selection and inclusion is based not on the poems, so much, or on the audience, but on the poet's reputation. They overlook the fact that many Native American poets—women and men—choose to publish their poems with small and alternative presses, select a smaller but possibly more attentive audience, and, by doing so, limit the range of their reputation— which is sometimes gained in the mainstream by hiring photographers or by sticking one's head in an oven like the perennially manipulative and self-proclaimed victim Sylvia Plath, one of the great self-pitying monologists of our millennial century.

Regretfully, these two scholars leave out more than one important voice in Native American poetry as easefully as they leave out the wonderful poems of Carter Revard or Ralph Salisbury. There is nothing new to this repetition of dominance and simulation of reality that comes out of a profound insecurity or uncertainty..

Like them, George Will's banalities result from insecurity. His debate over the remains, which he sees as uniquely factional, leads to a repetition of the argument over false correctives.

The respected and respectable Richard White tells the audience that the traditional view of the Alamo or Custer's "Last Stand" is primarily defensive, the innocents being attacked and massacred by the implicitly guilty.[5] These defensive disasters have been made into icons of tradition.

Bemused, White adds that now it's the Indians at Wounded Knee or Sand Creek who are being reinvented as innocents forced into a defensive posture as history attacks and massacres them. They, too, are mythic inventions of the same order, according to the way White tells it. The implication is that both versions are equally false, and yet this equalization is falsehood itself: Colonel George A. Forsyth was no innocent, no more than Chivington or Strong Arm Custer, who, given his lifetime subscription to the Buffalo Billed belief that Indians were savages to be subdued and eliminated, got a better afterlife than he deserved.[6]

At Sand Creek, the Cheyenne and Arapaho bands believed they had made peace with the whites:

> The army might have been justified in attacking the hostiles. Unfortunately, the ones who had surrendered were easier to catch. . . . [Major Scott J.] Anthony encouraged the Indians to remain near the post, in order—there is no doubt of this—to have them available for massacre. About forty miles northeast, on Sand Creek, a wide, almost dry watercourse, there were about one hundred lodges of two hundred men and five hundred women and children, ten lodges being Arapahos under Left Hand, the other Cheyenne under Black Kettle, White Antelope, and other peace chiefs. . . . [Colonel] Chivington marched [600-625 men] to Fort Lyon . . . joined [by] Anthony with 125 men from the garrison, saying, "I believe the Indians will be properly punished." . . . They marched all night and reached the camp at dawn on November 29 [1864]. Some of the women saw them, but Black Kettle said there was no danger. He ran a large American flag and a white flag up on a lodge pole in front of his tipi and he and his wife and White Antelope took their position under it. Then the soldiers fired. . . . "We, of course, took no prisoners," wrote Anthony. Terrible things happened: a lieutenant killed and scalped three women and five children who had surrendered and were screaming for mercy; a little girl was shot down as she came out of a sand pit with a white flag on a stick; mothers and babes in arms were killed together. The pursuit [of the fleeing] continued for about five miles. Then the soldiers turned back to the camp, stopping on the way to mutilate the bodies. . . . Chivington and his hundred days' men returned to Denver, where they exhibited more than one hundred scalps and were lauded as heroes. (Debo, pp. 194—95)

This is not historical revisionism, the rubric under which people dismiss the fact that their traditions are brutal, dishonest, and corrupt, and excuse the greed and murder that motivates them the way it motivated their ancestors. This is not reinventing the posture of the Cheyennes and Arapahos camped at Sand Creek as "defensive." It is recording the actuality. By implying that it is a reinvention, Richard White merely renews his subscription to the literature of dominance—which, take note, is not "the dominant literature" but the linguistic tricks that create an attitude that perseveres.

What Richard White implies is revisionist is not revision but revelation. He would be correct only if he illustrated how Sand Creek can be made an icon, a mythic competitor with historical time and a source for false historical consciousness, which can lead to many things: the belief that things have changed, that greed and commerce do not use brutal means to justify themselves; or to Indians staying near the fort, hoping the white flag of their identity cards will protect them while they, themselves, thin their own numbers into nonexistence. Why else does the federal government encourage the Laguna people to identify and certify Laguna people on the basis of their having one-quarter Laguna blood? Because many Lagunas are of mixed Indian blood and thus would be disqualified in this generation, being one-eighth Laguna and one-eighth something else. Because if the Feds can get the people themselves to hang around the fort, in one or two generations, there will be virtually no Laguna people left. They will have been annihilated, and the crazy thing is that they will have helped themselves be revised right out of history by peaceful acquiescence, and the federal government will be able to take away benefits, rights, and land belonging to the sovereign Laguna nation.[7]

◆ ——————— ◆

Recently, a friend told me about an Indian writer who had called people to ask how dark their skin was and if they carried in their pockets The Card, partly out of youthful thoughtlessness and perhaps partly because he smells commercial gain as long as he can be packaged and sold as Indian.

Nota Bene Descendants: the "Indian" writer is what gets sold, not the writing, and the writer is transformed here into the primary salesman, selling the writer's talent, which will be trivialized by commerce like the Indians on display in Buffalo Bill's Wild West Shows.

Indeed, this Indian person reproduces the self as "Indian" writer in the image of "Indian writer" that those editors and agents who tell him he has "commercial possibilities" already possess. He goes about imitating the imitation of the romantically represented noble idea much the way, as Richard White notes, that Indians like Sitting Bull acted out the roles of "Indians" in Cody's Wild West Show, and in doing so imitated the imitations of themselves.[8] His writing need not be good, and it need not have any connection to the oral traditions or the speaking truly and well of Native American storytelling—it may confuse the end of commerce, which is gain, with the end of story, which is unending process, and become an end to and of itself. He may lose sight of the fact that Talent is not only a means of exchange that integrates the self into a community and the individuals of the community with each other; Talent is also a burden—literally—a responsibility that must be wisely used and maintained.

He may well find himself like Coyote, who says,

"I'm the *Coyote*.
And I am lonely."
He says,
"I can't . . . use my powers anymore,
and people,
 they ignore me now
they don't depend on me
and nobody will pla-a-y with me
nobody will listen to my stories!" (Frey, p. 82)

This Coeur d'Alene story ends with the idea that if you give something to a white man that's going to do him some good, "he'll skin you alive!" (Frey, p. 91). What the mostly white and mostly still dominant mainstream culture of commerce wants are the authentic pelts of Indian stories, in this case, and in selling his pelts the writer may end up skinned alive, tied up and dead, needing Fox to step over him five times to bring him back to life. And even then, if he's like Coyote, he won't admit that he ever died and went to artifactual heaven.

This same writer is reputed to say that other mixbloods do not "write Indian"—whatever that means—and when called on to answer the question, says that their writing doesn't "speak to the Indian" in him.

Sort of like a young woman writer saying Flannery O'Connor doesn't "write woman"—is that it?—or Katherine Anne Porter doesn't "speak to the woman in me?"

Or Richard Wright doesn't "speak to the homosexual" in me—or is it that he doesn't "write black"?

Or Buchi Emecheta doesn't speak to the "African"?

Or Ngugi wa Thiong'o doesn't speak to the prisoner of politics in all of us?

Europeans are not the only people susceptible to confusing consumption with experience or the experience of being consumed with authenticity. And in this unimagined argument over authenticity, the issue becomes no longer an issue of imagination, which is a large part of identity or self-identification, but a problem of fantasy—a fantasy of blood and birth and ownership, a romantic nostalgia.

Consider the "Sweat Lodge," as told by Jim James, in which Sweat Lodge says,

> Whoever desires to construct me will have the right to do so.
> The one that builds me may pray to me for good looks,
> or whatever he may wish,
> the one that made me." (Frey, p. 158)

"Whoever"?

Evidently. As long as "who" treats the Sweat Lodge with prayerful respect. As long as he or she "makes" it, does not simply buy it or reproduce it but enters into the respectful construction and therefore meaning of it. As long as this making is personally involved and not a making only for public consumption.

Combine this with the Coeur d'Alene story "Cosechin," in which it is customary for the Indian who is going to use something from a tree (or fish or whatever) to "ask permission first . . . / 'Mr. Tree may I use some part of you / or I need it . . . for warmth for my children" (Frey, p. 177).

Last weekend, I was outside pruning some rather bony spruce trees, talking to the pair of them, explaining how I thought this would make them happier, help them grow taller and fuller, help them take advantage of their situation. My neighbor came over to see whom I was talking to in such a solicitous voice. After she left, it dawned on me that the argument can never be over who is Indian, who is an Indian artist, but over how—never over which images are whose but how anyone makes those images their own, with respect and bearing the burden of Talent's exchange and integration. Wasn't that why the Cherokees could adopt someone into the tribe and consider him or her fully a Cherokee—because in spirit they were? If so, then they were not Cherokee for the public but for themselves by integrative extension for their communities, and if they "taught" about being Cherokee after that, they did not organize new-age encounter sessions of forest excursions of tree hugging; they did it instinctively and humbly by example.

◆ ———————— ◆

The argument over who owns the past is an argument Bureaucrats want Indians to engage in, especially if they'll engage in it with other Indians. It helps them not only trick themselves, like our lonely Coyote, into thinking they have something other people want but, worse, trick themselves into believing that by providing that "thing" they can control not only the process but the result. The result for Coyote is that he is flayed alive, abandoned by the one he gave himself to, dead and needing Fox to bring him back to life by stepping over him ritually, respectfully, prayerfully, five times (and even then, Coyote, as charming and likable as our exemplary "Indian writer," refuses to admit to Fox that he was dead, claiming he was only asleep).

To frame the argument as an argument over the past, especially the "authentic" past, is to memorialize memorized images, stories, and meanings of the past, which is to memorialize Coyote as dead or flayed as though he were not dead, not flayed, which is to memorialize a fantasy. It is to come to inhabit a millennial, end-approaching delusion:

> Even as the erosion of millennialism caused people to contemplate the nation's past and future in terms of historical change and hence historical time, the proliferation of historical tales and anecdotes made mythical time—that is, heavy reliance upon sacred stories related to such moments as 1492, 1607, 1620, 1630, 1776, etc.—a genuine competitor with historical time and a complex source of false historical consciousness. Americans *believed* that they knew much more about the past than they actually did. Not only was the very basis of belief undergoing change, however; so was the place of belief itself in the nation's sense of its own traditions. (Kammen, p. 206)

After our first child was born, even though she was not particularly difficult, especially compared with other children, my wife and I used to videotape her during the day, and then, exhausted, glad when she was finally down for the night, we would watch the tapes and tell each other how delightful and precious she was, how much she was to be cherished.

America has videotaped itself from here to the moon. Some people like to watch the tape and tell themselves how delightful America is and how much whatever remains American is to be cherished.

In the past ten or so years, Native America has been getting video-taped (again) and the possibility exists that what is recorded (memo-rized) and stored (dead, but for the sentimentalism that passive audi-ences "feel" rewatching them) are the manners which the arguers over the past cherish.

In seeking the "real," Indians, like all Americans, may be creating a fake.

By memorializing the real—not just dates, but the intangibles of blood—we are memorizing stories and not remembering them. Frey says, "Stories are always remembered, never memorized. Memorization results in a rigidity that can inhibit participation in the story. Remember-ing encourages spontaneity and thus greater immediacy with the lis-tener; ... [it] reunite[s] with the reality of the story, ... reestablishes membership with the characters of the story ... for the listeners as well as for [the storyteller]" (p. 153).

The membering of identity demands re-membering. Member-ship de-mands re-membership. It cannot be legitimized by cards, numbers, or Stars of David; you may achieve the recognition by the community as a member of its story, but you cannot stop being a part of that community. It's this lat-ter that makes "Indians" fearful of Wannabes. People who Want-to-Be In-dian, Want-to-Be-a-Real Indian, or anything else never involve themselves in the processes, they do not re-member anything but nostalgias, and once membership is no longer popular—as it will not be—they not only let their membership lapse, they move on to better facilities, newer clubs. The com-munity is shunted aside in a process of disre- and dis-membering.

◆ ———————— ◆

In the Heard Museum, hidden in the glare of all those big paintings, is a color-pencil drawing by a woman, framed along with her penciled note saying how surprised and honored she was to have the curator ask to dis-play her work in a museum. It is a moving drawing, evocative, delicate,

and true—and true is all I care about, not whether the government certi-
fies her as authentic or she sells herself as Indian, or whether she has
"less" blood in her veins than one of the other represented artists.

A supposed Indian with the trumps of identity would not question
these paintings' authenticity or traditionalism. But a supposed Indian,
whatever machinations produced the ace of his identity, has already allowed the federal government to determine what is or what is not Indian
without considering that if he lets the government do that, he has accepted the government's final and inevitable statement that a particular
tribe or people are no more. That's what the government wants from the
Laguna people. It wants them to subscribe to the literature of dominance.
That's why the Santa Clara Pueblo invites the young people home.

Identity cards, like powwows with "traditional" dances and art museums with "authentic" paintings, may be a subscription to the literature
of dominance, not survivance. Survivance asks Indians to burn their
cards and dodge the B.I.A. draft or at least to doubt and wonder at them,
to refuse the federal definition of their antiselves in the absence of the
real, to stop harvesting the contempt of millennial imperialism.

> "For anything I see," said Dr. Johnson's friend, Old Meynell, "foreigners
> are fools." There has probably never been a time when the majority of
> Englishmen would not have agreed with this sentiment, adding, per-
> haps, that most foreigners are frivolous and lubricious rascals. Certainly
> at the end of the nineteenth century this insular mixture of contempt and
> suspicion was general at nearly every level of English society. No doubt
> a connection exists between England's imperial expansion at that time
> and the intensity of national insularity that accompanied it, . . . splen-
> didly isolated *from* . . . the great intellectual ferment on the continent.
> (Hynes, p. 307)

The ferment is intellectual, now, and it is also cultural and axial. A journalist's call for everyone to join his isolation and submit to his mixture of
contempt and suspicion of the so-called factions that are growing and
changing is a sign of his class, not his national, insularity.

The problem is that everything is connected like dandelions. Painting, speaking, dancing, and storytelling, like all the other things that

may be called "Indian" (or specifically called Nez Perce or Choctaw or Osage or Miwok or Costanoan), embodies change. Especially in the written literatures derived from a highly oral tradition in which the story told contained within itself the seeds of change according to audience, according to the corroborators who attended the telling and could interrupt and modify at any point along the storyline, according to circumstance. The story loses its ability to change when it becomes memorized, memorialized for recitation, when it loses its ability to accept its origin in change and growth, when it mythologizes time and ties event to the leash of the myth. Indian stories of survivance are comic as myths are never comic. To call traditional stories of creation, of adolescence, of living and dying, of the journey onward "myths" is to call them dead like the Latin Mass of Catholics or the anti-comedy of George Will calling on "us" to act like "him" in a hyperreality of simulated civilization and the ruined representation of renewed millennialism in which he wants "us" to believe that "he" knows more about the past than we.

Comedy, comic stories, do not search anxiously for the real thing and do not submit themselves to the melancholy of dominance. Doubt and wonder produce laughter. Doubt and wonder are comic, not tragic. Doubt and wonder mean that the argument is not over the ownership of the past but over the processes of the future informed by the changed and changing past.

Rachel Antonia Penn, six years old, saw two Quechua girls dressed up all in white one Sunday morning as she was riding the 85 Toyota with her mom. Wondering why they were dressed like that, she suddenly said, "I know, Mom. They're on their way to their First Confusion."

The Matachina Dance may have been the Pueblo People's first confusion, but they have made it their own, and it survives.

William Anthony Charles Penn, two years old and named for grand- and great-grandfathers with as many handles as William Penn Adair Rogers, bounced on the bed where I had folded his clothes, packing a suitcase for our journey, and began to knock the folded clothes on the floor.

"Stop," I said.

He didn't.

"Willy, stop! I'm serious."

He stopped bouncing up and down. "Don't get serious, Dad," Willy said.

"Okay. I won't," I said when I stopped laughing.

But how can I not when downtown Santa Fe is about as close to the real thing as Disney is to Pocahontas, a place the first immigrants to Golden may have emigrated to, and it makes Dave and me a little serious? I can't help it, overwhelmed by the truth, overrepresented by the made-for-tourist kitsch of the downtown square and the noise of clicking cameras as loud as a tour bus, of Umberto Eco's statement that, in seeking the authentic, Americans invent the absolute fake. Dave can't help it because he has friends from the pueblo who can no longer afford to live in the place that is theirs, has been theirs, and in all likelihood may well not be theirs in the future. Even if these friends of his were to change, they could not adapt, not to this—because to adapt to this you have to counterfeit the future and adopt a commercial fantasy, become a middleman or middlewoman who sells channels through crystal skulls purchased at Tiffany's or wears a Pendleton blanket in the National Museum of the American Indian and lectures tourists on how "they" have fucked up the world and now it's up to Indians to help them rescue it, or adopt unimagined poses like William Least Heat Moon and Jamake Highwater, or package and sell your "Indian" or "Indian writer" self to the mainstream and then deny that ever you have been dead. You have to trump with your identity card or trumpet "civilization" and call for a "Domestic Ethnic Studies" program because the "domestic" leaves it not only in your control but unchallenging and it, too, like American Studies can intensely study nostalgic fakes.

Jean Baudrillard writes in *Simulacra and Simulations,* "When the real is no longer what it used to be, nostalgia assumes its full meaning. . . . There is a proliferation of myths of origin and signs of reality; of second-hand truth, objectivity, and authenticity."[9]

These myths and second-hand truths are all around you, especially in Santa Fe, having proliferated around Taos with the strangely impassioned dullness of D. H. Lawrence's late sermons and the bright vaginal kitschiness of Georgia O'Keeffe's unimagined paintings and having flowed downward like water seeking its lowest level to be dammed in Santa Fe by middlemen, under-dealers in second-handedness who argue that in destroying the ability for people to live in Santa Fe they are actually helping Santa Fe move forward into the twenty-first century. As much as the *Song of Hiawatha*, Santa Fe is a memorial to dominance, to the manners manifested by the Dutch American who says on camera that we have to limit immigration to preserve America for Americans. *Ratio obscura*, indeed.

So when we claim that the world has changed, we are claiming that some people out there know all too well the attitude of dominance and how it works to continue the invention of manifest destiny with its emphasis on the axis east to west, its assumptions that without the generous contempt of the English or the sometimes self-hating contempt of the French, the burgermeister contempt of the Belgians and Germans this continent would never have had A or B, let alone X and Z, the continued stereo-mythologizing of the lazy and greasy Mexican or Guatemalan and his or her need of the C.I.A. at home and abroad, the refusal to understand that hundreds of years ago indigenous people began scientifically engineering better crops, like corn, by cross-breeding and grafting, and better ways to grow them by enclosing food crops with pest-repelling plants or irrigate them in tiers descending a hillside, or to realize that Bayer did not invent or discover aspirin but only patented and claimed what *indigenos* had already discovered.

American Indian people themselves, along with their cousins on a north-south axis, have the most difficult job of all. They have to maintain their knowledge and awareness of this attitude without succumbing to the instinct to mythologize history and life. They have to find a way to not get serious and to aim the argument not at the ownership of the past but the future, not at the images themselves but what the images mean, at the process not the artifact. They have to be careful not to revise history or tradition, and at the same time allow it to reveal itself—and tradition, like history, reveals itself not by mannered manifestations of artifactuality that try to tell us what we have been but by humorous suspicions of how we can continue to be.

NOTES

1. See "Indian America: A Gift from the Past," a film produced by Robin
    Cutler, Dave Warren, and Karen Thomas, and narrated by Wes Studi,
    Media Resource Associates, Inc. (Washington, D.C., 1994). This is an in-
    formative and thoughtful film about a Makah village, buried in a mud
    slide for hundreds of years, being revealed by the shift in tide and wind
    on the Northwest Coast. Recording Makah people talking about the
    recovery of their artifacts and tools, what they mean to them, and
    why they have built a museum to house them, the film is an excel-
    lent documentation of an instance of ownership of the past which needs
    no debate, although it may inform the way in which the debate may
    be approached.
2. See Gerald Vizenor, *Manifest Manners*, especially "Postindian Warriors of
    Survivance," for a description of the literature of dominance and the lit-
    erature of survivance.
3. See Patricia Hilden, Shari Huhndorf, and Carol Kalafatic, *Fry Bread and
    Wild West Shows: The "New" National Museum of the American Indian* (in
    manuscript).
4. I am grateful to my colleague and friend Professor John Coogan of the
    Department of History at Michigan State University for this and some of
    the following ideas.
5. These statements and implications are derived from a lecture Richard
    White gave on "The West" to an audience at Michigan State University
    in July of 1995.
6. See Evan S. Connell, Jr.'s *Son of the Morning Star*, as well as Jim Welch's
    Killing Custer, for views of Custer's psychology, his life, and his actions.
7. A young Ojibway woman came to my office to tell me how a professor
    from another department taught that Indians "asked for" what hap-
    pened to them by trading with the French for guns and kettles. She
    also apologized for not really being Ojibway because, while her father
    was enrolled, she was "only one-eighth" Ojibway, and even though
    she'd grown up among her father's people, she was not allowed to
    enroll. This was obviously painful to her, and I am forced to wonder,
    was her pain less—only one-eighth—than what her grandfather's
    pain would have been to hear the same professor say the same silly
    things? What will her father's tribe do when all the children have been
    denied? Where will the money—for that is what it's all about, isn't it?—
    go then?
8. See James R. Grossman, ed., *The Frontier in American Culture*.
9. Quoted in Vizenor, *Manifest Manners*, p. 25.

WORKS CITED

Connell, Evan S., Jr. *Son of the Morning Star*. San Francisco: Northpoint Press, 1984.

Debo, Angie. *A History of the Indians of the United States*. Norman: University of Oklahoma Press, 1970.

Frey, Rodney. *Stories That Make the World*. Norman: University of Oklahoma Press, 1995.

Grossman, James R., ed. *The Frontier in American Culture: Essays by Richard White and Patricia Nelson Limerick*. Berkeley: University of California Press, 1994.

Hynes, Samuel. *The Edwardian Turn of Mind*. Princeton, N.J.: Princeton University Press, 1969.

Kammen, Michael. *Mystic Chords of Memory: The Transformation of Tradition in American Culture*. New York: Knopf, 1991.

Krupat, Arnold. *The Turn to the Native*. Lincoln: University of Nebraska Press, 1996.

Vizenor, Gerald. *Manifest Manners*. Hanover, N.H.: Wesleyan University Press, 1994.

Welch, James, with Paul Stekler. *Killing Custer: The Battle of the Little Bighorn and the Fate of the Plains Indians*. New York: Norton, 1994.

On Mapping and Urban Shamans

Kimberly Blaeser

We mention those twin animals only every other year or so. I think about them more. I know you do too. The image stays. Especially in the fall, I picture their identical spotted markings. After all these years, we will likely never know just what they were. But we remember. An imprint. Nameless. Power. I still see them moving in unison, turning their heads for a look at us, leaping in time to some music, then smoothly away. Those spotted rumps. Your delight, twin to mine. And the strange awe that has not dimmed.

The current from their eyes has lighted other moments from other years. Lenny and I return from the Boundary Waters that late August feeling weakened by each mile we travel back into Illinois. We seek the solace of the forest preserve, walk off the twelve-hour drive on its paths. Coming to the rise of the hill, we suddenly enter their range. They see us and freeze. We do the same. Identically positioned, heads turned, necks craned, ears perked, they watch us from the edge of the cornfield. The raccoon darkness around their electric eyes painted by the same hand. Two small bucks so alike as to seem an illusion, one perhaps a reflection, a doubling of our tired vision. And then they move on cue, exact in the sameness of each motion. Turning, leaping, they cross the grassy path upon which we stand. Wind of their motion caresses us. Gone into the autumn woods. Lost and kept. Again.

I cannot leave the places where this can happen. And so I will never be an urban mixedblood. I have had my chances to live in cities: nine months in St. Paul when I was a graduate student, six months in Chicago on fellowship at the Newberry Library, several semesters of living teaching days only at one small apartment or another in Milwaukee. But the sightings and stories are different there.

Brenda and I drive together to a meeting in inner-city Milwaukee. We follow elaborate directions dictated to me earlier in the day. All goes well. We find the right street. Park close by. My notes say the meeting place is a second-floor room over a bridal shop. We congratulate ourselves on our arrival as we look for the shop. And then the scene turns city crazy because the whole damn block is bridal shops. We have arrived—in the urban twilight zone. Again.

No, I am not an urban dweller. When someone mentions cities, I routinely march out the stories of my Chicago days, all 181 of them. I parade the bizarre episodes, one after another like battle scars. How can so many ludicrous incidents happen within the three square blocks surrounding the Newberry Library, the "safe" zone of my fellowship days there? To the regulars in Washington Square park, the boarders at the YMCA, the cabdrivers, I must be marked as clearly as Hester Prynne, as clearly as any banded bird or tagged animal. With these urban natives I have strange conversations about gold chains, ground beef, and buses, but the culminating moment of my stay is my conversation with the Chicago police.

I set out to walk the two blocks to the library from my Chestnut Street apartment. Just after crossing the street I hear the noise, a moaning, groaning sound of someone hurt. Although I stop and look all about me, I cannot spot the injured person. Meanwhile other pedestrians stream by. Eventually I give up, walk on to the library, and put in my morning. At noon, on my way home for lunch, I hear it again. More determined

now, I look in doorways, along the curb, up and down the street, seeing
no one. A black woman, big in a dark wool coat, shakes her head and
clucks her tongue at me as if I were engaged in some disgusting activity. I am mystified.

Finally it occurs to me to look up. There he is. A naked man on a
wrought-iron balcony, caressing his erection and emitting the moans I
had mistaken for pain. Shocked, I rush back to my apartment and dial the
Chicago police. I speak to someone with a Hispanic accent. I give him
the location. I describe the scene. I repeat it three times at his request.
And then Chicago sinks in and I replace the receiver. He doesn't care. He
doesn't understand why I would call. No one has been murdered. There
has been no accident. All those lovely horses the police truck in and
mount on weekends symbolize something I with my rural-developed
sensibility will never quite understand.

I've learned to live by certain rules with regard to cities: First, avoid
them. If you can't avoid them, seek escorts. Try to enter and exit on the
same day. When this is not possible, seek escorts. Don't take public trans-
portation. When this is not possible, seek escorts. The rules go on like that.

Oh, I like the bookstores, the theaters, the museums. I like to be taken
to them and then taken safely home again. I didn't grow up appreciating
crowded streets, bright lights, or city noises. That hasn't changed. But
now I teach at an urban university. I won't live in the city, but on teaching days or for meetings I drive in. I spend two and one half hours in the
car each working day simply to avoid urban life. It isn't my heritage.

And yet, although I grew up on White Earth Reservation in Minnesota, I
lived the years after I started school in the "urban" part of the rez. Mahnomen, population 1,313 during most of those years, was not exactly a
reigning metropolis, but it was the county seat. It was the town where
most of the businesses were and most of the whites lived. The majority of
its streets were paved. It had curb and gutter, running water, a fire department, city police, a newspaper, two schools, and four churches.
Downtown was only three blocks long, but Main Street extended a full
ten blocks, twelve if you counted those blocks with houses but no curbs
or sidewalks. The residential streets in town averaged three blocks deep,

counting Main. You could find more houses in any direction—and we did each Halloween, but those were really considered on the outskirts of town. Railroad tracks fixed one "respectable" boundary as it tends to in small towns, and the fairgrounds road the other. But even those who lived "across the tracks" or "out by the fairgrounds" were accorded more status than those from outside Mahnomen, like the Twin Lakers, who included most of my Indian relatives. Farmers, of course, were exempt from the boundary classifications.

This status system was apparent even to a child, or maybe especially to a child. I understood that I was slightly more accepted because my parents lived in the main part of town, slightly less because one of my best friends came from "across the tracks," and even less because we spent so many weekends and holidays at Twin Lakes. Several of my little girlfriends would declare that although they had Indian blood, it was only a little fingerful. Mine, of course, was more than this. I remember how some of the white boys who were my friends in grade school, some who were even related to me, still asserted a kind of imagined prowess by speaking jeeringly of the tarpaper shacks out at the lakes. They would grow up and become the townsmen who breed that kind of arrogant humor.

I was most often quiet in these urban status wars. I understood the system; I simply wouldn't change. I might not have fared so well, but I was one of the bright children in our small class, and, encouraged by the nuns to explain the lessons to those who needed help, I developed a certain immunity. Academic status like job status, I learned then and would relearn again later, must be worked into the village class mapping.

Now that was in town. Out at Twin Lakes, I was again not quite the same as everyone else. My brother and I were allowed to go with our cousins to church school, where they made all kinds of wonderful things, sang songs, and really didn't seem to study anything at all. But going was not completely comfortable. Mrs. Tonce, the minister's wife and the teacher, knew we were being raised Catholic in town, and, with her repeated assurances of our acceptance in church school, she managed to create us as misfits. After he had built his birdhouse, my brother stopped going. I wanted to finish my beautiful macaroni artwork, so I lasted a little longer.

Those years, we knew most of the dogs that hung around the village houses, but though my brother ventured farther, I didn't know many of the kids besides our cousins, their friends, and the closest neighbors. Many I was warned against playing with because they were those "mean" Twin Lakers. My position out at the lake was constantly fluctuating; being from Mahnomen could carry either higher or lower status. Higher when we played school, lower when we played ball. Only during times like swimming at Pinehurst or Bass Lake do I remember feeling accepted on even ground. Most uncomfortable for me were those moments when, younger and blonder, in my ponytail and flowered barrettes, I was merely a doll my cousins proudly walked about but didn't want to get dirty. Wavering between innocent possessiveness and instinctive protectiveness, they treasured me. Years later I would understand and, in the academic status plays, have reason to distinguish that kind of affectionate championship from the kind that truly objectifies.

Growing to adulthood, I have discovered, is a long series of lessons about mapping, about lines of demarcation between people and places. But more important are the lessons about power and the sacred. As the years have worn on, I've come upon these lessons tangled oddly together like copulating snakes.

So they came with my first foray into the professional academic community when, as a graduate student in 1985, I traveled with a group of D'Arcy McNickle fellows from the Newberry Library into "Indian Country" Wisconsin. So much was strange to me on that journey. I didn't understand then, sometimes still don't understand, the intellectual objectivity that can separate us from the warm pulsating movements of our existence. My companions on the journey were established white academics with track records in Indian studies. Anthropologists, ethnographers, historians, they were witty, warm, and amiable, but somehow alien to me. They inquired about my home at White Earth, my childhood, my relations, our politics, tribal customs. But the questions presupposed an intellectual sophistication I didn't possess. I carried stories of catching whitefish last winter just below the ice, the poem about my Uncle Emet's speedy Studebaker, and bits of the old language still attached to people and the lanterns we gathered around. I had never extracted from the lived moments of my life theories and generalizations.

As we drove cross country, our van stopped at every historical marker erected upon the land. It stopped along roadsides for one member of the entourage to photograph American kitsch: bathtub madonnas, cutout animal shapes, wooden wishing wells. At the reservations we visited the tribal offices, schools, community meal programs, museums, treatment centers, and Indian craft stores. Family relationships, "subsistence" economy, community structure—life itself—I learned could be measured and mapped, could be studied. Then at WOJB radio station a young burly Indian man called me by name. As he told me who he was and we laughed about the last time we had seen one another, when he was ten or twelve and smitten with my younger cousin, and we were sliding down the hill by the ranger station, home became real to me again.

In those first conversations with the Newberry scholars I began to understand the positions available to me as an Indian in an anthropological system. I left West Walton Street an uninitiated informant and on the first day's drive became a casual object of study. That evening on the phone, within earshot of my female roommates, I tell Lenny, "I've never thought about my life like this before." Perhaps my discovery of the intellectual intentions behind the questions had already thrust me into the role of co-conspirator in the "study" of Indian life. I could interpret my world, translate it for someone else. For consumption and evaluation. Although I couldn't have explained it then, the sensations of that new place, privileged as it was yet confined, overwhelmed me. Sometime during that trip and the six-month fellowship that followed, another view opened. I could if I wished become myself the evaluator and classifier. If I chose to learn the social science methods, I could function simultaneously as the insider and the outsider. But with each advance in academic understanding and status, I heard the gates begin to click behind me. Now I know whatever choice I make, whatever position I might take, even should I adamantly reject the anthropological model, university flow charts, or the whole academic process, by my awareness of their existence I am already remade. Education enacts its own kind of removal. Happily stories breed return.

On that same Wisconsin Newberry journey we met a wonderful old storyteller whose own encounter with mapping seems symbolic to me of twentieth-century absurdities. A Bad River tribal member whose livelihood had always involved the hunting, fishing, and gathering guaranteed by treaties, he became caught up in the Wisconsin Chippewa tribes' battle for government recognition of those rights. During his many years, he told us, as he went 'bout setting nets for fish, he frequently ran afoul of the then rules of the Department of Natural Resources. Often he was arrested, had his equipment confiscated, went to court, was found guilty of violating state statutes, and paid a fine. "Every time I turned around," he laughed, "I was getting arrested."

After certain landmark legal cases had been decided in favor of Native American tribes and had upheld their treaty rights, the Lake Superior Chippewa, too, decided to challenge the law. But, suddenly, neither my storyteller nor his fellow tribal members could get arrested. "I tried for two years. I couldn't get arrested!" So they began an earnest campaign to accomplish what they had tried to avoid for years: to be arrested. The fishermen went so far as to put their names on their illegal nets. The nets would be found and confiscated, but no one came to charge them. Finally an arrest was made, and a target case wound its way through the court system. The tribe won. The Voight decision upheld treaty rights.

But in the negotiations that followed, an odd sort of compromise split the waters into parcels with certain sections being tribal waters, certain public, and they were separated by imaginary lines of demarcation. And so one morning my storyteller was out on the lake fishing when he was approached by another boat manned by the game warden. Once again he found himself accused of illegal activities with the familiar cant this time transposed to a new level of ludicrousness: "You're fishing on the wrong side of that imaginary line." And his response is perhaps the finest, wisest map for our time: "Well, god dammit! I imagine it's over here!"

This may be just another fish story. Or it may be a parable for our time with lessons about mapping and power. It might say life is absurd and we shouldn't take it too seriously. It might say that if you are a Native American you will always find yourself on the wrong side of that imaginary line. It might say that it is time Indian people begin to imagine clearly their own lines, against all authority. I know this: I may be perched uneasily on some borderline made especially for Indian academics, but that story gives me safe passage home.

Reading these attempts at tidy mapping in the various social and academic circles is to see extensions of America's grid dream. County and township maps carve into equal sections the countryside. These literal mappings of place externalize the wish to conquer and control. But power won't be contained. Not the power of human interactions, and not the power of the natural world. Older land maps prove Native peoples understood the life motion that withstands capture. Their renditions of the Arctic, for example, are not "to scale." They drew their relationship with places. Lakes where fish were in abundance grow big. Hunting grounds take prominence. These maps resist academic distancing, reflect personal engagement. Perhaps they are somehow inaccurate and unreliable; perhaps they are more accurate, more reliable; or perhaps the whole process of direction taking is subjective. The maps we require have much to do with our own way of reading and understanding the world. Perhaps the way we live now we need many maps overlaid like layers of earth to form our home, or like layers of clouds to filter our sky.

The standard flat maps print easily, fold neatly, and can travel in any pocket or glove compartment. But life pathways are harder to chart; the lessons of internal mapping, more elusive. I learned the way the two visions of place can come together in an exploration of Anza Borrego. In Southern California, a desert wilderness area of over one million acres, the region takes its very name from an odd mingling. The name of the Spanish explorer who headed a colonial expedition into that country in 1776 is Juan Bautista de Anza. The Spanish name for the bighorn sheep native to the region is *borrego*. One a symbol of the libidinous colonial legacy, one a symbol of stark desert physicality. Ambitious fantasies. Harsh realities. The sets of footprints crisscross and run double on the historical map of Anza Borrego. The land remembers both.

Such layering intensifies, expands the reality of the contemporary geographical maps. Hiking guides may star old Indian village sites, but the land itself carries more tangible markers. *Morteros*, hollowed bellies of rocks. Indelible signs. The boulders once used by Native inhabitants like the Kumeyaah and Cahuilla for pounding and grinding.

One morning Lenny and I follow our park map to find pictographs and *morteros*. A fog has settled heavy about us, hiding all but the closest rock faces, muffling every sound. Time itself seems masked and muted here. I think then of the seed gatherers, how they eked out a desert living by reading the internal rhythms of the land, traveling in yearly cycles to the many varieties of ripening plants. They used mortars and pestles to extract juice, crush nuts into meal, make flour. At the grinding site I stand, my hand within the rounded shapes of past lives, and wonder that the old voices have been kept so well in these badlands, returning now to rise and echo softly through the fog. Dimensions merge or fall away. We have traveled off the map. Realities converge in the space of memory. And I know this place.

Learning the land means learning not only its history but its motion. The natural desert landscape endlessly transforms itself through days and seasons, so no static map can give an accurate rendering. Yet I marvel at the mapmakers' attempts. Soon after our arrival we notice signposts and travel guides with labels for "ephemeral streams" and "flash flood" areas. The land at the designated places is dust dry with little more than small indentations or bits of debris to confirm the former presence of flowing water. But on our second day the rains come. Colors, flowers, and scents all awaken, and with them the streams. They fill and flow and soon certain roads begin to flood and become impassable.

We live every day immersed in evolving energies, but here the dramatic changes bear enchanting witness to the processes. On subsequent days we discover other mysteries. Oases and mirages. The real which seems implausible enough to be a vision; the vision which is only a trick of light. We learn to label realities with caution. The firm footing we tread can literally fall away. One moment, one day, it does. In the Fish Creek Wash hunting for wind caves we scamper in and out of deep gullies, up and over rock groupings, fascinated by the shapes we find. Then suddenly a foothold in the rock base gives way, crumbles beneath my boot, becomes sand. The ground's rock-solid base another illusion: sand hardened and shaped by wind and water acquires the lacquer and consistency of rock. Nature the master magician, supreme illusionist.

Soon we fall under her spell. The transformations of forms, the crossovers inspire our own creativity. We think movement, change. We think connection, relationship. Earthwork finally becomes our artwork.

Encrusted sandstone in the Borrego Badlands has a familiar squat round-ness. The roundness of bread loaves, of gourds, of pottery, of female forms in the Native art of the Southwest. I begin to understand how our experience, natural places, earth shapes and voices give us our aesthetic bearings. Our moral bearings too. Anza Borrego reminds me how marked is our earth, how marked are we by ancestral inhabitants. And the safe flat map of human existence is every moment forced to waver in the ephemeral space of an alteration, like a wash waiting to be filled. In that motion lies our power. Because I believe this, I resist separation from the places, events, and stories that continue to transfigure the pulse of spirit. Urban shamans cannot match this dream.

Oh there is sacred in the cities, learned sciences, and academies, but the pathways have become obscured in commerce, in endless competi-tion for academic status, for cultural capital, for position and power. Not the power of sacred motion or relationship, but power of another origin, measure, and destiny. And so the guideposts deviate. I read them now with caution. And I carry my own.

We plot our lives in various searches. Sometimes they work at crosscur-rents. Ties to tribe, place, families, belief systems, careers tug us in many directions. Their pathways may converge, run parallel; more often they diverge. For those of us from mixed cultures this is perhaps particularly true. We carry multiple maps. The roads on our maps have many forks. We must learn balance in our direction taking. But balance is the story the world chants endlessly. And so it comes if we let it, gently. No holding on with tightly clenched fists or teeth. Balance is a motion, a swaying rhythm.

The map of our bodies reminds us. In pregnancy I watch my body tak-ing its own shape. Performing each necessary and wondrous deed in its turn. One morning I wake and find every blue-veined path visible be-neath my newly translucent skin. I read a lesson in that map about the many paths our heart can feed simultaneously. I read another about the movement of our lives outward and the equal return inward.

Just now, migration is the pattern of my life. It takes me into class-rooms where students dutifully follow lines that have been drawn to dis-sect literature. Plot maps with rising action, climax, crisis, falling action, denouement. I suggest there are other figures that might be shaped by the words. I say let's look at the center, the centripetal forces, the weaving motion, the webbed relationships. I say draw me new pictures, new maps. Critics examine the tragedies of Indian stories. We look again for the triumphs and the comic. I ask how we can hear stories in different ways, how we can discover aesthetic or cultural values. I find my way in softly redrawing the perimeters of possibilities. The continual redrawing is also for me. It takes me back home. This is one branch, one vein, one motion in my life. I am finally learning that the trick to surviving is to keep it connected to all the others. That connection comes with story, memory, dream, heartbeat—all motion and relation.

Those twin animals. The magic of ephemeral streams. Old tales heard again in voices now gone. Mists, illusions, and visions. The world that cannot be easily carved and contained is the world I choose to inhabit. The other is the place I will visit, the maze through which I must carry the compass of stories to remember my directions.

Race and Mixed-Race

A PERSONAL TOUR

Rainier Spencer

The truth is that there are no races: there is nothing
in the world that can do all we ask race to do for us.

KWAME ANTHONY APPIAH,
In My Father's House

THE DREAM

*999 Afro-Americans arranged in a line—not by height or age—but chromati-
cally, from darkest to lightest, lightest to darkest. Colors blending slowly, im-
perceptibly, into one another. Not just colors, but lips, noses, and types of hair
too . . . light people with thick lips and wide noses, dark people with thin noses
and straight hair. Enter a white person to take her place in line. Does she go to
the end? No, for she isn't the palest one there—not by far. After much searching
she finally finds one who looks similar to herself, so much so that they could be
sisters. The only difference between them is that the black woman's eyes are blue,
while her own are brown. Meanwhile, the color line has begun to curve in on
itself—enveloping her, pushing her up against her near-twin—until it finally
engulfs itself as well and simply dissolves . . .*

Race is our historical curse, our great confusion. Race is what future generations will look back on with incredulity and pity, just as present-day

126

third-graders look back with amazed disbelief on the cosmology of learned medieval Europeans: "How could they have been so stupid?" My personal engagement with race and racial identity is a consequence of my own lived experience as a so-called mixed-race person. That experience has revolved around what we in this country refer to as the One-Drop Rule, the idea that any trace of African ancestry—one drop of black blood, so to speak—is enough to make a person wholly and unalterably black. My personal journey has taken me from unconscious acceptance of the One-Drop Rule, to what I thought was considered agreement with it, to, finally, a critical rejection of the rule and the racial categories on which it is based.

Questioning a concept so embedded and so naturalized as race always involves the breaking up of foundations and the toppling of superstructures that appear unassailable. In my case it involved appraising and ultimately rejecting everything I'd thought previously about identity. However, this is not to say that I feel myself a tragic mulatto—an overused and exaggerated term—for there is a vast difference between wondering whether one is black or white and questioning whether anyone really is.[1] It is the transition between these two modes of thought, the transition from being trapped within the constraints of an entrenched system of thought to challenging that system and ultimately transcending it that is the essence of my personal racial journey.

NEWS FLASH

> Grouped by the sickle cell gene, Yemenites, Greeks, New Guineans, Thais, and Dinkas all belong in one race, Norwegians and several black African peoples in another. Grouped by lactase retention, northern and central Europeans, Arabians, and certain west Africans share the same race, while other African blacks, east Asians, American Indians, southern Europeans, and Australian Aborigines all make up another race. Grouped by finger print patterns. . . .[2]

If there were a blood test that could determine definitively whether a person had any sub-Saharan African ancestors within the past 2,000 years, I doubt many white people would take it. Disruptions, disjunctions—it's so important that skeletons stay in their closets. Indeed, if there were a test to show the precise extent of European ancestry in individual Afro-Americans—just how much Irish and just how much English, for instance—I don't think many would really want to know, for it would be just the kind of interesting information that would complicate the very simple view most Americans have of race and identity.[3]

The scientific jury is in and has been for some time. Biological races don't exist, never have. Everyone is always already mixed. The Mediterranean slave trade of the ancient world moved sub-Saharan Africans into North Africa and Southern Europe, and moved Black Sea Europeans into North and sub-Saharan Africa. The later trans-Atlantic slave trade ensured contact between southern and northern Europeans, sub-Saharan West Africans, and the indigenous peoples of North and South America. Additionally, the still more recent phenomenon of passing has served especially well as a vehicle for the injection of African genetic material into unsuspecting white American families. Easily over a hundred thousand blacks have passed into white society, easily.[4] Keeping in mind that a successful act of passing is one that goes undetected, what white person can know that there is no African branch (or root) on her family tree? So many different people today carry so many different genetic heritages that in all likelihood when two white Americans mate they are transferring African genetic material without even being aware of it. If only they knew . . .

INTO THE MIX: BEGINNINGS

Mixed-race identity, or *mestizaje*, can be experienced in a variety of ways. It can be ignored, put in context, glorified, denied, and, as with race, reified. *Mestizaje* has, for me, always been just below the surface. As far back as I can remember, I've known I was mixed. That was the word my mother used—*mixed*. I don't remember my father talking about it at all. His work at sea took him away much of the year, so it's fair to say I grew up in a white household, albeit an immigrant one, specifically a German one. Psychologists and sociologists tell us that placing a child in this type of situation is a sure-fire recipe for identity confusion, but when I was young you could have fooled me. I was simply who I was. I knew I was unique the same way my friends all knew that they were themselves unique. All this business of either conforming to rigid identity types or being labeled confused is a pipe dream of psychologists desperately in search of a theory . . . but more on that later.

Though it didn't start out that way, our neighborhood of post–World War II attached houses in Queens, New York, eventually became a black neighborhood, so nearly all my friends outside of school were black. I don't recall this confusing me either, however; and in no sense was I torn by loyalties between my friends and home. In fact, I don't understand how such a loyalty dichotomy could even be possible. I was a little colored boy—*mixed*, if that level of precision was called for, and it usually wasn't. My nonblack school friends saw my mother from time to time, yet I was still a little colored boy to them. Racial issues certainly didn't complicate my life or cause me to hate who I was. Being called *yellow* by someone marginally darker than me was hardly a major psychological event. Indeed, when I was growing up in the early 1960s, having very dark skin color was what brought one the most insults and criticisms. From my own point of view, the two things I hated most about myself are still clear as a bell to me: (1) having an irredeemably strange name and (2) having a head that was flat in the back. These two things brought me more teasing than any child deserves. I'd gladly have traded anything for a normal head and a regular name.

As I recall, nearly all my friends had some aspect of identity that was in conflict with some imagined standard and therefore subject to teasing. Some were adopted, some were fostered; some were very poor, others were rather well-off; some were unhip, some had physical deformities, some were retarded mentally; some were ugly, some were gay, while some had seemingly nothing *wrong* with them and were teased precisely because of it.[5] I had an entire neighborhood of friends who treated me as well and as poorly as any other kid we knew. If one of them called me an Oreo or Frankenstein, I likely responded by insulting his mother, and then we'd probably go over to my house or his to play Monopoly, chess, Sorry, or slot cars.[6] Sticks and stones and all that

PSYCHOBABBLE AND THE SOCIOLOGY OF REIFICATION

That the Earth is flat is as easy to prove as driving a car. You never turn upside-down no matter how far you travel.

Too few people know the difference between racism (which does exist) and race (which doesn't). The reality of the former implies nothing about the latter. Unfortunately, though, it is much safer and much less complicated to believe that racism somehow proves race, even though racism no more validates race than did medieval European belief in a flat Earth actually make the Earth flat. Racism acts to support and perpetuate racist systems of categorization and social evil, much like Christianity supported and perpetuated the arrogant notion that the Earth was the center of the Universe while in no sense proving that false claim. The same goes for calling race a social reality, and treating it as if it existed simply because so many people think it does. It might seem reasonable on the surface to suggest that we ought to consider race to be real if people's belief in it affects their lives and others', for I could then say that race is de facto real under such conditions. But this would be to confuse the pathology with its (nonexistent) object.

Take the case of witchcraft, for instance. There have been sorry times in this world when people have believed so strongly in witches that in their paranoia they've put innocent persons to death. Yet the fervor of that belief is no reason to look back and agree with the unenlightened of those days that witches indeed existed among them. There is an important conceptual difference between recognizing that other people's mistaken belief in witchcraft may affect the way you express yourself publicly and acquiescing in the same belief merely because many other people do.[7] To accept the notion that other persons' beliefs can make race or witchcraft a reality is to believe that the Earth actually was flat during medieval times in Europe.

So the claim that race is a social reality is a mystification that takes us nowhere. When sociologists tell us that race is a social reality (their caveats notwithstanding), they perpetuate the myth of race and thereby become part of the problem, helping to ensure that the unreal is reified and that the truth becomes heresy. The analogy with flat-Earth thinking is perfect.

Even before elementary school I had a clear conception of the racial dynamics in my environment. My mother was white, my father was black, and my older brother and I were mixed. On another level I also knew that I was black and my brother was white. It was a fact of life, nothing at all confusing about it.[8] Nine years my senior, his looks, his hair texture, and the fact that the first seven years of his life were spent in Germany as a German all worked to channel his identity choices in certain directions, while my looks and my environment led me elsewhere. He never announced it (did he need to?), but there was no doubt he considered himself white. From his own phenotype to that of his various girlfriends to his musical tastes—and, I might add, his disparaging remarks about mine—it was both plain to see and utterly sensible, especially to someone who grew up as part of it. And this was in no way an identity crisis, for *he* certainly wasn't confused, and he's never to my knowledge been taken to be black by anyone who didn't know his background. It would be silly to even call it passing, which is a psychological phenomenon more than a physical one anyway. So, who, if not the individual, decides mixed-race identity? Do we really want to leave it up to color-struck psychologists and professional organizations such as the National Association of Black Social Workers?[9] Those of us who consider it vitally important to dismantle the racial categories put in place by racists long ago are frustrated, especially when so-called black intellectuals uphold the same illogical, racist categories and presume to dictate *healthy* identity choices for people other than themselves.

Psychologists inform us, on the one hand, that there are races and that there are stages of racial development (analogous perhaps to the cosmological formation of flat planets?). They assure us of the importance of telling mixed-race children in no uncertain terms that they are black, so that they will develop positive racial identities. Otherwise such children will grow to be confused individuals, marginal people, Oreos. On the other hand, people who question black and white racial categories are said by many black psychologists to be classic examples of confused identity development. People who question the racial categories that fly in the face of their own personal histories and everyday experiences are *diagnosed* by the psychologist ideologues as paranoid, schizophrenic, and in denial of their true identities. Conveniently then, disagreement with such prescribed racial identity is proof of faulty psychological development.

But the simplistic notion of possessing a distinct racial identity is, like the pompous idea that the Sun revolves around the Earth, a farce. There is no identity; there are identities, various and fluid. Depending on the situation and my mood I can identify as an American, German-American, Afro-American, Afro-German, male, New Yorker, Texan, Georgian, antiracialist, antisexist, academic, human, straight-ahead jazz loving, baby boomer. I can deploy these identities separately or in combination with full consistency. No one of them necessarily defines me more than any other; all of them come into play to constitute my whole personality. Moreover, some of my identities will be with me for life, while others will fall away, as my child identity became a past identity at adulthood.

Yet, many psychologists persist in declaring that there are such things as monoracial identities, that they are the primary category of personal identification, that they are crucial to our psychological well-being, and that each mentally healthy American has one and only one. I can't help wondering, though, why the uncritical acceptance of racial identity (like the one-time dogmatic belief in geocentrism and flat-Earth theory) is taken to be a sign of mature reasoning, while the questioning of imposed racial categories marks one as *confused*, which sounds ominously less like objective sociology or psychology than like the double-speak of religious dogmatists excommunicating those members of the flock who dare inconveniently to think for themselves. Consider the absurdity of the racial analysis: if the mixed-race person has difficulty identifying with the so-called black group, she is confused, fractured, and therefore sick; if she is well-adjusted and happy in identifying as neither black nor white but mixed, she is diagnosed as being utterly sick since the test of healthy identity for mixed-race persons is that they identify as black. And all the while the prospect of American blacks—with their centuries of European admixture—identifying as black only is taken to be a sign of robust psychological development, as if the healthiest person is the one who never, ever questions the identity imposed on her.

I prefer to see an unwillingness to accept racial categories as the *beginning* of mature identity development. Far from being confused about who I am, I'm certain it's the psychologists who haven't a clue about their own identities, much less about the identities of others. Simple reflection on the impossibility of racial categories turns the dogma of such identities upside-down by asking questions no psychologist or sociologist can answer. What is a race? How many races are there? Are any of them pure? Why can blacks be mixed but not whites? Why is a single drop of blood enough to make a person black but far from enough to make one a U.S.-government-recognized Indian? Aren't racial purity and mixed-race incompatible ideas? It is a curious phenomenon that Americans, black and white alike, are perfectly willing to accept the so-called racial passer as white until the ½, ¼, or ¹⁄₂₅₆ of African ancestry is uncovered. In what way, though, has the person herself changed on the basis of that new knowledge? If what we truly are concerned about are positive identities, then being positive about the various identities one *has* is the issue, not being positive about whatever mythical racial identity a racist society says one ought to have. And so I fantasize: a racist white politician suddenly discovers he is ¹⁄₂₅₆ black, which makes him therefore, according his own rules, all and only black. I can always hope.

MIXTURE, UNMIXTURE, DISSOLUTION

I grew through childhood and into adulthood without incident. There were no stares that I noticed when walking with my mother, no insults from passing cars when my brother would occasionally fetch me home for dinner, no social ostracism of which I was aware when the entire family went out to eat.[10] The dreaded racial identity crisis predicted by today's psychologists missed me somehow.[11] No longer a little colored boy, I was a full-fledged Afro-American, a presumably well-adjusted black male who (like most Afro-Americans) happened to be mixed in some degree.[12] It wasn't until I was in my thirties, teaching philosophy at a small northeastern college, that *mestizaje* began to surface and affect me. Initially, it was just a feeling that logically it made no sense to categorize myself as black or half-black when I was clearly half-white as well. And if some rule said I couldn't be white, then surely I couldn't be black either. It seemed to me strange and inconsistent that racially mixed people could be black or mixed but not white. What was the secret?

At about this time my identity development received a boost from my being exposed to two theories that shared as a central theme the idea that race is real and that blacks are superior to whites. The first of these, Afrocentricity, in addition to agreeing with the racist notion of the One-Drop Rule, claimed also that the one drop takes you all the way back to Africa. According to Afrocentrism, American blacks are in a proper relation to themselves only when they have placed Africa at the center of their being. Simply put, Afrocentrism is said to be natural for blacks, and Eurocentrism for whites. Of course, both *centrisms* are erroneous. Europe is no more at the center of all things for white Americans than Africa is for Afro-Americans. Afrocentrism is a tit-for-tat response to Eurocentrism and as such is every bit as flawed and racist as the fractured theory it proposes to displace.

The Afrocentrists stated that the Afro-American had a circular pattern of thought, was community-oriented, antimaterial, and had nonexploitive relations with nature (unless, of course, he suffered from confused racial-identity development); the white American was by nature individualistic, material, and had a linear thought pattern. I wondered, though, what was supposed to be natural for mixed-race persons?[13] Perhaps I had an oval thought pattern, or did it alternate between linear and circular depending on the day of the week? Even more difficult to understand was how I was to be material and antimaterial both at the same time. Afrocentric writers did not offer much in the way of clarification, the following analysis being a case in point:

> Africanity is a comprehensive theme shared by all types of Black families, a commonality tied to the African cultural heritage. The basis of that African cultural heritage is described as a oneness of being (everyone and everything is a part of the Supreme being) and the interconnectedness of all things.[14]

Given the crude, binary structuring of Afrocentric theory, even the most basic of questions concerning the extensive mixture of European and African genetic material in Afro-Americans, and why this should result in Africanity but not Eurocanity for Afro-American families are questions left unaddressed, presumably because they would only complicate the ideology at work.

The other theory I came across, the Sun People/Ice People hypothesis, said that the skin pigment melanin made blacks friendly and cooperative; while a corresponding lack thereof made whites hateful and evil by nature. The reason given had to do with the ancestors of black Americans living peaceful, communal lives under the friendly sun in Africa, while Europeans huddled barbarously in caves during the Ice Ages. Molefi Asante writes that "it is again the strong inherent desire in European man growing out of the nomadic, hunting context of Europe that makes him seek conquest of nature."[15] According to this theory, which along with Afrocentrism enjoys a sad but understandable currency among those it is meant to uplift, I was destined by nature at the very least to be friendly and evil at the same time. As an American of European *and* African descent it was unclear what I was to do.

What these two simplistic, essentialist, and thoroughly racist theories did for me was to make me see that there were some very deep and very serious inconsistencies involved in accepting racial categories—inconsistencies that were brought out especially by *mestizaje*. Slowly, what I'd taken for granted for more than three decades became a nagging philosophical problem. What was it about blackness that allowed it to be mixed with whiteness and yet stay black? And conversely, what was it about whiteness that caused it to be corrupted irretrievably by one drop of black blood, one black sperm, one black egg?

If there is such a thing as racial-identity development, then this is where mine began—with the first stirrings of skepticism toward the idea of race. For me, it was more than wanting to acknowledge both sides of my heritage, much more. Simply arguing that I was both black *and* white was not to the point, was not going far enough, for it was only an intermediate step on the path to rejecting race altogether. *Mestizaje* opened my eyes to the tyranny of the One-Drop Rule and forced me to question its meaning. I began to understand mixture that valued one component over the other for the racist hegemony it was. More than that, though, I found *mestizaje* capable of negating race altogether. *Mestizaje* is a contingent concept, its existence depending entirely on a prior notion of race. If you take race to be real, then either *mestizaje* is impossible or it is not. If *mestizaje* is impossible people are born either black or white only and not in-between. But it is precisely because American society recognizes some people to be born in-between that we have the One-Drop Rule.

We know that American society accepts the idea of *mestizaje* if by no other evidence than the mounds of laws and regulations generated in the past 370-odd years that govern the determination of racial identity in our society. We know because of words such as *mulatto, quadroon,* and *octoroon;* we know because of court cases; and we know because of blood quanta. We are all mixed—not just the visible mulattos—but everyone else as well. One does not walk down the streets of any town or city in this country and mistake the black inhabitants for West Africans. That has been impossible since the end of the African slave trade.

So, as long as people take race to be real, they also take *mestizaje* to be real; but this reality signals the impossibility of race, for race is nothing if not a rigid categorization. Race thought is safe thought, uncomplicated and familiar, while mestizaje is a disruptive, subversive threat to turn the whole universe upside down. Race, if you take it seriously, is pure stability and fixity. It depends on the words *white* and *black* having concrete and unchanging meanings. Race cannot allow ambiguity, fluidity, or mixture, for it then ceases to refer to something pure, something distinct. The absolute strength of *mestizaje* is the power it has—by its even being able to be thought—of dissolving race and everything associated with it, ultimately dissolving even itself.

It was, finally, with more than a bit of shock and disappointment that I came to realize that all my life I had—by accepting that I was black and by accepting that I was mixed—bought fully into a doctrine of white supremacy, had accepted that whiteness was purity and perfection, had accepted that blackness was something much less. How else to explain acceptance of the One-Drop Rule? By accepting the idea that because one of my parents was black and one white I was therefore mixed or black but not white, I was endorsing the most subtle and pervasive form of white supremacy ever to exist. The perfect hegemony is the one you never notice.

No, I'm not white, and I don't want to be. Nor am I mixed or black either, for the words are meaningless as predicates in the real world. Like the terms *unicorn* and *flat Earth* they describe fantasies, unrealities, wishes. My journey has taken me past constructions of race, past constructions of mixed-race, and into an understanding of human difference that does not include race as a meaningful category. Despite the psychologists' predictions, I survived my formative years as a mixed-race/black child in a so-called white household. I wasn't confused then about my identity when I thought I was mixed and when I thought I was black, but I was certainly wrong. Likewise, while the psychologists today may not be confused about who they think they are, they too are as wrong as they can be. Who is in denial of true identity? Is it the person who accepts and endorses a racist system of classification that has no scientific or logical reality, or the person who rejects the categorizations of others in favor of self-definition as a complex, genetically mixed, multi-identitied human being? Who indeed?

NOTES

1.   It is a special difficulty of engaging the topic of race that one often must utilize terms that have no meaning, such as *black* and *white,* if only in order to demonstrate that they have no meaning. Throughout this essay, the words *black* and *white* should be read as if they were contained in quotation marks and should be understood as if they read *so-called black* and *so-called white.* Nor is this inconsistent, or somehow an admission that race exists. That people indeed think they are white or black or Asian no more makes them so than thinking one stands on a flat Earth makes it so.

2.   Jared Diamond, "Race without Color," *Discover,* November 1994, 84–88.

3.   References to *America* and *Americans* are meant to be national, not continental, in character.

4.   F. James Davis, in *Who Is Black?: One Nation's Definition* (University Park: Pennsylvania State University Press, 1991), calculates that "passing probably reached an all-time peak between 1880 and 1925"(56). Estimates of

the number of black persons passing over into white society range from 2,000 per year to 12,000 per year during this time period. Even using only the lower rate, at least 90,000 blacks began passing as white during those forty-five years alone.

5. Lest the sarcasm slip by unnoticed, there is of course nothing wrong with any of these traits.

6. The Oreo reference would have been to being brown on the outside and white on the inside like the popular cookies, and the Frankenstein reference would have been to my head. Being teased about my head hurt me so much, while being called an Oreo didn't hurt at all. There is a difference that children can easily discern between insults and teasing that have some measure of truth to them and those that are just plain silly. Children are tougher than many psychologists are willing to give them credit for.

7. It's one thing to acknowledge that many people believe in a thing, whether race or witchcraft, but quite another to accept the thing as real on the basis of people's belief in it. The latter is what the social-reality concept entails.

8. I can only shake my head at all the psychologists and sociologists running around like Chicken Little, spreading alarms about imminent identity crises in the fragile lives of mixed-race and transracially adopted black children. It's a wonder any of us older ones survived at all without the benefit of these professionals' intervention.

9. The National Association of Black Social Workers is a premier evangelizer of racial religion. This organization has gone on record as opposing the adoption of black children by white parents on the grounds that such transracially adopted children would suffer racial identity crises, despite study after longitudinal study demonstrating precisely the opposite. The position of the National Association of Black Social Workers is that such children should remain institutionalized and in foster care rather than be adopted by willing white parents. The even more ominous side of this ideology is the group's assertion that transracial adoptions are tantamount to cultural genocide, as if the children in question are some sort of renewable resource whose fleeting chance to have a loving adoptive family is less important than their sacrifice on the altar of pseudoscientific, pseudopsychological, and pseudosociological racial mythology.

10. This is not to say that no such incidents ever occurred. Whether or not such things happened, I never noticed any and therefore was not subjected to the inevitable identity crises promised by the psychologists.

11. It's interesting to note, too, that other predictions of dire consequences made by today's psychologists were not borne out by my generation.

For instance, between kindergarten and the start of my Ph.D. program I had exactly one black teacher, yet, by all accounts, the lack of racial role models as teachers was of little, if any, consequence in my academic development. The same is true for my childhood contemporaries, many of whom are now successful doctors, lawyers, and entrepreneurs. There are good reasons for stamping out racial discrimination in teaching, but the role-model argument is a wrong-headed attempt at pseudo-psychology. Why not make specific demands for light- and dark-skinned black teachers? Why not insist on visibly and invisibly mixed teachers as well? Why should *black* alone be enough of a predicate, as if all Afro-Americans are exactly the same?

12. Afro-Americans are always already mixed; they are Euro-Americans as much as they are Afro-Americans. But it's a curious thing that in the United States even those blacks who are recognized specifically as mixed-race lose their mixed status when they have children and simply become black parents. A child with two white and two black grandparents is mixed if the maternal and paternal grandparents are of the same race respectively, but black if they are not. In what sense is the one child mixed and the other black? In what sense is neither of them white? The One-Drop Rule acts continuously to erase mixture and to perpetuate the mythology of distinct races.

13. Putting aside again the fact that most, if not all, American blacks are part European anyway.

14. Terry Kershaw, "Toward a Black Studies Paradigm: An Assessment and Some Directions," *Journal of Black Studies* 22, no. 4 (June 1992): 482.

15. Molefi K. Asante, *Afrocentricity* (Trenton, N.J.: Africa World Press, 1988), 81.

WORKS CITED

Appiah, Anthony Kwame. *In My Father's House: Africa in the Philosophy of Culture.* Oxford: Oxford University Press, 1992.
Asante, Molefi K. *Afrocentricity.* Trenton, N.J.: Africa World Press, 1988.
Davis, F. James. *Who Is Black?: One Nation's Definition.* University Park: Pennsylvania State University Press, 1991.
Diamond, Jared. "Race without Color." *Discover*, November 1994, 82–89.
Kershaw, Terry. "Toward a Black Studies Paradigm: An Assessment and Some Directions." *Journal of Black Studies* 22, no. 4 (June 1992): 477–493.

Visions in the Four Directions

FIVE HUNDRED YEARS OF RESISTANCE AND BEYOND

Arturo Aldama

> Identity for Native Americans is made more complex
> yet by the fact that the American Indian in the
> world consciousness is a treasured invention, a
> gothic artifact evoked like the "powwows" in
> Hawthorne's "Young Goodman Brown" out of the
> dark reaches of the continent to replace the actual
> native, who, painfully problematic in real life, is
> supposed to have long since vanished.
>
> LOUIS OWENS, *Other Destinies*

PREFACE: WHERE HAVE ALL THE WOLVES AND COYOTES GONE?

Summers, I always return to *el D.F.*, Mexico City, to see family, reconnect with my birthplace, and regenerate myself in the *cariño* and chaos of the largest city in the world. One of my favorite places to go in D.F. is the cobblestoned suburb and plazas of Coyoacán. In Nahuatl *coyoacán* means "the place or den of wolves." According to the plaque in the main plaza, Coyoacán is a ceremonial center founded by the Toltecs in the tenth century. Near the plaza, the Convento de Nuestra Señora de Los Angeles de Churubusco was built over a pyramid dedicated to Huitzilopochtli, the Aztec *teotl* (the spiritual force of the Sun), and the war in 1524. In 1847, it was here that eight hundred U.S. troops under the command of General Twigg were repelled more than ten times from the Convento by eighty

140

Mexican soldiers. Today, the convent houses the National Museum of Interventions, which catalogs more than 110 imperialist incursions on Mexican lands by the United States and France.

At the northeast corner of the Plaza Hidalgo, in the center of Coyoacán sits the Casa de Cortés, which became the invader's seat of power during the conquest and where the first major hero of anticolonialism, Cuauhtémoc, hereditary leader of the Azteca-Mexica peoples, was tortured after the "fall of Tlatelolco" in 1521. Nearby is the house of another revolutionary hero, Leon Trotsky, assassinated by Stalinist forces in 1940. Here in Coyoacán, as with other parts of D.F., Mesoamerica reveals its many faces through the cracks of the thin layers of colonial and neocolonial México.

Nowadays, Coyoacán is a center of Mexican counterculture. On the weekends, the squares, cafés, and bars fill to capacity, even though (or perhaps because) in 1996 people are struggling in a crisis so crippling that everybody's spending power has been cut by 50 percent. The cost of essential goods has increased markedly, between 15 and 30 percent. In Mexico City alone, more than two million people have been laid off in a period of only four months; those with jobs work three to five hours overtime at no extra charge to prove their indispensable worth to their employer. On Sunday afternoons artisans line the walkways of Plaza Hidalgo offering handmade jewelry and leather goods: Huicholes sell their peyote stitch belts, purses, and bracelets, and Nahuas from Guerrero sell their beautifully painted coconut shells and plates depicting village fiestas. Every twenty meters the *gente* circle around performances by mimes, comedians, Aztec dancers, and jazz bands playing such John Coltrane classics as "Giant Steps" and "Love Supreme." Under *los portales,* an open mike hosts urban punk bands who yell about the crisis, police violence, *los vecindades* (the projects), and streets full of trash, love, and desire. Here, I stand caressed by the polyphonous edges of history in a postmodern present, the dissonance of cultures in the making, a chaos of creation.

One afternoon, I walk on this cobblestone plaza, heading towards its center, a circular fountain with huge, dark, brass sculptures of wolves running after each other's tails mounted on its borders. I think about the wolves and the name *coyoacán.* The word *coyote,* used in both Mexico and the United States, has its origins in this Nahua term. I smile at some people playing guitars and think how wonderful it is to be in Mexico. Suddenly, a huge paddy wagon pulls up alongside the square. The door opens. A crew of civil paramilitary police, *granaderos* (literally, grenade throwers), rifles out in two lines. Usually recruited from the poorest barrios, these agents are trained to break up any kind of public protest violently. They heave tear-gas bombs, shoot rubber bullets, and wield their batons with metal cores. They beat protesters ruthlessly, dragging so-called subversives by their hair to interrogation centers.

The last soldiers out of the wagon take out maybe ten or twelve huge dogs that are a cross between Alaskan malamute and German shepherd. Their fur is a combined hue of gray-blue, white, and light brown. They have beautiful and piercing blue eyes, and fluffy tails reminiscent of their wolf ancestry. The *granaderos* begin heaving the dogs at the artists and musicians, as well as at the many families strolling around the plaza.

At that time, I had long hair with a cholo beard, square around the chin. I see the dogs and think about the impunity with which this paramilitary police operates—if they decide you're guilty, you're guilty. They will beat you unmercifully and report that you resisted their questioning, and that they had to use force to prevent you from fleeing. I stand up and casually leave, walking towards one of my favorite cafés, the Parnassus, a meeting place of writers, artists, historians, and leftist politicians.

Suddenly, I see a *granadero* move towards me. Dressed in a dark blue uniform with a black bullet-proof vest and white-lace combat boots, he has a sharply shaved crew-cut and piercing brown eyes. Even though I have nothing to hide, I feel my stomach tense and the adrenaline surge just as they did when the *chota* (cops) cruised through the Sacramento neighborhood in which I grew up, looking for Chicano/a scapegoats to fill the halls of "Juvie." The lucky ones got taken from the homes and shuttled out to the California Youth Authority camps, where if you didn't come in with your *carnales* and pledge *Norte* (North, color red) or *Sur* (South, color blue), or if you were not a huge giant of a *vato,* your ass would be kicked on a daily basis by either security-guard "counselors" or other *vatos* looking to take out their rage at neocolonial América on you.

He looks me square in the eyes to see fear and nervousness. He heaves the dog-wolf at me and my shoulder pack, which carries my books, including *Almanac of the Dead* (does life follow art or vice versa?). I don't reel back but let the dog sniff my bag. The *granadero* yanks the chain on his choker and moves away towards the fountain.

I look at the dog-wolves on choker chains and then at the sculptured wolves, a tribute to the founding of the area, and think of the name *coyoacán*, "the den of wolves," and wonder if these are the wolves of the 1990s. These powerful and gentle dreamers and dream guides can in a flash of an instant become the same dogs of fury that ripped the entrails out of Mexican peoples on the command of Hernán Cortés and other Spanish *conquistadores*.[1] Their gentleness, acute powers of observation, and overarching loyalty to their families are beaten out of them as pups. Selected to become attack dogs for the police, these wolf-dogs are trained to bite and tackle suspects when they sniff and detect herbs that have had (and continue to have) medicinal value in the Américas. These plants and their by-products are a multi-billion-dollar industry that dominates much of the politics, guaranteeing corruption and repression of people of color in this hemisphere.

INTERNALIZED COLONIALISM AND THE STRUGGLES FOR IDENTITY

In the contemporary era of postmodern and neocolonial social relations, the issue of identity for peoples positioned as others or subalterns by the violent histories of colonialism is crucial, urgent, and, in the case of cross-bloods and mestizos, "painfully problematic in real life."[2] We cannot discuss who "we are now" as Indian crossbloods and mestizos/as without understanding the violence of history and our strategic and spontaneous resistance to the forces of material and discursive colonialism.[3] In the Américas, we have the diverse nations of indigenous peoples named "Indians" through a geographical error, imagined and treated as savages, both noble and fierce, by the colonizing cultures.[4] Looking back over more than 500 years of history, we see full-scale invasions, genocide, rapes, usurpation of lands, broken treaties, and our stratification as social and cultural inferiors to the civilizing culture;[5] and we challenge the practices of representation that reify our positions as barbarians, exotics, illegal aliens, addicts, primitives, and sexual deviants; the essentialist ways we are invented, simulated, and vanished by the dominant culture; and the insidious internalized colonialism in our understanding of our selves and others.[6]

The issues of *mestizaje* (racial, ethnic, and cultural mixing) for Chicanos and Mexicanos and of the insidious processes of internalized colonialism—driven by more than 500 years of material and psychic colonialism—are complex. What aspects of our hybrid (mixed) identities are celebrated and suppressed, and in what terms? How do we decolonize ourselves without returning to a static and Utopian precolonial past? What strategies of decolonization allow our struggle for identity to engage the contradictory fullness of our mestizo/a and crossblood identities?

In the case of México and other Latin American countries, internalized colonialism on a national level translates into an internalized colonialism on a personal level. Ladinos—Europeanized mestizos—continue to denigrate and exploit contemporary peoples whose first language is Zapotec, Tzotzil, Yaqui, or Nahua, to name just a few.[7] In Ladino culture, the Mesoamerican societies of the Aztec and Maya belong in the past, to be resurrected only as tourist traps. The Mexican tourist council encourages such Toltec and Maya "ruins" as Chichén Itzá (a sacred center of extreme ceremonial complexity) to lure tourists with "spectacular sound and light shows." They want to dazzle foreign and national tourists with what they call the blend of the "primitive" and the "modern." The nearby Club Mediterranean complex (where the blond and the slender go to relax) sells itself as a jungle paradise with all the modern luxuries built right next to the ancient, "primitive," and "mysterious" pyramids.

At the same time, Eurocentric canons of beauty are imposed and circulated by the popular media: the *güero* (the blond) with European traits is venerated. Products that dye hair blond and contact lenses that make eyes blue are promoted and sold in great quantities. People save up their limited wages to try to remove the indigenous and African in expensive nose operations. If one appears more European, one has a greater chance of moving up in social rank and having higher-paying jobs.

In the United States, there are dual pressures for peoples of Mexican and Latino descent to assimilate into the mainstream Euroamerican culture at the expense of losing our language and cultural identity and of living in a state of enforced marginalization because we are Chicano/a and Latino/a. This marginalization translates into fewer jobs, more prisons, fewer educational opportunities, and English Only, codified by such acts as Proposition 187, which denies education and medical attention to "illegal aliens" in California. How do we challenge these forces of assimilation, marginalization, and internalized colonialism without suppressing issues of sexism and homophobia in our own communities?

The multigenre testimonial *Borderlands/La Frontera*, by Tejana/Chicana Gloria Anzaldúa, and the Americas-based novel *Almanac of the Dead*, by crossblood Laguna, Anglo, and Mexican Leslie Marmon Silko, challenge the practices of internalized colonialism and offer models for mestizos/as and mixbloods to de-assimilate from the institutions and practices of colonialist and neocolonialist power that depends on their denigration, exploitation, and erasure.[8]

As Greg Sarris, a crossblood Pomo/Miwok scholar, states in the prologue to *Keeping Slug Woman Alive*: "I use a myriad of voices and narrative forms to show how criticism can move closer to that which it studies."[9] Similarly, in *Teaching the Postmodern*, Brenda Marshall outlines what she means by "postmodernism" and the "postmodern moment," challenging the linguistic trap of the ending "ism" because it connotes that postmodernism is "complete, unified, totalized."[10] Marshall's argument extends to other "isms" such as sexism, racism, and imperialism. If we accept that imperialism is complete, for example, then there can be no opportunity for intervention and resistance. Marshall argues that postmodernism rallies against its own closure: "Postmodernism is about language. About how it controls, how it determines meaning, and how we try to control through language. About how language restricts, closes down, insists that it stands for some *thing*. Postmodernism is about how "we" are defined within that language, and within specific historical, social, cultural matrices. It's about race, class, gender, erotic identity and practice, nationality, age, ethnicity. It's about difference. It's about power and powerlessness, and, about all the stages in between and beyond and unthought of" (4). This open-ended approach liberates the literary and cultural studies to cross the borders of disciplines and genres, and provides critics ways to analyze the lived, the spoken, and the written in

their full and unwieldy selves. Marshall describes the act of a postmodernist critical intervention as a "postmodern moment": "The postmodern
moment is not something that is to be defined chronologically; rather it
is a rupture in our consciousness. Its definition lies in change and chance,
but it has everything to do with how we read the present, as well as how
we read the past. It is of this world and thus political" (5).

SOY NO MÁS QUE LOS CUENTOS QUE ME HACEN: I AM NO MORE THAN THE STORIES WHICH MAKE ME

I am a mestizo. According to simplistic myths of Mexican nationalism, I
am a product of the rape of Aztec women by Spanish *conquistadores, un
hijo de la chingada* (the son of the fucked one). The master narrative of the
Mexican nation considers the Adam and Eve of the mestizo to be La Malinche (Malintzin Tenépal) and Hernán Cortés.[11] Besides not liking how
this understanding of *mestizaje* leads to a general perception of Mexican
and indigenous women as betrayers of the race, I am not satisfied with
this definition. My family history betrays the simplicity of binary notions
of mestizo identity.

I was born in Mexico City. My father is Mexican, and my mother is
Guatemalan and Irish. I came to California when I was eight, first to San
Francisco and later to Sacramento. I was born *güero*, blondish with light
skin. My family loved me because I was the first to have blue-green eyes.
They thought I looked "less" Mexican, whatever that means, less than my
prieto (dark-skinned) father and more *güero* than my mother, who is light-
skinned with dark brown hair and coffee-colored eyes.

According to my *abuelita* on my father's side, I am a descendant of
Basques, Africans (four generations back), and probably Otomis and
Chichimecas. My Mexican family comes from Guanajuato, which in
Otomi means "the place of frogs," the center for the 1810 Revolution of
Mexican Independence, led by some of my ancestors, the brothers Juan
and Ignacio Aldama. The basket in which counterrevolutionary forces
hung the head of Juan Aldama is still there on the northeast corner of the
great granary of the Alhóndiga in Guanajuato. In the other corners there
hang the baskets for the heads of the other revolutionary leaders: Captain

Ignacio Allende; Father Miguel Hildago, whose "Grito de Dolores" inspired the revolutionary uprising where the possessions of *gachupines* (members of the Spanish bourgeoisie) were ransacked and the people killed by the masses of Indian and mestizo peoples; and Mariano Jiménez, who led many successful insurrections against the Spanish royalists.[12] Descendants of the Aldama family eventually moved to Mexico City.

My mother is Guatemalan (Spanish and Mayan) and Irish, born to migrant farmworkers in Los Angeles. My Guatemalan grandmother came to Los Angeles as a refugee. Along with her seven brothers and sisters, she was raised by her mother, who sewed for people and never learned English. My grandfather, a lanky man (with his cowboy boots he is over six feet tall), must have married my grandmother, who is less than five feet tall, because he thought that she would never question his authority. However, she divorced this violent man, himself orphaned by parents who fled hunger and persecution in Ireland.

My Irish grandfather once chased me and my brother out of his trailer because he didn't want "no damn thieving Mexicans" in his house. And so, as a crossblood, I learned to negotiate contradictions early in life.

The summer after her high school graduation, my mother left her high school sweetheart, whom everybody thought she was going to marry. Then, without telling anyone, she left the small farm in Folsom, California, with its deadly hot summers, cowboy hats, gun racks, and Sunday picnics dedicated to shooting squirrels off trees. She caught a Greyhound to Mexico City to study art and find herself. There she met the man who became my father. He was heavily involved in student and worker strikes, marches, and actions. She became involved in the all-night organizational meetings, taking turns to crank the hand-operated printer to put out fliers denouncing the latest act of governmental repression, running from the tanks and *granaderos*, visiting friends in jail, and attending funeral services.

COLONIALISM, VIOLENCE, AND THE OVERCULTURE

I want to remember the ancestors of the Américas, renamed Abya-Yala, the spirits, the animals, the violence of history, and the strength of physical, cultural, and spiritual resistance that began during the first conflicts of the colonial encounter in the Américas and continues today.[13] The historical testament *The Devastation of the Indies: A Brief Account,* first published in 1552 by Fray Bartolomé de Las Casas, a slave owner and an advocate of peaceful colonization, describes the brutal Christian acts committed against the tribal peoples of the islands, now called the Caribbean, and against the Mayas of the Yucatan peninsula: "They attacked the towns and spared neither the children nor the aged, nor pregnant women nor women in childbed, not only stabbing them but cutting them to pieces as if dealing with sheep in the slaughter. . . . To others they attached straw or wrapped their whole bodies in straw and set them afire. With still others, all those they wanted to capture alive, they cut off their hands and hung them around the victim's neck, saying 'Go now, carry the message,' meaning, Take the news to the Indians who have fled to the mountains" (33–34). Casas relates the following incident, in which a boy in the Yucatán resisted being taken back to Spain, to be paraded around as an exotic prize of plunder: "The boy still said No, he did not want to leave his land and the Spaniard unsheathed his dagger and cut off the boy's ears, first one, then the other. And when the boy said again that he did not want to leave his land, the Spaniard cut off his nose, laughing as did so, as if he had administered a punishment as trifling as to pull the boy's hair" (82). As I read these accounts of colonial desecration, a disturbing thought occurs to me: *My Mexican and Guatemalan ancestors were probably on both sides of the sword, on both sides of the fires, those who lit them and those who were slowly burned to death by them.*

These acts of atrocity and barbarism by the colonizing culture are not just limited to México and Latin America. In the stolen territories now called the United States, I need only to think about the massacres of the Cheyennes at Sand Creek in 1864 and the Lakota peoples at Wounded Knee in 1890. After most massacres in the westward expansion of the United States empire, cavalry soldiers paraded and sold such "trinkets" of war as Indian fingers, breasts, testicles, and teeth—not to mention offering rewards for Indian scalps during the California Gold Rush.[14]

The desecration of the Other by torture, rape, and dismemberment is still in full force today. The difference is that now the Other—usually *campesinos,* indigenous peoples, students, people of color, women, and

poor people struggling against conditions of extreme repression and exploitation—is the Subversive, the Terrorist, the Gangbanger, the Crack-
head, or the Communist. One needs only to read the testimonies of
such women as Quiché activist Rigoberta Menchú, AIM activist Mary
Brave Bird, El Salvadoran member of the mothers of the disappeared,
CO-MADRES, María Teresa Tula, or about the murder and dismemberment of Micmac activist Anna Mae Pictou Aquash, to understand that
this brutality continues.[15] The massacres, wholesale rapes, and violent repression that echo with the violence of the Conquest of the Américas are
now called counterinsurgency.[16]

The torture of individuals—Inquisitions of the twentieth century—is
now called interrogation or intelligence gathering.[17] To induce confession,
CIA-refined science uses techniques of pain dating back to the Inquisition—techniques developed by the great fifteenth-century inquisitor general Tomás de Torquemada—as well as the most advanced surgical, elec-
trical, and video technology. The modus operandi are electrocutions,
incisions, and violent beatings that are extremely painful but leave few
marks. Additionally, audio and video re-creations or simulations of loved
ones and comrades being tortured or confessing to their crimes against the
state are used to induce and intimidate the insurgent "subjects" into confessing what the state has decided is their crime. These "scientific" techniques, along with other methods of repression, are taught by U.S. military advisers to the members of a given military regime on the field,
fighting, in their words, "the communist terrorists" (for example, in El Salvador and Nicaragua), or they are taught in a more systematic way to officers of Latin American military regimes lucky enough to attend the
School of the Americas, whose campuses are in Georgia and Florida. The
scrivener's pen of the Inquisition is now replaced by ready-to-sign type-
written forms and video cameras that record the subject's "confession."
These victims of torture are dressed in clean shirts and made-over with
cake powder to cover the bruises and scars.[18] Videotapes of torture are
prized commodities on the underground market that circulates snuff
films, child pornography, and materials about bestiality and necrophilia.

This is the ground of my discussion of identity in a real world of social
relations where the lives of the Others—Chicanos, Latinos, Indians,

blacks, Asians, gays, and lesbians, to name a few—still have little meaning in the cultures of dominance—the "Übercultures," as Patricia Hilden calls them. I like the way this term resonates directly with the fascist culture of dominance in wartime Germany, and I can't help thinking that at the height of the Nazi genocide the officers of the Third Reich loved to show off the lamps made from stretched Jewish skin.

Overcultures operate in multifaceted ways; power circulates and disperses on multiple fronts and layers. Its trajectories end and regenerate themselves in the complete abjection and desecration of the Other, as seen with the skin lamps, pickled testicles, and the Asian teeth that rattle in Emo's medicine bag in Leslie Silko's *Ceremony*.[19] However, the Otherization travels in more subtle ways and begins (?) when children have contact with the agents and institutions of the Überculture, teachers, social workers, immigration officers, and the police.

I remember the first couple of years of school in the States. Having just arrived from México, I did not speak English. My blond-haired teacher with perfect teeth loved Chinese kids because they were so quiet and studious, and she wished Latino kids were more like them. She did not know what to do with me, so I was put in the back of the class and told to play with blocks, clay, and make scissor cutouts for at least a semester and a half. From the second day of school on, I became very nervous during the last fifteen minutes of class, when my thoughts began to focus on getting home without getting my ass kicked by a group of marauding second graders, white, mainly Irish American, who hate "greasers, spics, and dirty Messicans, who don't speak American." *They wanted to kick me back to México, and I wanted to go.*

One day, when I could not walk to school because there were shootings in Golden Gate Park, I asked my mom why everybody hated me so much and why nobody understood me. She told me that I had it easier than my brother because he was darker, like my father, and that all I needed to do was learn English as fast as I could. I told her I did not like how English sounds, and she got mad at me. Anything that reminded Mom of México reminded her of Dad and their failed marriage.

By the end of my first year in school, I was put in a special education class, which meant more games, listening to records, and hanging out with other Latinos and African Americans, some with developmental disabilities. In the third grade, when I was living in Sacramento, an older Latina who loved my melodic-sounding English gave me an intelligence-quotient test and determined I was gifted. Then I was put in another small class, mainly white, exempted from boring requirements, and told to play more games—word games, math games, and visual-spatial puzzles—and given individualized diction lessons: "Speak American!" . . . "You are so smart, but I can't understand you when you talk too fast or slur."

My peers in the gifted class, mainly white, talked all the time about their swimming-pool parties, summer camps, birthday parties, and tennis clubs. I was never invited. I didn't want their friendship or their things anyway. I wanted to be outside with my friends (Mexican, Italian, Vietnamese, and African) who hung out behind the trailers practicing the latest Kung Fu moves on each other, telling barely understood dirty jokes heard from the older kids, taunting the playground monitors, and talking about how far we could jump on our recently converted Schwinn motor-cross bikes. Even though, at the end of the fourth grade, other tests showed that I had a college-level vocabulary, my favorite words then were *shit* and *fuck you!*

AUTOCOLONIALISM AND RESISTANCE

In his essay "Another Tongue," poet and theorist Alfred Arteaga calls the most extreme response to material and discursive colonialism "autocolonialism."[20] For Arteaga, autocolonialism occurs when the colonized subject made Other, or subaltern, "effaces or denigrates him/herself from within. In the endeavor to mimic the monologue of power, the Other harmonizes with it and suppresses difference" (17). Two concrete examples of autocolonialism are Hispanic border-patrol agents, hired to chase, detain, and deport "illegal aliens," keep the border "clean," the Other out, and preserve the United States for "real" Americans, and GOONs, Guardians of the Oglala Nation, assimilated Lakotas, hired to harass and shoot militant and traditional Lakotas. Their official purpose is to ensure that the Lakota nation at Pine Ridge has a "smooth" transition into progress and civilization. Similarly, present-day Mayan soldiers capture, torture, and kill their own people in the name of freedom and democracy.

Arteaga's term echoes the psychic or psychological effects of colonialism on the colonized. In *Black Skin, White Masks* the Antillean psychiatrist Frantz Fanon describes how internalized colonialism functions as he clarifies the dialectics of negotiating identity in a colonial context: "The colonized is elevated above the jungle status in proportion to his adoption of the mother country's cultural standards. . . . He becomes whiter as he renounces his blackness, his jungle."[21] Fanon gives specific examples of Senegalese officers of the "French colonial army" who are to translate to the troops and "convey the master's orders to their fellows," gaining a "certain position of honor" as a result (19). In his chapter "The Negro and Psychopathology," Fanon provides a map for understanding the schizophrenia produced by the psychic violence of colonial relations which equate "immorality" with blackness: "Moral consciousness implies a kind of scission, a fracture of consciousness into a bright part and an opposing black part. In order to achieve morality, it is essential that the black, the dark, the Negro vanish from consciousness. Hence a Negro is forever in combat with his own image" (194).

Jack Forbes, a Powhatan-Renate historian of indigenous peoples in the United States, México, and the Caribbean, takes this issue of colonially produced cultural schizophrenia one step further in *Columbus and Other Cannibals: The Wétiko Disease of Exploitation, Imperialism, and Terrorism*. Forbes states that the overriding characteristic of a *wétiko*, a Cree word, is "that he consumes other human beings for profit, that is, he is a cannibal" (55). Forbes ranges his discussion of violent *wétiko* systems from medieval Europe to death-squad repression of peoples in Central America. In the case of tribal reservations in the United States, he considers how the *wétiko* disease drives "Indian agents" to sell their people's land to business interests, as in the Oklahoma oil rush. Forbes argues that the "secret of colonialism" lies in the internal divisions created by a colonial administration, dividing "the conquered masses (who are usually a majority population) into rival groups with a small sector (the *ladinos*, or *mestizos*, or light mulattos in the plantation south of the United States) being used to kill, lash, and control their more oppressed relations" (68).

Forbes describes how Ladinos, mestizos, and others who assimilate into the European value system reenact the denigration and exploitation of their own peoples in order to take part in the "profits." They are given the "privileges" of raping and beating their own peoples without "fear of prosecution" (69). However, Forbes argues that the *wétikos*, the Ladinos, "are brutalized as they brutalize. They are steadily more corrupted until finally an Indian machete or bullet ends their career" (69).

When I was in Mexico City one summer, I described internalized colonialism to my dad and uncle. The family stories began breaking out. My uncle Jorge laughed, saying, "Hey, if you want to talk about internalized colonialism, you should have seen your great-grandmother Pita. . . . She was really something."

I remember a very old woman who invited me to come over to sit on the floor next to her on her favorite chair when I was four or five years old. She would stroke my hair and feed me *dulces* while she fed herself small, green, marinated serrano peppers. Priding myself on my five-year-old ability to handle hot chilies, and wanting to be like my *querida* Pita, one day I popped a few of the serranos in my mouth. I screamed and cried for at least an hour. Nothing except milk could put the fire out in my mouth. I also remember what my *abuelita* told me about Pita and her Cinderella-like story. She was poverty-stricken, the owner of only one dress, the oldest of her brothers and sisters. One day Pita was stopped in the street by an officer in the army who stepped out of his carriage to introduce himself as Captain Juan Aldama III. They were married shortly after.

But back to Jorge's story: Pita blessed *Dios y la Virgen* when her only son, my grandfather Arturo, was born light-skinned. In Pita's mind, her son had possibilities. He could even be considered a *gente de razón*. Later, she cursed God when all of Arturo's seven children were born with dark skin. With utmost solemnity, Pita tried to wash away and purify this "shame" and "disgrace" in her grandchildren.

Jorge said, "Oh man! . . . To make me whiter, Pita literally rubbed my skin raw with a pumice stone when I was little, . . . from when I was four to nine."

"And the funny thing is," I replied, "your skin turned even darker and redder because Pita irritated it so much with her relentless scrubbing."

We all burst into laughter.

Then I looked at my dad, who is darker-skinned than my uncle, and timidly asked him if he was subjected to Pita's purgatorium. They both laughed, looking at each other, and Jorge said, "Oh no, your dad was saved from the baths. "

"Why?" I asked.

Jorge replied, "Pita thought that your dad was such a cute and thoughtful child with a nice smile that made him a good person."

(I say to myself, "Good person means good Mexican and good Indian.")

Then I asked about Tía Julieta, my dad's youngest sister, the darkest of my aunts. Both Jorge and my dad said, "She was somewhat saved because Leonora, the oldest sister, with brown-green eyes, was Pita's favorite granddaughter and Julieta was Leonora's favorite sister."

DIRECTIONS: OLD (NEW) VISIONS

I remember that even deer can pass in one of my favorite stories that the Nootka-Cowichan storyteller Johnny Moses told me. It was about Father Anthony, one of the first Catholic missionaries to try to convert the Nootka (Nu-Cha-Nu-ulth) people on the west coast of Vancouver Island in what is now British Columbia, Canada. Father Anthony learned the Nootka language and began baptizing the people with Christian names and teaching the people the "proper" conduct of God's true faith. One of the rules was to eat only fish on the Friday before Easter.

The story goes that there was an old man, recently baptized as Robert but the people call him Old Man Bob. Bob, a man of prayer, became a devout member of the new faith, not seeing any contradictions between it and the medicine ways of his people. Father Anthony was always scolding him about the rules, even though Old Man Bob always prayed real strong in the services.

Anyhow, one day Old Man Bob is walking along a stream on his way back home, happily singing to himself, "Uhm I got me a deer and I am going to eat good tonight. . . . Uhm I got me a deer and I am eat good tonight"

(Johnny tells the story first in Nootka, then in English, with a hilarious use of voices and faces as he assumes the different personages.) Father Anthony heard of Old Man Bob's great find; yet it was the Friday before Easter. Father Anthony comes to scold Bob yet again. "You must follow God's commands, and eat only fish on this Friday; otherwise it is a sin!"

Old Man Bob looks at the deer and thinks of the stew he is planning to make, looks a little sad, and then smiles and tells the priest, "Sure. No problem. If you want me to eat fish, I'll eat fish."

The Father, a little suspicious because of how quickly the old man agreed, leaves, planning to make a surprise visit later. That night when Father Anthony comes back, he smells freshly cooked deer and is really, really mad. Old Man Bob looks up at Father Anthony and smiles. With a gleam in his eyes, Old Man Bob throws water on the venison stew four times and exclaims, "I baptize you fish."

On a plane to present my first paper at the annual National Association of Chicano Studies conference, held for the first time in México, I am part of a large group of Chicanos from Berkeley—professors, graduate and undergraduate students. It is my first year in graduate school, and I get seated next to one of the newer Chicana sociology professors. I try to ask her about her research, classes, and community work. She answers my questions in monosyllables, and then all of sudden she looks at me and says, "I don't know why you are coming to this conference."

I say, "Yeah, I feel pretty nervous about presenting a paper for the first time."

She continues, "This conference is for Chicanos, and you are not a real Chicano."

I'm shocked, go quiet, and fall into her trap of defending myself. "What do you mean?"

She says, "You have had too much privilege to be a Chicano."

Sure. Men in both Mexican and Anglo cultures are more privileged than women. I have always had to work. I have had to put myself through college. Our family lived on welfare until my mom got enough child-psychology credits to be a bilingual teacher's aid.

Then the professor goes on to tell me that my family history—immigrating from México, hunger, police harassment—does not fit the sociological pattern of immigration. We are outside her sociological norms. In her method of legitimization, we simply do not exist.

Since then, I have begun teaching my own classes in Chicano literature, culture, and history, and have had more than a few first- and second-year Chicanas from East Los Angeles and South Central come to my office in tears because in Professor J.'s classes on the Chicano family, they were not Chicana enough.

One student's father was Mexican and her mother Puerto Rican. She grew up in a longstanding Chicano barrio in Los Angeles. When she asked about how she could reconcile the aspects of her Puerto Rican identity with her Chicana identity, she was told that she should leave the class on La Chicana and take a Latin American Studies course. She started crying in the seminar, and Professor J. used her as an example to the rest of the class of feminine weakness, saying, "The reason that Chicanas are not respected as critical analysts is because they fall too easily into unnecessary emotional weakness."

Professor J. is herself a crossblood. Her father is a famous Cambridge-trained English biochemist. Professor J., who is short and *morena* (dark-skinned) takes after her Mexican mother. What sociological models of immigration or family structure explain her experience and determine her identity?

She can pass.

But what if you don't want to pass? In *The Other Side* crossblood journalist and poet Rubén Martínez addresses the dialectics of negotiating multiple identities in multiple cultural spheres, México, El Salvador, and Los Angeles.[22] Martínez sees himself standing at the gateway of cultural forces, without a center or movement: "I have lived in both the North and the South over my twenty nine years, trying to [be] South in the South, North in the North, South in the North, and North in the South, and a rage arises from within as the ideal of existential unity crumbles. I cannot tell whether what I see is a beginning or an end. My quest for a true center, for a cultural, political and romantic home, is stripped of direction"(3). Martínez states that when he was thirty, he was "a world traveler, healing the wounds between cultures, between ideologies, between selves and others" (4). Martínez negotiates his multiplicity by signing "treaties" with his "various selves—Mexican, Salvadoran, middle class Angeleno, barrio dweller, poet, journalist, et cetera" (4), which, if a mirror of how all U.S. treaties have been broken with Native nations, implies a fragility and uncertainty. Martínez clarifies that this book is a search for "home," which he has "lost and found countless times. . . . Wherever I am now, I must be much more than two. I must be North and South in the North and in the South" (5).

I am inspired by Martínez's struggle to bring the North into the South and the South into the North. The spheres I travel in are México City, San Francisco, and Berkeley. However, I try to bring the North and South into the East and West; a challenge to find a psychic and cultural center in the four directions. As a crossblood, I am always translating and negotiating cultural realities, bridging Chicano with Native American and Latin American, with varying degrees of success.

Even when I'm looking for an apartment around the Mission San Francisco, every place that I apply for gets offered to more "qualified" tenants. I have good credit, a steady job, and excellent landlord references, but, to most landlords, Chicanos and Latinos mean extended family (overoccupancy), noise complaints, frequent police visits, empty bottles everywhere, INS raids, and drug houses. I finally get a call back on a first-story flat, three blocks up from Mission Street. The landlady wants to "meet" me and my roommate; she lives upstairs. (Are we good Mexicans and Latinos?) Her apartment has masks from Oaxaca and Guerrero hanging in straight lines all over her flat. I ask her about them, and she informs me that she goes to México a lot. I tell her that I was born there, and that my dad's family is still there.

"Oh really. . . . You sure don't look Mexican."

Oh no, here we go again. I don't fit her invented images of Mexican. I exist outside the blinders that limit her understanding of *mestizaje* in México: the villages of *güero campesinos* in Jalisco and the Afro-mestizo towns on the coast of Guerrero and Veracruz. I assure her that I am, and ask myself, "What México does she go to?"

After I explain that I take after my mom, she tells me that I must not have Indian blood, a descendant of Spaniards. "Oh thank you for deciding who I am; I feel more secure in the world knowing that I am catalogued in its appropriate place." Then I wonder, "Do I want the apartment bad enough to put up with this bullshit?" For crossbloods, small talk is always an interrogation of identity: "Imagine that, I thought all Mexicans are . . . " "Oh I have a friend who is Mexican . . . " "I always wanted to learn Spanish . . . " "Mexicans are such nice people, so humble and considerate." "Oh yeah, then why don't you learn something from them!"

Then, she goes on to say how people always mistake her for Latina because her ancestry is Romanian and Jewish. And even though she once married a Puerto Rican, she can only speak a very limited Spanish. I tell her that I am expecting a long-distance call, and can we discuss the details of the lease. She is eager for the deposit, which is twice the monthly rent, the maximum amount legally allowable; and, tired of looking, my roommate and I move in two weeks later.

Border discourse is in the vanguard of cultural studies. It is "in" to have multiple subjectivities, articulate multiple consciousness, and resist multiple marginalizations. However, living on the edges of any overculture is painful and violent. I feel my self most reflected in other mixed-bloods who are not in denial of their identity: those who negotiate the overculture's gaze and resist the position of "I can pass, so why bother?" No matter how hard this gaze fixes and catalogues you into its own zones of comfort and discomfort, we will never fit. I'm glad.

> This land was Mexican once
> was Indian always
> and is.
> And   will be again[23]

In addition to linking Chicanos with peoples of the Caribbean and Latin America, Ray Gonzalez's *Without Discovery* links Chicanos with Native Americans.[24] As he says in the preface, "Five hundred years have passed, and these writers know it. Five hundred years of native and foreign languages have already created voices of mixed cultures, the true sound of the Américas, as its artists and writers mark history with honest visions of what it means to be citizens of the Américas, not American citizens" (x). Gonzalez concludes the preface by arguing for the primacy of native writers and voices at "the final years of the twentieth century," those who "prove the true mark of history," which Gonzalez states "comes from individuals living and writing their own stories" (xi)—individuals like Francisco Alarcón, whose essay "Reclaiming Ourselves, Reclaiming America" considers the survival and persistence of the Mesoamerican culture in the contemporary politics of Chicano/a identity.[25] "For many of us," Alarcón says, "our America has been taken away from us. Our America has been invaded, occupied, whitewashed, gagged, suppressed, sanitized, and at best, ignored" (34). But "Mesoamerica has survived and is alive, well, and all around us." The vitality of Mesoamerica "cannot be reduced to museum artifacts, bones and stones." It is found in the "flesh and spirit of many contemporary Native and Mestizo peoples" (35) and "one of the most pressing changes that need to happen is our recognition and celebration of a cultural face of ours that has been suppressed and denied for so long: our living Mesoamerican heritage" (36).

Challenging linear conceptions of history, Alarcón argues that "this awareness of our Mesoamerican past should be projected into our present and our future in radically new ways" (36), and he argues that in hegemonic América the dominant culture needs not only to be aware of the Mesoamerican but to engage with the *carne* and *hueso* (flesh and bones) of this world: "America must be able to see, hear, touch, taste, and smell this America" (37).

In "Chicana Feminism," Norma Alarcón considers how the Mesoamerican past projects itself into contemporary Chicana identity.[26] She argues for a decolonization that challenges not only cultural hegemony but also systems of patriarchy in Anglo, Chicano, and Mexicano cultures. Considering how Chicanas were excluded from leadership in the male-dominated "Chicano political class" of the 1960s and 1970s, Alarcón, eager "to redefine the economic, racial, cultural, and political position of the people" (248), argues that the "patriarchal" practices of exclusion in the Chicano movement were congruent with gender practices in México (249). However, in the 1980s there was "a re-emergence of Chicana writers and scholars who have not only repositioned the Chicano political class through a feminist register but who have joined forces with an emergent woman-of-color political class that has national and international implications" (249).[27]

After considering how the name *Chicana* is "consciously and critically assumed" to dismantle "historical conjunctions of crisis, confusion, political and ideological conflict" (250), Alarcón considers Chicanas' relationship to a precolonial past and concludes that this process of decolonization is not a recovery of "a lost 'utopia' nor the true essence of our being" (251) but an embodiment of the selves multiplied and dislocated by conquest and colonizations. Understanding Chicana/Indigena identity as an interplay of "plural historicized bodies with respect to the multiple racialized constructions of the body since the 'the discovery' "(251), Alarcón lists these constructions as "criolla, morisca, loba, . . . china . . . and mulatta," depending on the degree and type of racial *mestizaje:* African, Spanish, and Otomi, for example.

In *Borderlands,* Anzaldúa offers strategies for decolonization that not only challenge Euroamerican, Spanish, and Mexican cultural hegemony but also confront sexism and homophobia in the Anglo, Chicano, and Mexican communities. To her, the U.S.-Mexican border *"es una herida abierta* [is an open wound] where the Third World grates against the first and bleeds. And before a scab forms it hemorrhages again, the lifeblood of two worlds merging to form a third country—a border culture" (3). The inhabitants of this borderland are the "prohibited and forbidden: *Los atravesados* live here; the squint -eyed, the perverse, the queer, the troublesome, the mongrel, the mulatto, the half-breed, the half dead" (3). When people cross into the United States, the "Gringo" treats them as "transgressors" and "aliens" with or without "documents." Anzaldúa warns Indians, blacks, and Chicanos not to enter the border zone: "Do not enter, trespassers will be raped, maimed, strangled, gassed, shot" (3).

In addition to describing how the U.S. border with México enforces the marginalization of the Other through violence, Anzaldúa considers how cultural denigration travels from Anglo institutions of power to the Chicano community, who in turn join with their oppressor to denigrate indigenous cultures. "Within us and *la cultura chicana*, commonly held beliefs of the white culture attack commonly held beliefs of the Mexican culture, and both attack commonly held beliefs of the indigenous culture" (78). She calls for a plural subject that potently challenges the multiplicity of oppression in general, and in specific repels the multiple attacks on Mexican and indigenous cultures. This rebellious subject of re-sistance, the "new *mestiza*," "copes by developing a tolerance for contra-dictions, a tolerance for ambiguity." Anzaldúa describes the mestiza in ways that underscore a capacity for trickster-like transfigurations. "She learns to be an Indian in Mexican culture, to be Mexican from an Anglo point of view. She has a plural personality, she operates in a pluralistic mode" (79).[28]

Out of the painful interstices of multiple marginalization, Anzaldúa creates a way to account for the contradictory totality of the self in one's own terms; she has become *la nueva mestiza* who rallies against the mono-logic construction of identity. *Mestizaje*, then, becomes more than just a simple racial and cultural mixture of Spanish and Indian: it is an ethnic, sexual, and political challenge to re-vision systems of being that celebrate the multiplicity of consciousness—what Yvonne Bejarano-Yarbo refers to as a creation of a "third space, the in-between, border, or interstice that al-lows contradictions to co-exist in the production of a new element (*mes-tizaje* or hybridity)."[29]

Because I am a Chicano, my journey for decolonization can longer be just about confronting race, class, and cultural hegemonies but must also be about confronting sexism and homophobia.[30] I grew up in a working-class neighborhood in Roseville, California, that was mainly Mexicans, "Ok-ies," bikers, and truckers. It was a hot, dry land of inflatable pools, water-melon-flavored Kool-Aid, government-issue cheese, Twinkies, glow-in-the-dark white bread, handmade tamales, and men constantly working on cars, trucks, and choppers. My neighbors, born-again Christian truckers from Missouri, had pigs in their backyard. I thought they were cool be-cause, in addition to having industrial-size boxes of the latest multicolored cereals, their mom had a special arrangement with the local McDonald's. She would buy bags of 100 frozen, regular-size hamburgers, and the kids, eleven in all I think, could eat them whenever they wanted to.

There in my neighborhood, to be a man is to be tough, a "hood"; show no fear. My friends and I were always being challenged by older broth-ers, their fathers, and *tíos* (my adopted role models since my parents di-vorced) to prove we were not "sissies" or "fags." We learned to fight first each other and then the kids from the next housing tract. We sneaked out at night and lit bonfires in the street, daring each other to jump our bikes over them. Once, Chris Martinéz, whose mom is Yaqui and whose dad is second-generation Chicano, had the brilliant idea of seeing who could jump over his dad's pride and joy, a nicely polished, pin-striped, electric blue, highly detailed, long-nose Cadillac. He leaned the ramp, a half sheet of plywood, on the back of the trunk, and you had to clear the entire car, landing on the street in front of the hood. On the third jump, Chris's back wheel slammed into the hood, and he nose-dived onto the street. He got such a whipping that we teased him for a week because he couldn't even sit on his bike seat.

THE WITCHERY OF COLONIZATION

In Silko's *Ceremony*, the crossblood shaman Betonie answers Tayo's concern about the hegemony of white culture, "their wars, their bombs, their lies," by saying that the belief that "all evil resides with white people" is a "trickery" of "witchcraft" (132). Betonie continues by telling Tayo that "we can deal with white people, with their machines and their beliefs. We can because we invented white people; it was Indian witchery that made white people in the first place" (132), and then Betonie tells the story of how white people were created by a witch whose story "set in motion" the invasion of the Américas.

In *Ceremony*, the witch is nameless, "no one ever knew where this witch came from/which tribe" (134). However, in *Almanac of the Dead*, Silko names the witch and his allies through the character of Yoeme, which in Yaqui is the sacred name of "the people."[31] Silko interprets how the arrival of Cortés coincided with the prophecies of the return of Quetzalcoatl and the relatively friendly way that he was welcomed by the ruler of the Aztec empire, Montezuma:[32] "Yoeme alleged the Aztecs ignored the prophecies and warnings about the approach of the Europeans because Montezuma and his allies had been sorcerers who had called or even invented the European invaders with their sorcery. Those who worshipped destruction and blood secretly knew one another" (570). In both novels, Silko subverts official practices of history which understand colonialism and cultural domination as linear materialist movements of manifest destiny from east (Europe) to west (Américas), and North (Alaska) to South (Argentina). Silko's interpretation of the invasion of the Américas relocates the ultimate agency in the tribal peoples and the generative power of stories and ceremonies; they create and counterbalance witchery. In doing so, Silko disrupts paternalistic views of native peoples as passive victims. This subversion of historical understanding and method places Western civilization and its notions of cultural superiority literally on its head. For Silko, the Western empire is a puppet of witchery and blood sorcery.

Silko's understanding of colonialism challenges us to rethink native and white identity: If white people were created by Indian witchery, are they not somehow Indian too? Are mixed-bloods contaminated by the witchery of white blood? Are all white people agents of witchery? If so, why does Silko have characters such as Emo, a Laguna full-blood who thrives on death and violence *(Ceremony)*, or Menardo, who denigrates his identity as a Mexican-Indian (Mayan) and whose "Universal Insurance" guarantees the smooth operation of right-wing terrorism and Ladino and foreign business interests in México and Central America *(Almanac)?* Perhaps, Silko is forcing us to think less about who we are racially and our relative percentages of Indian, Anglo, or Spanish blood quantums, to name a few, and to think more about where we stand in relation to the witchery of the Destroyers (the *wetíko* psychosis), whose worship of blood transcends blood quantums.

A POSTMODERN POSTSCRIPT

Every time I look down my street in Berkeley, I am confronted by a billboard announcing the family entertainment *Indian in the Cupboard.* This billboard is a picture of a young boy, maybe eleven, holding in the palm of his hand a young Indian "buck," with a perfectly muscled red-brown body, dressed in clothes of the Plains, with wrist ties. This boy emanates a white light, a halo around his head, that explodes out into the rest of the billboard.

I think about the racial semiotics of light, and dark, as well as the play in sizes, and I ask myself if this shrunken caricature of a colonially contrived simulation represents how native peoples are currently invented in the mainstream of Euroamerica? *Dios mío!* When will the violence of representation stop?

NOTES

1. Bartolomé de Las Casas, *The Devastation of the Indies: A Brief Account* (Baltimore: Johns Hopkins University Press, 1992; originally published 1552).

2. Louis Owens, *Other Destinies: Understanding the American Indian Novel* (Norman: University of Oklahoma Press, 1992), 4. Notwithstanding the reasons why Niranjana (1992) chose the term *postcolonial* to support the indigent "forces against colonial and neocolonial domination in these societies" (8), I chose the term *neocolonial* because I want to emphasize that colonial-like relations of power are still operating in communities and nations that have supposedly liberated themselves from colonial rule. Tejawasini Niranjana, *Siting Translation: History, Post-structuralism, and the Colonial Context* (Berkeley: University of California Press, 1992), 8. For example, see Ward Churchill, *The Struggle for the Land: Indigenous Resistance to Genocide, Ecocide and Expropriation in Contemporary North America* (Monroe, Maine: Common Courage Press, 1993), a series of case studies of contemporary neocolonial encroachments on and appropriation of tribal lands. Also, for a discussion of how the term *postcolonial* creates an intellectual elite, denying the continued hyperexploitation of ex-colonials, see Aijaz Ahmad, "Politics, Literature and Postcoloniality," *Race and Class* 36, no. 3 (1995): 1–21.

3. My use of "we" in this essay is specific to the Native American crossblood and mestizo contributors to this book. Also, I assume or imagine a community of readers who directly relate to or sympathize with the struggles for crossblood native identity more than 500 years after the brutal invasion of the Americas.

4. See Robert Berkhoffer, *The White Man's Indian: Images of the American Indian from Columbus to the Present* (New York: Vintage Books, 1979), 1–4, for a discussion of *Indian* as an invented term and its consequences for diverse tribal peoples. For discussions of the term *savage*, see Hayden White's "The Forms of Wildness: Archeology of an Idea" in his *Tropics of Discourse: Essays in Cultural Criticism* (Baltimore: Johns Hopkins Univer-

sity Press, 1978), 150–83; and for discussions of how the term *savage* was deployed to describe peoples of the Americas, see Lewis Hanke, *Aristotle and the American Indians: A Study in Race Prejudice in the Modern World* (Chicago: Regnery, 1959), and Olive Patricia Dickason, *The Myth of the Savage and the Beginnings of French Colonialism in the Americas* (Edmonton: University of Alberta Press, 1984).

5. See Tzvetan Todorov, *The Conquest of America: The Question of the Other,* trans. Richard Howard (New York: Harper & Row, 1984), 133–34, which estimates the loss of seventy million lives between first contact and the middle of the sixteenth century through murder (inside and outside warfare), bad treatment, suicides, and diseases.

6. See Robert Blauner, *Racial Oppression in America* (New York: Harper & Row, 1972), for a discussion of how communities of color are segmented into internal colonies in the United States, providing cheap and unprotected labor. For a discussion of how this segmentation of internal colonies applies to Chicano communities, see Mario Barrera, *Race and Class in the Southwest: A Theory of Racial Inequality* (Notre Dame, Ind.: University of Notre Dame Press, 1979), and Rudolfo Acuña, *Occupied America: A History of Chicanos* (New York: Harper & Row, 1981). However, for the purposes of this essay, I am interested in how the values of the colonizing culture are internalized, rejected, subverted, and mimicked by peoples living in the aftermath of sieges by colonial empires, as discussed by Frantz Fanon, *Black Skin, White Masks,* trans. Charles Lam Markmann (New York: Grove, Weidenfeld, 1967), Jack Forbes, *Columbus and Other Cannibals: The Wétiko Disease of Exploitation, Imperialism, and Terrorism* (Brooklyn, N.Y.: Autonmedia, 1992), and Gloria Anzaldúa, *Borderlands/La Frontera: The New Mestiza* (San Francisco: Spinsters Aunt Lute Press, 1987).

7. The Ladino hegemony in Mexico is currently being challenged by the Zapatista army. To read their communiqués and interviews, see Ben Clarke and Clifton Ross, eds., *Voices of Fire: Communiqués and Interviews from the Zapatista National Liberation Army* (Berkeley, Calif.: New Earth, 1994).

8. Anzaldúa, *Borderlands/La Frontera.* Leslie Marmon Silko, *Almanac of the Dead* (New York: Simon & Schuster, 1991).

9. Greg Sarris, *Keeping Slug Woman Alive: A Holistic Approach to American Indian Texts* (Berkeley: University of California Press, 1993), 7.

10. Brenda K. Marshall, *Teaching the Postmodern* (New Brunswick, N.J.: Rutgers University Press, 1992), 5.

11. For a discussion of Malintzin as *la chingada* (the fucked one) and Eve of the Mexican people, see Octavio Paz, *The Labyrinth of Solitude: The Other Mexico,* trans. Lysander Kemp (New York: Grove, Weidenfeld, 1985), 78–89. Rolando Romero, "Texts, Pre-Texts, Con-Texts: Gonzalo

Guerrero in the Chronicles of the Indies," *Revista de Estudios Hispanicos* 26 (1992): 332–62, traces how Gonzalo Guerrero, a Spaniard who shipwrecked off the Yucatan coast in 1511, actively assimilated into the Yucatec Mayan society (eight years before the arrival of Cortés). Contrary to the myths of Mexican nation-making and the genesis of the mestizo, Guerrero's children were not products of rape, miscegenation, or La Malinche's supposed betrayal of Mesoamerican peoples. See also Adelaida R. del Castillo, "Malinztin Tenépal: A Preliminary Look into a New Perspective," in *Between Borders: Essays on Mexicana/Chicana History*. ed. Adelaida R. del Castillo (Encino, Calif.: Floricanto Press, 1990), 124–47.

12.   Victor Turner, *Dramas, Fields, and Metaphors: Symbolic Action in Human Society* (Ithaca, N.Y.: Cornell University Press, 1974).

13.   See Pedro Ceinos, *Abya Yala: Escenas de Una Historia India de America* (Madrid: Miraguano Ediciones, 1992). Ceinos explains that the use of the name *Abya Yala* (the Americas), a term from the Cuna peoples of Panama meaning the "Earth in its full maturity," spread to many indigenous peoples defending themselves against invasion by the Europeans. In similar ways to Eduardo Galeano's trilogy *Memory of Fire*, trans. Cedric Belfrage (New York: Pantheon Books, 1985), this study chronicles over 600 historical scenes of strategic resistance to the colonial invasion from first contact to 1990.

14.   Richard Drinnon, *Facing West: The Metaphysics of Indian-Hating and Empire-Building* (New York: Schocken Books, 1990).

15.   Much of my commentary here is informed by María Teresa Tula, *Hear My Testimony: María Teresa Tula, Human Rights Activist of El Salvador* trans. and ed. Lynn Stephen (Boston: South End Press, 1994), and Rigoberta Menchú, *I, Rigoberta Menchú: An Indian Woman in Guatemala*, ed. Elizabeth Burgos-Debray, trans. Ann Wright (London: Verso, 1993). Also see Elaine Scarry, *The Body in Pain: The Making and Unmaking of the World* (Oxford: Oxford University Press, 1985).

16.   Susanne Jonas, *The Battle for Guatemala: Rebels, Death Squads, and U.S. Power*, Latin American Series (Boulder, Colo.: Westview Press, 1991).

17.   Scarry, *Body in Pain*.

18.   See Turner, *Dramas, Fields, and Metaphors*.

19.   Leslie Marmon Silko, *Ceremony* (New York: Penguin Books, 1977).

20.   Alfred Arteaga, ed., *An Other Tongue: Nation and Ethnicity in the Linguistic Borderlands* (Durham, N.C.: Duke University Press, 1994),

21.   Fanon, *Black Skin, White Masks*, 18.

22.   Rubén Martínez, *The Other Side: Notes from the New L.A., Mexico City, and Beyond* (New York: Vintage Books, 1993).

23. Anzaldúa, *Borderlands/La Frontera*.

24. Ray Gonzalez, ed., *Without Discovery: A Native Response to Columbus* (Seattle: Broken Moon Press, 1992).

25. Francisco Alarcón, "Reclaiming Ourselves, Reclaiming America," in *Without Discovery: A Native Response to Columbus*, ed. Ray Gonzalez (Seattle: Broken Moon Press, 1992).

26. Norma Alarcón, "Chicana Feminism: In the Tracks of `the' Native Woman," *Cultural Studies* 4, no. 3 (1990): 248–56.

27. One of my students who is a member of Mecha (Movimiento Estudiantil de Chicanos de Aztlán) recently told me that Mexica and Native American elders are being invited to give talks and hold sweat lodge ceremonies during the student empowerment conferences.

28. In this section, Anzaldúa considers the oppression of women for only 300 years instead of 500 years. Why? Weren't women brutalized from first contact? Christopher Columbus's journal entry on December 11, 1492, gloats about how he "thrashed" an Indian "harlot" to succumb to his will and raped her (Todorov, *Conquest of America*, 49). Perhaps Anzaldúa wants to draw attention to the fact that many tribal cultures that were (and are) matriarchal and matrilineal resisted the imposition of racist Spanish and Anglo systems of patriarchy (for 200 years?) and were able to maintain more egalitarian gender roles? For example, the Zapotecas in Oaxaca, Mexico, are still a matrilineal culture. For a discussion of how colonialism affected women and the roles of gender in North America, see M. Annette Jaimes, ed., *The State of Native America* (Boston: South End Press, 1992), 311–37.

29. Yvonne Bejarano-Yarbo, "Gloria Anzaldúa's *Borderlands/La Frontera*: Cultural Studies, 'Difference,' and the Non-unitary Subject," *Cultural Critique* (fall 1994): 11.

30. See Will Roscoe, *The Zuni Man-Woman* (Albuquerque: University of New Mexico Press, 1991), which draws into question how much of violent homophobia is a product of colonialist cultures and their transported codes of gender, masculinity, and femininity.

31. Ruth Warner Giddings, *Yaqui Myths and Legends* (Tucson: University of Arizona Press, 1959).

32. See Miguel León-Portilla, ed., *The Broken Spears: The Aztec Account of the Conquest of Mexico*, trans. Angela María Garibay and Lysander Kemp (Boston: Beacon Press, 1962), for a discussion of prophecies; and for a discussion of Montezuma's ambiguity, see Todorov, *Conquest of America*, 63–98.

Between the Masques

Diane DuBose Brunner

When I was a child I was afraid of shadows. So afraid I needed to sleep with a night-light. I didn't like the shadow games my friends played either as they made strange shapes on the wall with their hands. These were monstrous to me. Shadowy shapes lurked, taunted, made me look under my bed and make sure my closet door was closed before I slept. Now that I understand shadows are particular images created by the effects of light at various angles to persons or objects, I am no longer afraid, yet I still ponder the significance of shadow.

Identities are much the same; that is, various angles of perspective and value can create images that violate, thus scarring both the body and the spirit. Indeed, we are frequently seen not as fluid bodies with functional anatomies nor as the dwelling place of the spirit but as fixed images (perhaps media representations) that are spatially bounded in categories of race and gender. Mikhail Bakhtin refers to this fascination with difference as a curiosity.[1] And he says that the only thing that will keep us from con-

168

tinuing to fix identities in this way is love—the sort of mutual respect that produces the kind of intimacy that requires that we take time to know the particulars of another's life and our own.

What is true and what is real, the "true-real," escapes what is false in language and therefore escapes dominant culture, is free then to signify a reality that is neither subject nor object, neither free nor open signifier, but is body that is spirit, soul, mind. This concept is based in the notion that language can violate, reproducing images that reduce bodies to isolated and fragmented race, class, and gender dwellings, making humans refugees in their own bodies. Insofar then as language represents through images, it has the potential to do violence to the body—it plasticizes the real body, objectifying the body as art, not as a body but as a discourse about a body. The plastic force of language reveals the political in language, and the political reveals mythologies that resign women and men to categories.[2]

In this regard, shadows may reveal the plasticizing effects of language as perceived through different angles of vision, or they may be the "true-real," seeking symbiosis in a body that confounds simplistic renderings of identity. They may, indeed, be constructed as the illegitimate offspring of internalized perceptions of others, creating the interfaces between—the child literally dying to be recognized, to have her or his existence legitimated. In other words, shadows may be unconscious repressions taking shape, creating form out of formlessness, while they simultaneously cloak the fact that their existence is a "yoke" on personhood. To come out of the shadows and dance for all the world is to engage in performance, to shadow play, indeed, to extinguish the shadow because the repression that created it is now open and capable of being dealt with. Yet dancing a shadow play of desire and resistance may be the ultimate paradox. Ironically, shadows may contest what they give form to, but in its very existence as shadowy figures shadow play exists because repression has not been undone. The seductive play of shadows illustrates the complex contradictory notions of desire and resistance with/in formations of identity and place.

Between my masques is a shadow play dancing an unquiet self. For neither my family name nor my married name betrays my heritage. My olive skin and dark hair could belong to anyone. What does betray? How I think? How I see the world? Or the conflict, the writhing under these masques that echoes my Cherokee grandmother's words, "Don't push the river; it flows by itself." Her words are tracks, imprints in the gene pool of life that tugs my soul. Grandmother's tracks have followed me from her home in southern Alabama to Florida to Georgia, and here to Michigan, where I struggle to know this interracial daughter of Cherokee, French, and Scots-Irish descent. I find my center in her words, but the conflicted nature of warring personalities is nauseating as I tear at my masques.

Dealing with the tensions produced by my own position in a society that justifies domination and, therefore, subordination, my writing, performing, invoking art becomes a forbidden pleasure. As the squirming, signifying body (re)positions itself over and over under the masque, writing becomes a sorting activity. Traditional Western representations of women and men tend to bear out the extent to which imagination—posited in this instance as historical discourse that inserts itself as "real" and thus becomes an object of desire—controls frameworks of gender and race as both are co-constructed. The performance of my unquiet self is a mimetic (re)appropriation of the "I" society would make of me. As a clandestine outlier, I mime patriarchal violation to invoke a new mythos. This (re)articulation requires fighting my way out of the abyss, looking beneath the masque, confronting the face.[3]

Day in, day out, I sit before my computer staring into that black hole of a screen, trying to type the words that match my visions, my dreams. Tearing at the layers of masques I wear is exhausting work, but work that does not leave me ready to sleep when I close my eyes at night. Breathless and filled with angst, I rush from my bed, searching for the door, for a window, for air. Image-like hallucinations plague my half-sleep.

Over a beer one afternoon, I tell my Mexican psychotherapist friend about feeling like I'm on the edge of an abyss and that waking breathless is what prevents my falling in, tumbling forever into nothingness. He tells me I've read too much Freud. I say, but no, there are palpitations; my chest feels like a herd of elephants is sitting on it, and I'm not asleep. But I can't wake up either. He says it must be depression; I say always the excuse, heh! He says that'll be ninety dollars, please. We laugh, leave. Nothing changes.

I sit again. Write again. I know it's me underneath, squirming. Tearing away at the masques.

Bakhtin's primary interest in bodies, however, seems more connected to the role of spirit, to the fragility of human-ness and to its capacity for "real" dialogue when that intimate side is present. Indeed, for Bakhtin it seems that the spiritless pursuit of dialogue is like the spiritless pursuit of identity. Embodying one's identity spiritually, however, suggests the place of perspective, taking and framing value. In this regard then, Bakhtin suggests love adds both ethics and aesthetics to the identity making/marking act. And these ideas, according to Caryl Emerson, did not begin with dialogue and carnival but with the idea of architectonics in the early 1920s. They began with Bakhtin's discussion of the split between culture and life, Emerson argues:

> An ethical and creative subject must engage in [the] far riskier, more humbling, present-tense practice of "participative" thinking. To do so requires that I actively "enter in" to the other's position at every moment, a gesture which is then followed *not* by identification but by a return to my own position, the sole place from which I can understand my "obligation" in its relationship to another. Only then will I nurture an "I" of my own.[4]

Emerson goes on to say that we do not easily come upon wholeness in the wider context. Rather wholeness is found in response to what we make of the world. The responsive act empowers us to "initiate a whole in ourselves" that forges identities rather than accepting how others imagine us. The "I" here is a socially responsible "I" accountable for all that she or he says, does, and makes of herself/himself. It is not a victimized "I" nor a blaming "I." It is not an isolated "I" but an "I" that connects and recognizes responsibility and even obligation in that connectedness.

If (re)mapping begins in "real-life worlds" and spreads outward spherically, then perhaps (re)articulation of human-ness as body, mind, and spirit may be heard as a culture cry that moves beyond the successive layering of masques and myths to express identity. If that cry arises from the desire for mutual respect, then the sound that's heard may be the sound of the resilient spirit invoking art, voicing an identity that moves beyond oppressive and even violent representations.

A bigoted man, my father, he wanted work so he kept his native side hidden. Playing the white man's game, he cursed black people as he spoke of their plight. Oppressed and then oppressing, he seemed to gain satisfaction in believing he was superior to some. Since he professed to disdain "mixed marriages" (which he thought of only in terms of white people marrying black people), he could never have admitted that he himself was half-breed, a product of interracial marriage. We were all mixed bloods. This was the job-layoff, working-class, greasy-overalls father I knew. The other one was my storytelling grandmother's son. Factory time seriously constrained my fisherman father of Cherokee and French descent.

Hardly anyone could understand how he could sit on his little fishing boat for an entire day patiently waiting for a bite. Few, especially my mother, could understand how he could love to rise so early and hurry up to sit and wait. Those were his rhythms. Fishing time was, indeed, for my father ceremonial time. It was his time of renewal as much as his fun. After being laid off the railroad in the early fifties, he lived out his life fairly attuned to those rhythms—a mechanic and fisherman until he died. He loved naps and sitting under the oak tree in our front yard.

He sat under this tree and spoke to every passerby. "Hey, DuBee, how ya doin'," someone would call out as they'd drive by.

"Oh, fair to middlin'," he'd say back. I'd heard those exchanges hundreds of times from my bedroom window. One day a reporter from our small-town newspaper drove by, and as usual my father threw up his hand in a "howdy-do."

Noticing a baby in a stroller, the reporter asked if might take a picture. That photograph remains my favorite. My father is sitting with my nine-month-old son, Chris, who is now twenty. They're not looking at one another or speaking; they're just *being*, something, despite other harsh ways, my father was very good at.

No one seemed to value that much, least of all my mother, who worked every second from the time she arose until she went to bed again at night. She wouldn't think of lying down for a nap. Her work ethic kept her pushing; his was more relaxed, yet he could take apart a tractor and put it back together almost before you could blink. (Once he took two grapefruits for pay.) How much was his work valued? Probably not much more than the schools in which I've taught have valued concepts of time that children have, which often run contrary to school time. Indeed, children's learning often occurs in very different time frames, almost never in forty-minute blocks of discrete curriculum. This problem of value is part of the same issue that resides in my teaching now at a university. How we value, what structures of valuation we choose in valuing are a part of the larger questions with which I wrestle.

Both in our literatures and in my work with teachers, the questions that stir me most, however, are those related to the essentializing habits of intellect that contain rather than open. In other words, identity politics push us to essentialize—to say, "I alone can speak for my culture." But to what culture do I belong? My collective self belongs to many cultures. For, indeed, I am both an individual and a collection of selves residing in one body, and I am in solidarity with a number of groups.

Fragmented by much, I struggle to unknow the harsh distinctions of essentialized color lines. For if I must essentialize, then I am nowhere. Counted out. Zero. My loss is great. For the grandmother's spirit is my spirit, seeking to negotiate a world of divisiveness, of either/or. Indeed, to be interracial, to gingerly step with feet in two worlds, is a most complicated project.

Her tracks are in my senses. She warns not to push, but I do. The river flows by itself. But I am of two minds, and I push anyway. I overlap; I am contained yet uncontainable. I push and I wait, push and wait. The past is part of my today, and today will be part of my tomorrow.

Elite and very conservative corporations with powerful influence assure those of us in academic settings that regardless of what we attempt they can and do wield the power to maintain a stratified society that weighs time and human resources against a profit margin. So perhaps bell hooks and Cornel West's suggestion that the spirit of Play with a capital P "serves to mediate the tensions, stress, and the pain of constant exploitation and oppression" may be our immediate hope for derailing the pathological linearity of the symbolic order.[5] Further, in his political tract theorizing and imagining the end of Western civilization and freedom from Judeo-Christian thought, Milan Kundera writes, as bell hooks does, of yearning as transformation; that is, he "yearned for yearning."[6] The Czechoslovakian intellectual Kundera writes about laughter as both a uniter of persons and a sacrilege—as in the particular passage which describes "bod[ies] shaking with laughter" in the throes of orgasm and "in church when the priest raises the host."[7] Moreover, Kundera writes of the ability of laughter to shake us free (even if "just for the moment"):[8] "Laughter [is] stronger . . . than that inhuman world our civilization imprisons us in."[9]

Laughter, one of the body's literacies, like Play, may be key in moving from linearity to circularity. Humor may make the unbearable bearable. It may cut across races and ethnicities, classes and sexualities, differences both public and private. When, and perhaps only when, the full experience of any moment includes the body and the mind, self and other, significance and insignificance, pleasure and pain, laughter and tears, when we can move from having everything to having nothing, from being everything to being nothing, then perhaps we can think in terms of freedom. As Kundera states explicitly:

> Cross the border and you hear that fateful laughter. And if you go on farther, *beyond* laughter . . . [you will not see] that the border is a line dissecting [one's] life at a given point, [nor] that it marks a turning point in time, a definite second on the clock of human existence. No, in fact, I am certain the border is constantly with us, irrespective of time or our age; external circumstances may make it either more or less visible, but it is omnipresent. . . . [Yet] it takes ridiculously little, an insignificant breeze, to make what [one] would have put down as [one's] life for one minute seem an absurd void the next.[10]

Laughter, however, does not mean trivializing various hardships caused by economic and political strife, but as hooks and West suggest of Play, it is one of the body's ways to cope. It may be a way of articulating that which it is not possible to articulate through purely linguistic means; it may be a way of inviting wholeness in the self divided, so that strife ceases to take control of one's being even if only for a moment. It may be a letting go of material significance and a release of tensions that bind to the sort of exploitation materialism contains.[11] It may be in this space that the unquiet self who laughs and Plays experiences a time-out in which conversion becomes possible[12]—not so much a religious conversion as a healing or renewal of the human spirit that gives one the capacity to reinvent/re-present one's self and the world. This conversion lies in the imaginative and in the performative—a space that is always open, where neither time nor truth/Truth is linear, a poetic discourse that short-circuits the hard-wired systems of thought in which patriarchal fetters bind traditional Western ideologies.[13] In this space "the sacred and the sensual . . . live very near one another in the psyche, for they are brought to attention through a sense of *wonder*, not from intellectualizing but through experiencing something . . . that for the moment or forever . . . takes us to a pinnacle, smoothes out our lines, gives us a dance step, a whistle, a true burst of life."[14] The unquiet self can be discovered; indeed, it already (always) resides in the body's own literacy, where performative action may give way to transformative critical reflection.

As a child I wanted to dance, but as a child of working-class parents who not only couldn't afford lessons but also didn't value dance, I had to pretend. Up and down the front porch of my house, I'd swirl on my toes through splintered boards and all. I came to see that pretending was like rehearsing; like imitating, pretending is a form of knowing/showing through the body or mimesis. I'd choreograph great ballets in my head at age five, but by the time I was age ten school and the society that was now my world had taught me that since I hadn't taken dance, I couldn't dance, and since I wasn't a dancer and really didn't know classical music, I hadn't choreographed anything. At age twenty-nine I took dance for the first time. I imagined much that I couldn't do. But the dance was still in my head, in my senses. The sense memory my body retained added much to my study, but too many years and too much flesh had created limitations that didn't allow me to match with my body what I thought/felt I could do. So today running has replaced dance, and teaching/writing has replaced other art forms. But the lessons of childhood play and schooling experiences have taught me much about how and under what conditions we imagine ourselves.

Now I like to run long distance. I don't compete; I don't usually run with other people; I don't even do it just for the exercise. I do it because I like the way it feels, the way it makes me feel, the way it allows me to feel the inner rhythms of my body. The deep breathing I do is meditation—a much-sought-after form of solitude. I lose myself in a long run. Regardless of whether I listen to headphone music or to the music of my own breathing, when I run time changes. I enter a different temporality, one that is circular and includes past, present, and future. Both the movement and the music work to help me see possibilities; I begin to compose, a form of expression not unlike the dancer or the tai chi artist.[15] At this point I feel as though everything is possible.

For me running lies between the "not yet" and the "not that"; in its physicality, it evokes traces of the semiotic that Michael Wood says can be found in "poetry and painting, in games and dreams."[16] Within this space I challenge the old logics, especially much of the gender logic. Furthermore, running provides a break in routine; it's play. Music, a long stretch of road, a steady pace, my legs lifting and falling, heart thumping, lungs breathing in and out: all these combine to suggest that not just dance but also other forms of movement can alter one's perception of time and one's relationship to the universe, of who one is and what one is capable of. With the fluidity of tai chi or the hoop dance, my mind and body are no longer distinct in this moment of desire and resistance—desire for a clear head and a peaceful moment, resistance to wondering why I train so hard if nothing outside myself (like a race) is at stake. It is a time when the object (that's me) is caught in the subject's gaze (that's also me), when the self becomes other to itself (as Julia Kristeva suggests, both "subject of utterance . . . and object of the subject of enunciation"), negotiating the border identity that resides at the edges of my being.[17]

Formations of identity that include the self with the other, a (re)presentation in each occurrence, are constructed in time-out-of-time moments. Such moments seem to derail sameness and create a space for otherworldliness. In this space and time, the mind and body may be no longer distinct. Yet how my identity forms when I run and how constructions of identity occur when I dream may be quintessentially different from how I identify at any other time—precisely why, for me, (re)presenting identity is both performative, spatial, and temporal. That is, at other times I identify as a hurried mother trying to pace a busy work schedule, looking for time to share a moment with my fifteen-year-old daughter. And on other occasions, I identify as an eccentric teacher believing my only freedom lies in the degree to which I can convince folks that my eccentricity is really an avant-garde artistic nature.

One theory I tell myself is that if the corporate world wants automatons, they've found the best way to produce them. Slot them into rushed schedules where no one has time to think; the result is conformity and, perhaps, higher profit margins (productive stress, they call it)—perfect little worker bodies. The now-corporate university has discovered this as well. But at what price? And for whom? So eccentricity is a luxury I sometimes give myself, not really one I can afford, however.

Gloria Anzaldúa suggests we wear so many masques we lose track of who we are. I wear the masque of teacher, of scholar, of researcher, of mother, of sister, of daughter, of woman who is all this and more. I call these selves masques because they bear only a faint resemblance to the one who feels the difficult and delicate balance of interracial identity that produces contradictory personalities of a conflicted nature. The sexual representations co-constructed with ethnic identity make that unmasked self all the more difficult. In fact, I don't know if I would recognize me without all the selves that are, indeed, masques to be worn and removed at appropriate times.

Masques can, indeed, provide a sense of invisibility, covering public and private identities. Shadows that emerge as dream-like figures (or nightmarish ones) seem to suggest the importance of continuing to masque "true-real" identities. Masques make it seem as if one is living without borders; masques help one to survive the border lands of consciousness if not the physical border land. Improvising with masques makes it possible to live not as a refugee but as one who might be free. But masques confuse. They provide a sense of what is. What appears is what counts. Masques make it possible to avoid looking inward (which would, I perceive, amount to a "true-real" break), to examine our own dwelling place—the body—so that we might not continue to be alienated within our own place of dwelling. To examine what may be stored between the layers of masques then is what I find most interesting about Anzaldúa's notion.

As I recall from the days my mother sewed, interfacing is a mesh-like, rather stiff fabric stitched inside the outer fabric of a garment to give it body and form. It's that interfacing that keeps the layers together. And so it's the interfacing that gives a masque body and form. Indeed, it may be what's stored in the holes of that mesh of threads that prevents my discarding the masque, that makes it difficult to crack through and thrust out.

I visited my grandmother until I was ten years old. Dreaming, I hear her words. Waking, I remember.

I see the little girl sitting at her feet listening for the story. The storytelling grandmother sits as always in the middle of a large, mostly unfurnished room. A wheelchair fashioned from a wooden framed chair is always the same. A handmade lap robe of pieces of flour-sack cloth quilted together covers her swollen legs, which barely touch the floor. With her toes she moves the chair ever so slightly. The range of her mobility is now confined to the center of the dimly lit room where the girl always finds her. Though her health is poor and her demeanor is no longer pleasant to most, she is still the one the girl comes to for the story. Before she begins, she turns for the ritual glance to her left at the sepia-toned, oval portrait. A robust woman with gently graying long hair pinned up in back, wearing a rough-edged sack dress, breasts free, emerges barefoot through a field of tall grasses with a smile that equals the sun. She looks down at the little girl and begins. Once there were many stories, now there is one. It is always the same, but the girl, confused by its meaning, returns again and again to the feet of the storytelling grandmother:

"In my day I was formidable."

"What's formidable, Grandma?"

"I was a force to be reckoned with. I was fearless. I loved the outdoors."

"Did you run and jump and climb like me?"

"Yes, and I rode and I hunted. During planting season, when other women offered prayer sticks to the moon, I offered prayer sticks to the sun."

"What's a prayer stick?"

"It's an offering to our ancestors for a good harvest."

"So why were you different?"

"I wasn't different; I was who I am."

"But how, why?"

"Because that was my true nature; it was in my blood. People can possess many spirits."

"But what spirits, Grandma, and how and why?"

"You ask hard questions, child. Do not ask how and why. Someday, I'll tell you those stories. But for now I want you to understand something else. The spirit in children is special. Not to be trampled. Listen to your heart. Try to resolve difference. Be a warrior; carry those who struggle. Try not to erect barriers where none are needed. Don't push the river, it flows by itself. Who you are now is who you are and who you will be when you are grown up, is who you will be. Don't push against your feelings; they are like the river; go with them. Be strong and quick. Dance and make the world green."

NOTES

1. Mikhail Bakhtin, *Toward a Philosophy of the Act,* trans. Vadim Liapunov and Michael Holquist (Austin: University of Texas Press, 1993).
2. Patrick McGee, *Telling the Other: The Question of Value in Modern and Postcolonial Writing* (Ithaca, N.Y.: Cornell University Press, 1992), 180–84.
3. Gloria Anzaldúa, "Tlilli, Tlapalli," in *The Graywolf Annual Five: Multi-cultural Literacy,* ed. Rick Simonson and Scott Walker (St. Paul, Minn.: Graywolf Press, 1988), 39.
4. Caryl Emerson, "Bakhtin at 100: Art, Ethics, and the Architectonic Self," *Centennial Review* 34, no. 3 (1995): 412.
5. bell hooks and Cornel West, *Breaking Bread* (Boston: South End Press, 1991), 77.
6. Milan Kundera, *The Book of Laughter and Forgetting* (New York: Knopf, 1980), 227.
7. Ibid., 224.
8. Ibid., 30.
9. Ibid., 224–25, 228.
10. Ibid., 217.
11. For a thorough discussion of the human spirit and materialistic bondage, see, for example, Chogyam Trungpa, *Cutting through Spiritual Materialism* (Boston: Shambhala, 1987).

12. Cornel West, *Race Matters* (Boston: Beacon Press, 1993).

13. Julia Kristeva, "Word, Dialogue, and Novel," in *The Kristeva Reader*, ed. Toril Moi (New York: Columbia University Press, 1986).

14. Clarissa Pinkola Estes, *Women Who Run with the Wolves* (New York: Ballantine, 1992), 342.

15. George Sheehan once wrote, "I cannot write without running, and I am not sure I would run if I could not write." "The Best of Sheehan," *Runner's World* (July 1994), 24.

16. Michael Wood, "Time of the Assassin," *London Review of Books* 17, no. 2 (Jan. 26, 1995), 18. I perceive that Heidegger's use of the term *habitus* means a feeling of placelessness in an environment of alienation emerging from domination. See Martin Heidegger, "Building Dwelling Thinking," in *Basic Writings of Martin Heidegger*, trans. A. Hofstadter (New York: Academic Press, 1968), 323–39.

17. Kristeva, *Kristeva Reader*, 46.

From the Turn of the Century to the New Age

PLAYING INDIAN, PAST AND PRESENT

Shari Huhndorf

Recently, a friend and I attended the Newlife Expo in New York City. The Expo, which tours major cities throughout the United States twice each year, is one of the primary venues for the latest New Age trends including, of course, the movement's widespread fascination with Native America. Countless booths featured things Indian—medicine wheels, feathers, and Native-inspired spiritual aids, most of them obviously fake—all marketed to enthusiastic seekers of traditional wisdom. But, for us, the highlight of the Expo was a popular workshop on "Plains Indian Spirituality." Here, dozens of eager seekers of Indian wisdom purchased tickets and packed the room to hear the speaker, an earnest young (white) man, instruct them in "traditional" Native ways.

The story he told was a familiar one, merely a repetition of an age-old pattern of white men going native. During a visit to the Comanche reservation some years ago, he was adopted by an elderly medicine man (the last of his tribe, of course) who, apparently finding no worthy Comanche person to inherit his knowledge, instructed him in ancient Indian wisdom that was "dying out." Now he was committed to sharing these important teachings, such as the "true" meanings of the vision quest and the medicine wheel, with the non-Indian world. In his presentation, these "traditional" teachings resonated with New Age concerns, rendering them virtually unrecognizable to anyone with even a casual acquaintance with Plains practices. Nonetheless, the audience, many of whom had donned feathers and beads and other pseudo-Indian apparel for the occasion, was enthusiastic. "Do Plains Indian have any techniques we can easily learn?" one woman queried, obviously hoping to better her own life with a minimum of effort. Ironically, although the friend who accompanied me to the event is visibly Indian and was born and raised on a Plains reservation, not a single one of these seekers of "authentic" Indian wisdom addressed him either during or after the event, although he drew a number of curious stares. Clearly, the audience viewed the non-Native speaker as the authority on Plains spirituality.

This event and countless others like it attest to the widespread phenomenon in modern American culture of "playing Indian," especially popular in New Age circles. New Age guru Lynn Andrews is only the best known of the numerous spokespersons of the movement who market spurious "traditional" knowledge, frequently for shockingly high prices. Andrews claims authority to speak about such matters based on her "transformation" into an Indian medicine woman; nor is she the only one to claim an "Indian Identity."[1]

Popular culture also provides abundant opportunities for indulging such fantasies. Kevin Costner's box-office smash *Dances with Wolves* describes the metamorphosis of Lieutenant John Dunbar, a Civil War soldier disillusioned with the greed and corruption of European society, into a "Sioux" newly dubbed "Dances with Wolves." That the film touched a responsive chord in its vast audiences is attested to by its immense popularity.

Is this widespread popularity of "playing Indian" evidence of a new respect for Native peoples, as many claim? Or is it a particularly insidious (because it's rarely recognized as such) form of colonialism, designed to appropriate Indian things and erase real Indian identities? The answer, of course, isn't always clear. Costner, for example, employed a number of Indian actors in his film and drew the public's attention, however fleetingly, to the genocidal history of the United States. Nevertheless, while a few Indian actors secured temporary employment during the filming, Costner amassed a fortune as the film grossed tens of millions in ticket sales and as his career skyrocketed after the film won the 1990 Academy Award for Best Picture.[2] Similarly, little of the vast sums spent on Indian-inspired New Age paraphernalia ever makes it into Native peoples' hands.

The continued economic exploitation of Indians, however, is only part of the problem. One fundamental issue at stake is who will define "Indianness" (even, at times, to Native peoples). Such is the appeal of these romantic images of Indian life, always disappeared or disappearing, that their consumers cling to them tenaciously, even when confronted with the disparity between these representations and the lives of most (if not all) contemporary Native people. Many of my students, for example, cite New Age and popular-culture images as their reasons for studying Native literature (one proudly claimed to have seen *Dances with Wolves* eight times!) and are consistently surprised at the failure of most Native writers to conform to their expectations. Some of them even refuse to recognize these writers' works as "authentic" because of this disparity. In a sense, these highly visible would-be Indians breed a deep-seated and persistent ignorance about the realities of contemporary Indian life. But Native peoples are affected in other ways as well. The flood of wannabe Indians has only fueled the fires of the "identity wars" which are creating such divisiveness among Native groups and deflecting attention and energy from other concerns.

This phenomenon of "playing Indian," of course, is not new. Throughout the colonial era, members of the colonial culture donned Native clothing and emulated Native practices for various reasons at different times. However, around 1900, there developed an increasingly widespread desire to assume "Indian" identities. The growth of this phenomenon occurred remarkably soon after the end of the Indian wars (the Wounded Knee massacre of 1890, of course, being the last military assault upon an Indian group), and in many ways this then-recent history of military conquest determined the forms this fascination took.

In a certain sense, this emulation of Indian ways is but one of the many striking examples of what anthropologist Renato Rosaldo has termed "imperialist nostalgia"—that is, the "agents of colonialism" yearning "for the very forms of life they intentionally altered or destroyed." Such imperialist nostalgia, Rosaldo argues, "uses a pose of 'innocent yearning' both to capture people's imaginations and to conceal its complicity with often brutal domination" (1989, 69–70). In the case of Native America, as well as other colonized cultures, these nostalgic yearnings also constitute part of an ongoing colonialist project. They not only transform colonized subjects into images in some way useful to the colonizers (they become, in other words, another resource to be exploited) but also contribute to the invisibility (perhaps even disappearance) of Native peoples. By defining "Indianness" in particular ways, the colonizers render many Native lives unrecognizable as "Indian," even at times to Native people themselves.

So we need to examine the turn-of-the-century manifestations of this phenomenon of "playing Indian," demonstrating its collusion with earlier forms of colonizing Native America. In the turn-of-the-century United States, these fantasies were merely the latest expressions of the changing needs, projections, and fantastic imaginings of the dominant society, a continuation of the exploitation that originated centuries earlier and has continued to the present day.

◆ ——————— ◆

Throughout the era of conquest, Indians were, for the most part, vilified in Euroamerican representations in an effort to justify the genocide of Native peoples and the stealing of their land. Their cultures were imagined, in Roy Harvey Pearce's words (1988), as the "savagism" that had to be annihilated in order to establish European "civilization" in the New World. However, as the military conquest neared completion, dominant Native images began to change in keeping with the new requirements of the colonial society. The form many of these representations took was a romanticization of Indian life (or, rather, some stereotypical notion of it). Idealized images emerged which positioned "Indianness" as a remedy for many of the problems besetting American society, and, as a consequence, many Euroamericans began to emulate Native life, often by joining one of the many clubs with Indian themes.

Indian-inspired men's and boys' clubs began to spring up around the middle of the nineteenth century and proliferated in the following decades. One commentator, writing in 1897, described the last third of the century as the "Golden Age of Fraternity"; during that period, up to one-fifth of all adult males belonged to one or more of the 70,000 fraternal lodges in the United States (Carnes, 1989, 1), many of which had Indian themes or sponsored Indian-type activities. As early as 1842, anthropologist Lewis Henry Morgan founded the Grand Order of the Iroquois, a secret society of men dedicated to collecting data on Iroquois life. In their gatherings, which were opportunities for them to "shed inhibitions and live, if only for an evening, the life of the 'noble savage,'" members would "dress in Indian regalia and utter the 'war whoop'" (Bieder, 1980, 350). Later in the century, among the patriot groups that emerged and proliferated was the Order of the White Crane, "named for White Crane, the Hereditary Chief of the Ancient Tribe of Ojibway Indians." Members of the group had to be either "royal descendants of Aztec or Toltec kings [!], or else of colonial settlers who had arrived prior to 1783. Potential members without royal Indian blood had to be of 'Aryan' stock" (Kammen, 1991, 249).

The widespread fascination with ritual during this era found an outlet in the activities of many of these groups. Mark Carnes (1989, 1) describes an initiation ceremony of the Improved Order of Red Men, a fraternal organization founded in the 1860s:

> Slowly the young man walks toward the sacred campfire. He hesitates, and glances back at the tribal elders, who urge him forward. Thunder rumbles in the distance and lightning pierces the darkness, revealing tribesmen seemingly asleep by a teepee. As the youth approaches, the tribesmen leap to their feet, bind him with a rope, and carry him into the bushes. There they give him a ritual loincloth and moccasins and smear dyes on his face. Several nights later he is brought back to the camp and bound to a log. . . . Suddenly, an elder, knife in hand, rushes toward the bound figure and subjects him to an ordeal. The tribesmen and elders then gather round, eager to embrace the newest member of their secret society.

This "Indian" ritual, created by a committee of white men in Baltimore, took place in a lodge room and used lamps, gaslights, and a gong for its effects.

Largely an urban and middle-class phenomenon, the rise of groups of this type and the activities in which they engaged are indicative of the anxieties about masculinity which plagued many Victorian men; Carnes observes that "nearly all the orders were exclusively masculine institutions, and their rituals were closely linked to issues of gender" (1989, 14). Although by the end of the century five and a half million adult men belonged to fraternal organizations, the most mainstream and influential of these Indian-inspired clubs were those which emerged in the context of turn-of-the-century youth movements in the United States, most notably the Boy Scouts and its predecessor, the Woodcraft Indians.

Youth movements were a widespread series of experiments begun in the 1870s and designed to combat what was increasingly perceived as "the boy problem" in white, urban culture.[3] As a variety of factors such as immigration, labor unrest, and the rise of suffragism challenged the political power of the middle classes, the desire arose for a means of controlling an increasingly unruly and diverse urban populace. Meanwhile, the middle classes feared that their own boys, freed as they were from the necessity of physical labor, were becoming "too soft," physically and morally flabby, perhaps even effeminate. Ernest Thompson Seton, founder of the Woodcraft Indians and, later, chief scout of the Boy Scouts of America, commented that Americans had grown "degenerate. We know money grubbing, machine politics, degrading sports, cigarettes, . . . false ideals, moral laxity and lessening church power, in a word 'City rot' has worked evil in the nation" (quoted in Macleod, 1983, 32). Many believed these conditions had created the "boy problem": a 1916 survey found that most newspaper editors blamed "urban immorality and lack of recreation for the unruliness of modern youth" (Macleod, 1983, 33). Leaders and supporters of turn-of-the-century youth movements sought to stem social degeneration through programs that would inculcate boys with Christian morality and discipline.

Originating in part from popular concerns about the decline of manliness (a middle-class value associated with the capacity for social control), the vast majority of youth movements served young boys, not girls. By 1910, there were twenty times as many organizations for boys as for girls (Macleod, 1983, 51). Moreover, in those movements that did provide activities for both sexes, girls and boys were usually separated. While girls' work stressed domesticity, boys' clubs emphasized physical fitness and outdoor life and sometimes militarism. In the scout movement, which was oriented towards boys but later added a girls' division, the groups' symbols were interpreted differently for the two groups: while the boys' campfire signified the rugged frontier experience, for the girls it was interpreted as the domestic hearth. Evoking a by-now-familiar paradigm opposing the corrupting and enervating influence of city life to a wilderness experience productive of virtue and strength, boys' organizations sought to moderate the effects of urbanization with a dose of primitivism and a sampling of life on the frontier.

For some, Indians provided an ideal model for manly virtues in boys. In the1890s, American psychologist G. Stanley Hall and his students produced their revolutionary and widely celebrated theories of childhood development, most notably the "recapitulation theory." According to Hall, children repeated the epochs of human history in the process of their development. Following the then-current anthropological model which asserted that culture proceeds through a fixed series of stages before culminating in (white, middle-class, Western) civilization, Hall contended that children repeat "savage" patterns of behavior in the successful maturation process. Just as "most savages in most respects are children," he pointed out, so too are children like savages: "The child is in the primitive age. The instinct of the savage survives in him" (quoted in Bederman, 1995, 78). In Hall's theory, boys' attraction to the habits of feral men such as frontiersmen and savages was natural and should be encouraged.

This regression into savagery, however, was not an end in itself but was instead a means of playing out and ultimately overcoming boys' primitive instincts as they grew into manhood (which would in turn enable them to dominate women and to subjugate "real" savages on the imperial frontier). Ultimately, Hall's concern was with the maintenance of white, male civilization (and its attendant dominance over others), which weak men could not but fail to sustain. Hall believed the failure of adolescents to live out their instincts would result in the "retrogression, degeneracy, or fall" both of the individual and, ultimately, of civilized society (Macleod, 1983, 99).[4] Gail Bederman writes (1995, 94):

> By taking advantage of little boys' natural reliving of their ancestors'
> primitive evolutionary history, educators could "inoculate" them against
> the weakness of excessive civilization. . . . By shoring up the collective
> masculine power of the civilized races, Hall believed he could not only
> save civilization from degenerating; he could help move civilization to-
> ward a millennial perfection.

Hall believed that the regression into savagery provided the only means
of overcoming hypercivilization and, ultimately, of preserving civilized
society; "the boy who reads frontier stories till he is almost persuaded to
be an 'Injun,'" he writes, "is merely being vaccinated against savagery
later in life" (quoted in Bederman, 1995, 97). Significantly, his recapitulation theory was explicitly male-centered. Girls did not have the savage
instincts boys did and were not required to enact the same regression in
the maturation process.

The Indian as model of manliness was inspired by a familiar stereotype. At the turn of the century, memory of the Plains Indian wars was
still fresh in the minds of the American populace and, with it, the reso-
nant image of the (male) savage Plains warrior. In the public imagination,
the feathered war bonnet, tipis, and the culture of the horse and the buffalo became synonymous with the whole of Indian life. Indian images
were fraught with contradiction: Indians were both noble and savage,
dignified and pitiable, warlike and childlike. In a peculiar reversal of values, it is the warlike stereotype which rendered Native peoples worth
emulating in the context of the turn-of-the-century crisis in masculinity.
While "civilized" white men were becoming soft and effeminate as a result of the ease of modern life (Theodore Roosevelt denounced "the over-
civilized man, who has lost the great fighting, masterful virtues"; quoted
in Macleod, 1983, 45), Indians, the stereotype seemed to demonstrate, had
always managed to maintain their virility through constant warfare. One
historian writes: "It was an imperial habit of mind to divide non-Euro-
peans into martial and non-martial races: the martial races kept their
virtues sharp by war, the non-martial races were soft and 'over-civi-
lized'" (MacDonald, 1993, 135).

Applying the ideas of his contemporaries regarding adolescence and
the regenerative potential of the wilderness, Seton initiated the Wood-

craft Indians as "an orderly endeavor to systematize and direct [boys']
fever for 'playing Indian'" (MacDonald, 1993, 141). Seton was a natural-
ist and writer of animal stories who moved to the United States in the
1880s. His fascination with Indians found a practical application in his
idea for rehabilitating young boys who had vandalized his property by
teaching them Indian ways. "I suppose that every boy in America loves
to 'play Injun,'" he later wrote (quoted in Rosenthal, 1984, 65–66), and he
conceived the Woodcraft movement as a way of harnessing young boys'
interests to something productive. During the 1880s and 1890s, Seton
wrote essays in magazines such as *Forest and Stream* in which he developed the Woodcraft idea. In 1902, after publishing articles on the idea in
the *Ladies' Home Journal,* Seton organized his first group of "Indians," the
Blue Heron Tribe of New York State. After further systematizing his plans
for the movement, he published the first handbook of the Woodcrafters,
the pamphlet "How to Play Indian," in the following year. As his ideas
developed, he expanded the pamphlet into a book, *The Birch Bark Roll,*
which was published in several editions through the 1920s.

For Seton, Woodcraft was recreation with a serious purpose: that of in-
augurating boys into manhood, which in turn would serve as a means of
ameliorating many of the ills affecting society as a whole. In *The Birch Bark
Roll,* Seton writes that "half of our boys go wrong, make a failure of life,
are more or less of a burden on society, and in a large and unnecessary
proportion, become criminals." The root of this problem, in his view, was
the ease of modern life and the loss of the necessity for physical labor.
Evoking the specter of the fall of the Roman empire, he warns of the consequences of living a life of comfort: "Through the ability to do have peoples prospered and nations become great. When the Romans put in the
hands of slaves the doing of everything, they thereby lost the power to
do, and were defeated by themselves in their national life and then by
their enemies in battle. . . . So the Woodcrafter of today will learn to do, if
he would be happy and healthful" (Seton, 1927, 115).

As the official handbook of the Woodcraft Indians, *The Birch Bark Roll*
contains organizational instructions for the movement, sanctioned activities, important knowledge for members, and the qualifications for attaining official Woodcraft honors. "Indianness" pervades every aspect of

the handbook: the basic organizational unit for Woodcrafters was the tribe. Each tribe selected a totem, and tribal offices included chief, wampum keeper, shaman, and dog soldier. After having achieved a high rank in the tribe, members selected Indian names; a partial list of names in the 1927 edition of the handbook includes Plenty Coups, Deerslayer, Tatanka, and Little Eagle. Woodcrafters camped in tipis, donned feather headdresses, "scalped" each other (one's "scalp," a tuft of horse hair, could be lost in competitive games), counted coup, and smoked peace pipes. *The Birch Bark Roll* also instructs readers on how to play Indian games and perform Indian dances (such as the Shoshone Dog Dance and the War Dance) and contains a number of Indian songs (including the Zuni Sunset Song, the Songs of the Peace Pact, and—perhaps most disturbing and ironic of all—a Ghost Dance Song).

After their initiation into a tribe, members organized outdoor, recreational activities. Seton was an enthusiastic advocate of summer camps, and *The Birch Bark Roll* includes a great deal of instruction on outdoor life. Woodcrafters were supposed to know the proper use of a knife and an ax, how to identify animal tracks and follow spoor, the names of common varieties of trees, flowers, and birds, and the meanings of various weather signs. Woodcraft honors were awarded in such activities as fishing, farming, hunting, building shelters, and campcraft. Seton's outdoor orientation was motivated by his conviction that experience in nature would endow the boys with health, moral character, and, perhaps most important, manliness. "We want the simple life, the primitive life, the outdoor life," he writes, "but there is only one perfect place for these happy combinations, that is summer camp. The physical advantages of this primitive life can scarcely be over-estimated." Camping out, Seton instructs his readers, is an effective remedy for a variety of ailments including nervous breakdown, anemia, constipation, selfishness, irritability, and, perhaps the most grave, effeminacy. "Is [your boy] inclined to be a sissy and afraid to play the part of a man?" he queries. The remedy: "Send him to camp" (Seton, 1927, 160–61).

Seton echoes a familiar late-nineteenth-century theme of nature as an arena of regeneration and renewal for sick bodies and sick societies. This panacea for individual ills, he believed, worked on the national level as well: the outdoor movement was essential to continued national life (Seton, 1927, 159). That many of Woodcraft's prescribed activities bore little, if any, resemblance to the activities of tribal people (his "Indian" inspiration was, after all, the novels of James Fenimore Cooper) seemed not to bother Seton. Instead, he writes that primitive play, which was merely signified by "Indianness," was a "natural" part of boys' behavior; that it might not resemble the practices of real "primitives" mattered little (quoted in Rosenthal, 1984, 27):

> No large band of boys ever yet camped out for a month without finding it necessary to recognize leaders, a senior form, or ruling set whose position rests on merit, some wise grown person to guide them in difficulties, and a place to display the emblems of the camp; that is, they have adopted the system of Chiefs, Council, Medicine-man and Totem-pole. Moreover, the ideal Indian, whether he ever existed or not, stands for the highest type of primitive life, and he was a master of Woodcraft, which is our principal study. By Woodcraft we mean nature-study, certain kinds of hunting, and the art of camping, but we added all good outdoor athletics to our pursuits.

Although Seton claimed that his "foundation thought was to discover, preserve, develop, and diffuse the culture of the Redman" (Murray, 1937, 16), his objective was actually to give white boys an arena in which their instincts were allowed free rein. Playing Indian, he believed, would help boys mature properly and teach them to be men.

As a movement, the Woodcraft Indians never really got off the ground. Most often, its programs were used to supplement the work of the newly founded YMCA. Seton's greatest claim to fame lies not in his role as chief of the organization but in his influence on the work of Lord Robert Baden-Powell, founder of the Boy Scout movement.

Seton met Baden-Powell in 1906, when Baden-Powell was considering initiating a youth movement in Great Britain. As an officer in the British Army during the Boer War, Baden-Powell had found the quality of recruits and the nature of their training so inadequate as to endanger the British empire. He devised a system of training designed to remedy these failures. His "Aids to Scouting" was completed in 1899, during the siege of Mafeking. Returning to England in 1903, he began to adapt his program to meet the needs of young boys. After reviewing Seton's *The Birch Bark Roll,* he responded, "We are going on with my scheme like your Woodcraft Indians!" (quoted in Murray, 1937, 32). Like Seton, he envisioned the Boy Scout movement as a means of combating national problems not through social programs but instead by training individual boys in manliness. In this way, he believed, the nation would be stabilized and imperial virility maintained.

While Seton's Woodcrafting was modeled solely on his stereotypical vision of Native American life, Baden-Powell's influences were more diffuse and his relationship to Seton's Indian model ambivalent. Baden-Powell's program stressed outdoor recreation, and who better to inaugurate young boys into this experience than Native peoples? "Savages understand how necessary it is that boys should be trained to manliness and not allowed to drift into being poor-spirited wasters who can only look on at men's work." Baden-Powell's "savages" of choice were the Zulus (a result of his tenure in South Africa) and American Indians (due, in part, to Seton's influence). The diversity of the sources of his inspiration seemed to matter little;[5] what was important was that his natives (like all natives, in his view) be manly and close to nature. "Give me the man who has been raised among the great things of Nature," Baden-Powell continues; "he cultivates truth, independence, and self-reliance; he has generous impulses; he is true to his friends, and true to the flag of his country" (Baden-Powell, 1924, 72). Like *The Birch Bark Roll,* Baden-Powell's *Scouting for Boys* emphasizes camp life, knowledge of animals and plants, and outdoor activities such as tracking. In the opening pages of the handbook Baden-Powell writes that "by the term 'scouting' is meant the work and attributes of backwoodsmen, explorers, and frontiersmen" (9). The activities listed therein are designed to teach the skills appropriate to life in the woods.

The frontier myth provided an "alternative ethic" by supporting "the frontiersman as a cult figure," using "'primitive races such as the 'Red' Indian and the Zulu as examples of martial virility," and elevating the imperial Scout to the status of "national hero" (MacDonald, 1993, 5). The Scout uniform was modeled on frontier clothing, and Scouts emulated life on the frontier in their recreational activities. In the movement, the frontier idea and a stereotypical vision of "savage" life were elided: "if only civilized boys could be trained to duplicate the savage life, then they might have everything that the savage had not yet lost—virility, hardiness, martial spirit" (MacDonald, 1993, 132). It was the constant struggle posed by life in a savage wilderness that taught boys to be men. As one observer commented, every family "should possess *Scouting* in default of the chance of going on the war-path with a Red Indian" (quoted in MacDonald, 1993, 23).

In playing savage, however, Boy Scouts were not actually supposed to become savages. Rather, savagism was, ironically, a way of attaining the highest virtues of white civilization (nationalism and imperialism); the regression into the savage stage enabled civilized boys to grow up and subdue real savages. In the movement there was a good deal of ambivalence about the appropriateness of presenting natives as role models: because they embodied a lower stage in the evolution of humankind, many believed they could not represent the highest model of manhood. Baden-Powell was particularly ambivalent about Seton's use of the Indian as role model. Indians were useful for teaching some things, but as one commentator writes, overall "the Indian was lazy, drunk, too much of the native; a quite unsuitable model for civilized boys" (MacDonald, 1993, 142). Boy Scout publicity in 1914 contained Indian themes—among them a picture of a Boy Scout and an Indian brave gazing at the landscape from their vantage point on a hillside, as well as a sketch drawn by Baden-Powell entitled "The Genesis of Scouting" depicting a warrior hunting a buffalo (MacDonald, 1993, 143). However, unlike Seton, Baden-Powell believed the Indian theme to be of limited use in his project of moral indoctrination.

Concerns about using "savage" races as role models extended to debates about whether imperial subjects (in many cases, the very groups being emulated) should be allowed to become Boy Scouts and, if so, whether their status should be different from that of white boys. Deploying Victorian ideas associating race and civilization, Scout leaders debated whether their training was suitable for native children; the training might even, many feared, lead to revolutionary impulses on the part of imperial subjects. In South Africa, a compromise was ultimately reached on this issue. Units were created to accommodate different ethnic groups: one for blacks, another for Hindus and Moslems, and one for "half-castes." Thereafter, Scouting took on a self-conscious colonizing mission of training native children in their appropriate roles as imperial subjects.[6]

When the Boy Scouts of America was established in 1910, Seton was appointed chief scout of the organization. However, a number of factors led to his ouster in 1915. Seton opposed the heavy militaristic and nationalistic orientation of Baden-Powell's program and clung to his individualistic Indian model, while Baden-Powell tended to resist Seton's Indian enthusiasms. Ideological differences between Seton and Baden-Powell, in combination with lesser factors such as Seton's British citizenship, ultimately led to Seton's ouster from the organization in 1915. Yet the popularity and influence of the Boy Scouts of America steadily increased. According to annual reports, its membership tripled in the following five years, and in 1981 over sixty-six million men and boys were or had been members at some point in their lives (Rosenthal, 1984, xi).

◆ ─────── ◆

The relationship of Seton's Woodcrafters and, later, the Boy Scouts to Indians was contradictory and ambivalent. Although the use of Indians as role models for boys has appeared to some observers to be a sign of admiration and respect, examination of the kinds of images used and the attitudes of participants towards them paints a different picture. The Indian role model had little to do with any recognizable form of Native American life but was instead inspired by stereotypes depicting Indians as beings who were warlike, close to nature, and always relegated to the past with no relevant role in the present (except to rejuvenate white society). Furthermore, the inspiration for their use in these movements derives from the belief that they represented an earlier—and inferior—stage of civilization, in some way equivalent to the difference between adolescence and manhood. This view partially accounts for the ambivalence demonstrated by many of the Indian-inspired organizations' participants towards the images they deployed. Since Native peoples inhabited an earlier (and inferior) phase of cultural development, they did not exhibit the "superior" virtues of "civilization." They could, however, aid in the progress of civilization by providing, in limited ways, a model for some of the attributes it had lost. Of course, part of the ambivalence demonstrated by leaders such as Baden-Powell was the product of outright racism—their acceptance of more obviously negative Indian images which seemed to render Native peoples completely unfit to be role models for children.

It is ironic that youth movements in the United States, with their penchant for playing Indian, arose at a time when real Indians were becoming less and less visible in American culture. Not only were Native Americans generally perceived as a vanishing race, but government policies were designed to ensure that this was the case. Assimilationist policies, as well as the implementation of new criteria for determining identity (such as blood quantum), were intended to complete the genocide of Native peoples through the abolition of Native cultures as well as through statistical extermination. As Indians seemed to be disappearing, more and more non-Indians felt compelled to emulate them. These nostalgic gestures were not motivated by a desire to sustain Native peoples and cultures but were instead predicated on the idea of their disappearance. Furthermore, they reinforced the idea that Indians were vanishing by popularizing stereotypical versions of Native life which bore little, if any, resemblance to the lives of contemporary Native peoples.

Contemporary imitators of Indianness exhibit some uncomfortable similarities to their turn-of-the-century forbears. The object of New Age desires is, of course, Indian spirituality to sate the spiritually bankrupt Western world rather than the "manliness" of Indian "warriors." Nevertheless, the pattern remains the same: the object of desire is a nostalgic invention intended only to serve the needs of the dominant culture. New Age, as Sherman Alexie has noted regarding the men's movement, "blindly pursues Native solutions to European problems but completely neglects to provide European solutions to Native problems" (1992, 30). In a sense, it even exacerbates these problems by blinding its consumers to the realities of many contemporary Native peoples' lives.

During a recent event at the New York Open Center, this conflict between New Age desires and Native realities came to the fore. The event, entitled "Finding the Good Path," featured a well-known, local Native artist. Open Center promoted her presentation as an exploration of

Native solutions to the problems facing the West and promised an "interfaith ceremony." "As the western world faces serious fundamental problems," the publicity queried, "what can we learn from native peoples that will help us discover a better relationship with the natural world and with each other?" The artist's presentation, the publicity strongly implied, would supply some badly needed Indian solutions to Western problems.

To the dismay of the audience, the artist's presentation did not address these problems at all. Instead, she discussed slides of her interesting work, much of which draws on the history of the colonization of Native America. The audience members, apparently baffled by her failure to conform to their expectations, were virtually silent during the question period. Eventually, one complained that she had been misled by the publicity since no "traditional" Native knowledge had been shared there. The artist replied that she had never seen the publicity but that it apparently had been misleading. Encouraged, another audience member persisted, demanding, "What is the Native American remedy to healing our planet before it's too late?" The artist politely said that she did not have the solution and anyway Native people hadn't caused the problem so she couldn't see why they should have the solution. At this point, the questioner became visibly angered by this apparently arbitrary withholding of Native knowledge, which she obviously believed she was entitled to receive. "I came here to meet Native Americans because I don't meet any in my daily life," she announced. "It's time for cultures to start sharing!"

The consequences of this current fascination with Indianness for Native people are unclear. One could argue that the visibility being chic brings is a good thing. However, as it did at the turn of the century, this hypervisibility creates a kind of invisibility as well—especially for the people and the issues that don't conform to its stereotypes.

NOTES

Conversations with Dean Curtis Bear Claw, Patricia Penn Hilden, Roy Huhndorf, Carol Kalafatic, and Francis Peters helped to shape my thinking on the issues discussed in this piece. I also wish to thank William Penn, Carol Kalafatic, and especially Patricia Penn Hilden for their comments on and criticisms of the essay itself.

1. See, for example, the "autobiography" of Andrews (1981) and see also Mauricio (1981).

2. See, for example, two compelling critiques of Costner's enterprises: Seals (1991) and filmmaker Victor Masayesva's *Imagining Indians* (IS Productions, 1992).

3. My brief discussion of American youth movements is based on the work of Macleod (1983).

4. For a discussion of Hall's theories and their relationship to youth movements, see Bederman (1995), especially Chapter 6, "Adolescence and Gang-Age Boyhood: An Ideology for Character Building," as well as Chapter 3, "Teaching Our Sons to Do What We Have Been Teaching the Savages to Avoid: G. Stanley Hall, Racial Recapitulation, and the Neurasthenia Paradox"; and MacDonald (1993, 132–35).

5. Baden-Powell's beliefs echoed contemporary theories of social evolution postulating the fundamental commonality of all "primitive" societies. Tylor writes (1958, 6): "Surveyed in broad view, the character and habit of mankind at once display that similarity and consistency of phenomena which led the Italian proverb-maker to declare that 'all the world is one country.' . . . To general likeness in human nature on the one hand, and to general likeness in the circumstances of life on the other, this similarity and consistency may no doubt be traced, and then may be studied with especial fitness in comparing races near the same grade of civilization. Little respect need be had in such comparisons for date in history or for place on the map. . . . As Dr. Johnson contemptuously said, . . . 'One set of savages is like another.'"

6. Rosenthal (1984, 256–57). Rosenthal discusses the contradictory nature of Baden-Powell's thought on the subject of race, which, he writes, "combine[d] the most pernicious kind of racism with sincere aspirations for world harmony." In exploring the subject, he compiles a number of disturbing excerpts from Baden-Powell's writing on the subject of the natives of Africa and Australia (255–60).

WORKS CITED

Alexie, Sherman. "White Men Can't Drum." *New York Times Magazine* (October 4, 1992): 30–31.

Andrews, Lynn V. *Medicine Woman.* New York: Harper & Row,1981.

Baden-Powell, Sir Robert. *Scouting for Boys: A Handbook for Instruction in Good Citizenship through Woodcraft.* London: C. Arthur Pearson, 1924.

Bederman, Gail. *Manliness and Civilization: A Cultural History of Gender and Race in the United States, 1880–1917.* Chicago: University of Chicago Press, 1995.

Bieder, Robert E. "The Grand Order of the Iroquois: Influences on Lewis Henry Morgan's Ethnology." *Ethnohistory* 27/4 (Fall 1980): 349–61.

Carnes, Mark C. *Secret Ritual and Manhood in Victorian America.* New Haven, Conn.: Yale University Press, 1989.

Kammen, Michael. *Mystic Chords of Memory: The Transformation of Tradition in American Culture.* New York: Vintage Books, 1991.

MacDonald, Robert H. *Sons of the Empire: The Frontier and the Boy Scout Movement.* 1890–1918. Toronto: University of Toronto Press, 1993.

Macleod, David I. *Building a Character in the American Boy: The Boy Scouts, YMCA, and Their Forerunners, 1870–1920.* Madison: University of Wisconsin Press, 1983.

Mauricio, Victoria. *The Return of Chief Black Foot.* Virginia Beach, Va.: Donning, 1981.

Murray, William D. *The History of the Boy Scouts of America.* New York: Boy Scouts of America, 1937.

Pearce, Roy Harvey. *Savagism and Civilization: A Study of the Indian and the American Mind.* Berkeley: University of California Press, 1988.

Rosaldo, Renato. *Culture and Truth: The Remaking of Social Analysis.* Boston: Beacon Press, 1989.

Rosenthal, Michael. *The Character Factory: Baden-Powell and the Origins of the Boy Scout Movement.* New York: Pantheon Books, 1984.

Seals, David. "The New Custerism." *The Nation* (May 13, 1991): 634–39.

Seton, Ernest Thompson. *The Birch Bark Roll of the Woodcraft League of America, Inc.* New York: Doubleday, 1927.

Tylor, Edward Burnett. *Primitive Culture.* New York: Harper & Row, 1958.

Troublemakers

Rolando Romero

Mother, father,
there's no passing the cup
I'm going to be a troublemaker
when I grow up.

DEMETRIA MARTÍNEZ,
"Troublemaker"

At a 1993 conference at the University of California, Irvine, Hernán Vidal, of the University of Minnesota, stated that once at a dinner during a professional gathering, out of the ten Spanish departments from different U.S. universities represented at his table, seven were in receivership—the equivalent of bankruptcy, where the dean of the school finally decides that the internal turmoil prevents the department from handling its duties and appoints an outside chair to carry on administrative tasks. Commenting on Vidal's statistics, Jane Gallop, a colleague in the Modern Studies Program at the University of Wisconsin–Milwaukee, asked me if I could provide an explanation. Why do departments that house Latinos seem to create most of the friction, often generating rumors of discrimination? We could easily blame the Chicano hot temper, though in my explanation the machinery squeaks most where the university does not oil the pieces properly; left unattended, the machinery will grind to a halt. Departments that go into receivership are grossly mismanaged, violate university policies, and show extreme favoritism toward certain groups. Since favoritism affects U.S. Latinos negatively, they characterize department policies as discriminatory. In effect U.S. Latinos who understand administrative functions will demonstrate how certain practices exclude them. Their colleagues thus characterize them as saboteurs of the discipline for exposing the inequities of the system.

In the spring of 1994 U.S. Latinos accused several universities of racial and ethnic insensitivity. News reports on charges of discrimination focused on the University of California at Santa Barbara, the University of California at Davis, the University of California at Los Angeles, Cornell, Michigan State University, and our own UW-Milwaukee. UW-Milwaukee appointed a committee to look into allegations of racial discrimination on campus when two legislators protested to the president of the University of Wisconsin system that administrators did not respond to complaints of sexual and ethnic harassment. These issues surfaced after both the national news and the television program 20/20 showcased the Cecile Pillsbury case of sexual discrimination. The *Los Angeles Times* mentioned the UW-Milwaukee campus area in an article that focused on the purported discrimination against a group of African American youngsters to whom the International House of Pancakes refused service.

Likewise, the University of California at Santa Barbara made national news when the renowned Chicano scholar Rudy Acuña, author of *Occupied America*, alleged discrimination in the university's hiring practices. Professor Acuña filed the lawsuit against both the campus and the University of California system. Not surprisingly, in support the students at UCSB went on a hunger strike.

Similarly, the students at Cornell took over Day Hall, one of the administration buildings, because someone damaged the sculpture by artist Daniel Martínez, part of a Latino art exhibit entitled "Revelations/ *Revelaciónes.*" The Latino students converged on Day Hall to lodge a complaint with administrators over the lack of protection for the sculpture and the lack of a formal public statement condemning the vandalism. Some of the students refused to leave the building and thus found themselves taking it over. Though the vandalizing of the sculpture motivated the conflict, the unrest had been building because of the administration's inability to form a Latino studies program. The Cornell students demanded a discussion on the low numbers of Latino faculty, lack of progress on filling faculty positions, few courses on Latino issues, and a paucity of library resources in this area.

Michigan State University went through a similar battle. Latino students, demanding that the university name one of its buildings in honor of César Chávez, stormed into a board meeting and crushed grapes on the meeting table. The students also demanded the establishment of a committee to look into the safety of eating grapes sprayed with pesticide since the United Farm Workers union had pressed for a boycott of grapes on health grounds, a contention that the growers deny. The students at the University of California, Los Angeles, performed a similar though perhaps less obvious act when demanding the establishment of a Chicano studies department. The students presented the chancellor with a brick, a gesture the chancellor did not understand. The brick alluded to Alejandro Morales's *The Brick People*, in which the author documents the participation of Mexican labor in the manufacture of bricks which were used in many public buildings in Los Angeles and Orange County, including some buildings at UCLA..

THE INSTITUTIONAL GAME

In most of the cases of Latino discontent Spanish departments—which have become hotbeds of interests that the universities have been able neither to control nor to understand—figure prominently. One of the earliest conflicts, for example, occurred in 1990: Chicano students and faculty accused the chair of the UC Davis Spanish department of favoritism toward Spanish students. The case gained national prominence when Chicanos went on a hunger strike against the UC Davis administration. Such conflicts can be explained easily in terms of internal dynamics. Traditional Spanish departments reflect the Eurocentrism of U.S. education, where a preference towards peninsular literature is the rule. Latin American interests stand second in line, with faculty assuming that because they represent the "origin" of U.S. Latinos, they can speak for them, often condescendingly. The third group, U.S. Latino faculty, only now is beginning to make its presence felt and refuses to play by the old rules of exclusion. Non-Latino professors, also represented in the faculty, feel increasingly victimized by the tenants of affirmative action.

The usual makeup of a class in the Spanish Department is half Latino and half non-Latino. Some faculty specializing in Spanish literature who still hold to a notion of language purity (which has been negated at least since Vulgar Latin gave rise to the Romance languages) make disparaging comments to U.S. Latino students—who come to Spanish departments expecting to find answers to questions of cultural identity. The departments do not represent the three major groups—U.S. Latinos, Latin Americans, and Spaniards—equally. Spanish departments have housed Latino affirmative-action hires reluctantly and thus become "Hispanicized" under the magic of a philosophy that ignores questions of teaching, research, and political and philosophical methodological approaches to literature. They view U.S. Latino culture condescendingly, as not worthy of serious study. If the students want faculty to teach courses on U.S. Latinos, the institutional argument goes, anybody can teach them. A professor once commented that if he could teach French, German, and Latin American literature, why couldn't he teach Chicano literature? Arguments like this show great disdain. U.S. Latino literature already forms a canon that often encompasses not only Spanish literature but Latin American as well. Superficially addressing nondominant cultural issues allows the university to forgo hiring specialists in the area; thus whereas Latin American and Spanish writers trek through the campus as visiting professors or lecturers, U.S. Latino writers still do not set foot in those institutions because the faculty does not engage in critical debate with the writers represented in its courses.

The news about Acuña's lawsuit against UCSB was not surprising. Ingrained problems of exclusion at the university fermented the lawsuit; the lawsuit was not the cause of the internal turmoil. As a graduate student at UCSB I experienced some of the problems firsthand. At UCSB students like me who wanted to specialize in Mexican and Chicano literature were at a loss because the Spanish department did not offer courses in either field. When the department finally hired Chicano scholar Bruce Novoa to teach both Chicano and Mexican literature, a group of students suggested that he teach a course on Mexico. The Spanish department responded that the professor needed to address the students' needs much more broadly. This argument made little sense when graduate students were spending two academic quarters studying one single Spanish author (such as Luis de Góngora or Miguel de Cervantes) or one single Spanish book. Though the rules of the university stipulated that if a group of students showed interest in a course, and a professor was available and willing to teach it, the faculty member could automatically teach the course, the department denied the request.

A 1993 fund-drive packet from UCSB included a copy of the faculty newsletter 93106. It shows the nationally recognized dean of Chicano literature, Luis Leal, with both the chancellor of UCSB and former Mexican president Carlos Salinas de Gortari. The caption reads: "After delivering the keynote address at the world business conference in San Francisco on September 20, Mexican President Carlos Salinas de Gortari . . . met with Chancellor Barbara S. Uehling and UCSB Chicano literary scholar Luis Leal. The Mexican government has donated $120,000 to UCSB's campaign to establish the Luis Leal Chair in Chicano Studies" (1). Ironically the Acuña lawsuit forced UCSB to come out in support of a discipline it had chosen to ignore. Leal could not work with Spanish and Portuguese department graduate students at UCSB because the department had instituted numerous rules in order to hide its deficiencies—graduate students could work only with its faculty, even though they were not experts in the field.[1]

At UCSB since all the requirements were heavily skewed toward their area, the students specializing in Spanish literature finished the academic course requirements for the Ph.D. while, at the same time, advancing their dissertation research. As a result, they moved forward much quicker than the students specializing in Latin America. Also, since the university paid top salaries to specialists in Spanish literature (who knew very little of issues affecting U.S. Latinos), the department mainly attracted students interested in the literature of Spain. In order to justify the investment, not only were Spanish literature students (protected by the "rhetoric" of quality and "genius") the only ones working with those professors, but, to provide those students with fellowships, the "qualified" U.S. Latinos were encouraged to apply for the so-called target-of-opportunity fellowships. Subsequently the department and the university developed a rhetoric that those fellowships were not as valuable as the "academic" ones given to the students of peninsular literature. To this day, the UCSB Spanish department proudly points to the fact that it places its Ph.D. students at institutions like Yale, the University of Illinois, Columbia, and Princeton. The department does not mention its Eurocentric bent (the Spanish Yale specialist in Chicano literature, for example, is the only professional in the area who did not have to remain in the Chicano closet at UCSB), thus hiding its dismal record with U.S. Latinos; the magic of "Hispanicism" protects the UCSB statistics. UCSB alumni survive in academia by developing a network that does not include their alma mater. Spanish departments could have benefited from a truly Hispanic representation of all three major groups, but the internal turmoil caused universities to stop funding non-U.S. students. The universities now financially exclude foreign students from many programs.

Providing the inside track to people specializing in Spanish literature has deleterious professional consequences. The U.S. Latino researcher has been trained to work in the closet and to first conduct exhaustive, repetitive research in Spanish and Latin American literary discourse. Though I am considered a specialist in Chicano and Mexican cultures, my transcript shows only one course on Mexico, which I took while pursuing my master's degree at the University of Texas. It shows no courses in Chicano literature, since the Spanish departments never offered them. My undergraduate, master's and Ph.D. transcripts, however, show several courses on the Generation of '98, Spanish Realism, and Spanish Naturalism (Spanish departments mislabel repetition as carefulness). A case can thus be made that the Spanish department did not train me and my fellow Latinos to survive in the fast-paced competitive arena of academia, leaving only the door of "university service" open to us. Not following the fast track of academic engagement relegates minorities to the service ghetto, where they effectively become the workhorses of the university (serving on committees, meeting the academic needs of the community). The U.S. Latino will concentrate on the research he/she wanted to conduct from the beginning only after jumping the hurdles. Traditional departments view U.S. Latinos as wild horses that they need to train and contain before allowing them to step on the track. Whereas Spanish departments train the specialists in Spanish literature as sprinters, they train U.S. Latinos as long-distance runners and hurdle jumpers.

THE CRYING GAME

Unfortunately, given the power structures and dynamics of Spanish departments, Vidal's unofficial statistics were not surprising. Discrimination against U.S. Latinos by Spanish departments has become an article of faith in Chicano academic discourse. Renato Rosaldo quotes the complaints of a Spanish professor before the University of Arizona Academic Senate in which he compares the hiring of Chicano/as, which up until then had been limited to the "Mexicanized" Spanish department, to a "cancer" that had the potential to spread throughout the whole university.

> The truth of the matter is that my unfortunate department was thoroughly Mexicanized back in the sixties. The university's president and provost would apparently like to make that mistake universal. I call upon all my colleagues to extirpate a deep rooted evil in one department to prevent its spread through the entire institution.

Displaying his reluctance to place Chicanos "in positions of authority in government and education, the Professor puts up an invisible sign: 'No Mexicans Allowed'" (Rosaldo 143).

During my tenure as a Ford Foundation Fellow at the University of California at Irvine in 1993–94, I attended the discussions held at the Humanities Institute and have since seen that they reflect the presentation of minority issues at similar centers around the country. I attended lectures by Chicano/a critics (Chon Noriega and Cherrie Moraga) who spoke from a venue opened to them by these centers, which value personal experience. Experience, nonetheless, only justifies lackadaisical attitudes towards issues concerning nondominant groups. For if we valorize experience, who can blame us for not researching the minority issues we espouse so dearly but that we have not experienced? One author is all that is necessary to understand that experience, which we will then represent a thousandfold in the "minority literature," "literature of the oppressed," or "testimonial literature." Witness how many texts have come out speaking about the "collective unconsciousness" of Chicanos, postmodernist theories notwithstanding. Education, though, should never focus on experience but on the analysis of experiences. The "writing from experience" approach thus also denies the very essence of education.

The "crying game" has also turned into a card in the academic poker game. The multicultural debate allows the university to argue for its representation of issues dear to minorities, though it does nothing more than maintain the hierarchy of power and control while giving the impression of openness. The issues presented under those conditions mimic the old rules of exclusion. The inclusion of one or two members of nondominant cultures in Benetton conferences and research institutes allows a faculty to associate with the "subaltern" (to use Gayatri Spivak's terminology) or the "colonized" (to opt for Edward Said's), while at the same time perpetuating the oppressing establishment behind a criticism of essentialism. Critics argue that these research institutes espouse nondominant issues to give the appearance of representation now that the power, at least in terms of numbers, rests with nondominant groups. As proof of lack of interest minority scholars point to the fact that when they organize conferences following their own academic agendas, pursuits, and questions, humanities centers deny minority speakers institutional support by their lack of participation in these conferences.

Humanities institutes have been most adamant in the discussion of "political correctness," an issue that Latinos/as have not taken up. Political correctness has nothing to do with "minority" issues. As the demographics of the typical university change, the turmoil created by the "PC" supporters and detractors translates into a battle for control. The critics of a more inclusive curriculum already feel excluded since students themselves cast their votes with the classes they take. The defendants of a Western European curriculum feel victimized by the lack of enrollment in their classes, especially in geographical areas like the Southwest where the "minority" students make up a large part of the student population.

Humanities institutes frequently associate with English departments, and thus they discuss issues the English departments consider important. Yet foreign-language departments have criticized English departments for monopolizing the teaching of literature in this age of multiculturalism. Duke University professor Walter Mignolo argues that, as a subject of epistemic inquiries (a "Third World" subject), he felt baffled by assertions taken as truth in English departments. Mignolo contends that, as a professor of Latin American literature, he was surprised to read a Harvard English professor who claimed that Third World literature had been neglected, "since one of the things I did during those fifteen years was to teach third-world literature to American students." Thus, Mignolo argues that he came to the conclusion "that both the literature and the role of entire foreign language and literature departments were being, and may still be, ignored. For what is the function of a Latin American litera- ture department or program if third-world literature counts only when it is integrated to the English curriculum?" (Mignolo 16).

Specialists in Chicano/a discourse admit the English departments have been the most supportive of Chicano/a causes. English depart- ments, nonetheless, have a vested interest in the debate. If Spanish and Portuguese departments or Chicano Studies departments house the U.S. Latino professors, then the English department bears no responsibility for the representation of U.S. Latino issues. Not surprisingly, the English department at UCLA supported the institution of the Chicano studies de- partment "in principle" but not in practice. The creation of a Chicano studies department takes away the power of the "traditional" disciplines to appoint to Latino studies the people they want. In a sense, traditional departments would lose the power to govern from outside the field, as they have commonly done. A Chicano studies department advances self- determination and self-governing, and traditional departments will not easily give away that power.

Chicano studies programs have been ineffective because they have functioned as a representative body on Chicano issues for traditional de- partments. Since the Spanish or the English or the history or the sociol- ogy or the political science departments must approve the appointments in conjunction with Chicano/a studies, the appointees always reflect a compromise, a blend of specialties the Chicano studies department, act- ing on its own, probably would not have chosen. Since the minority stud- ies programs gather minority faculty hired by various traditional de- partments, the minority faculty hired represents more the interests of those conservative departments (otherwise there would have been no need for a special program to deal with issues affecting minorities in the first place) than the interests of the minority groups. Thus, as is the case at UC Irvine, the minority population makes up the majority of the student body, but the faculty does not reflect its ethnic make-up. In a sense, a minority chooses faculty for the majority. Minority studies programs also falter because they do not foster faculty interaction. A building (or an office or a telephone) does not a program make. If the university does not require its minority studies faculty to discuss issues on a day-to-day basis (who gets the teaching assistantships, whom will they hire, what sort of academic background should appointees have, whom will they bring in as a visiting professor), the faculty cannot face questions important to its own profession or to the university as a whole. University administrators turn minority studies programs into rubber stamps by assigning them minimal budgets and few positions. At worst, in places where "minorities" constitute the majority of the student body, administrators who deny the discipline self-determination engage in what Jorge Castañeda has called the process of "dedemocratization" and other critics call academic apartheid. The university that spreads out its minority faculty throughout the campus without the ability to self-govern effectively gerrymanders the discipline.

THE SILENCE GAME

Academic political games force minorities, afraid to be labeled as "troublemakers," to not represent their views. Thus the status of minorities in an academic climate of exclusion forces minorities into silence. Silence comes about as the unstated consequence of racial incidents. As with exposing child molestation or physical abuse in a family, suddenly racial incidents place the victim in a position to expose the dirty secret of the house, in the process sending to jail a member of the household. Furthermore, exposure entails a mix of emotions that the victim hardly understands. Exposure requires a detachment the victims lack, as they usually feel too emotionally incensed by those occurrences to trust their judgment. Ironically the academic victims become silent because they believe that anger denies their intellect. Having heard negative comments over and over again about the "quality" of their research, they believe that showing their emotions corroborates dominant assessments of their field of study. In the victims' mind, anger denies their training. Racial incidents viscerally poke at the heart, unsettling the mind's attempt to classify. Was it prejudice or not? Can victims just label the racial incident as ignorance and proceed on their way, quenching their anger? Can the blame fall just on the callousness of one single person? Or might the institutional climate foster the insensitivity? When racial incidents take place at the university, what does it tell the victims about an educational system supposedly designed to train future generations to interact in society? Those incidents poke at the unhealed wound that forces victims to look at the condition of the body and, ironically, remind them of their humble humanity and of the fact that no education will completely do away with the anger and the pain ("What do you call a Chicano with a Ph.D.?"). So they keep silent, or maybe they share their anger with their partner, but life treks on, with the tenure clock marking the step.

Although "minorities" sometimes impose the silence upon themselves, the institution also forces them into silence. Graduate students in Spanish departments, for example, seldom produce dissertations written in English. Though many of the issues affecting Latin American/Spanish and U.S. Latino discourse have connections with critical questions discussed by English departments, the Spanish department's foreign-language requirements (perhaps in an attempt to secure a market that otherwise would not be there) are skewed in favor of an Ibero-peninsular vision (Spanish, French, Portuguese), even though an American one would make much more sense (English and Spanish). The suppression of the English language for comparative purposes in Spanish departments also effectively silences a powerful voice of U.S. Latino culture.

The fact that English department students tend to satisfy the foreign-language requirement with languages other than Spanish teaches them to apply to the Spanish language attributes of "economic"" or "use" value. The question of aesthetic value is separated from use value. Roby Rajan argues that "attempts to hold the economic at bay have historically taken the form of various kinds of refusal to submit to the principles of rational calculation, profit, and instrumentality that would make them unassimilable to the economic. Strategies of transcendence such as Kant's have tried to carve out spheres of absolute value that lie above and beyond contamination by the economic" (Rajan 4). Rajan, with Smith, argues that aesthetic value is defined in "contradistinction to all forms of utility."

Chicanos also see the multicultural syllabus as another attempt to silence their voices. The high ahistoricity of the multicultural approach to teaching effectively denies the groups that have traditionally studied the field the opportunity to show their expertise in the area. The discipline in fact becomes appropriated by the same faculty who previously denied its existence. Under those conditions, it is not uncommon to see the self-hatred of writers such as Richard Rodríguez represented in the curriculum, without the benefit of a more rounded context of Chicano cultural production.

Unfortunately, silence immediately lowers morale in the work environment. Only gossip vents frustration because silence closes the avenue of communication. It is not surprising that no complaints are filed at the Office of Affirmative Action. The affirmative action office exists not to handle these types of complaints but as a step in the process of documentation if a person wants to take legal action against the university. It falls in the infamous category of internal review boards, which, at least in the cases of alleged police brutality, do not perform their function until higher political bodies assign independent commissions to look into the problem (witness the Rodney King beating lawsuit against the Los Angeles Police Department, which triggered the civil disturbances in the city). In other cases of harassment, the Affirmative Action Office on the UW–Milwaukee campus claimed that it lost many of the files of people lodging complaints against the university.

THE HIDING GAME

Academics also play another game, closely related to the silence game. At UCSB, I recall that in order to take a course on Mexico with Leal I pretended to take an independent studies course with a member of the Spanish department's faculty who then officially assigned the grade recommended by Professor Leal. My first published paper came out of this course, and my professional career thus began in the closet. Since every institutional act reverberates, I have often asked myself what results from "hiding" a specialty. If the professor's actions show that a student can take a course in a specific field only by hiding, how can the professor convince the student that the discipline merits serious study?

In my opinion, the hiding game exposes the fabric of racism. In openly classified acts of prejudice (for example, the swastikas tagged on synagogues) racism functions only in the absence of the perpetrator. I recently saw a graffiti mark on one of the toilet stalls (a "private space") at UC Irvine. Right next to a swastika were the words "No More Asians." When identified, enunciators of the racist slurs defend their text, arguing they were misinterpreted. California Republican State Assemblyman William J. Knight circulated a racist poem (labeled by *Harper's* as "Ode to the New California") about Latinos crossing the border to collect welfare. The poem characterized the immigrant from Mexico as lazy, as overbred, as a welfare parasite who takes over the "White" neighborhood forcing "Americans" to move out. In this incident, "after members of the legislature's Latino caucus complained that the poem was racist, Knight argued that it was 'clever' and 'funny,' and said he 'didn't mean to offend anyone.'" The disclaimers in these cases never admit to the racist act, only to media misrepresentations and victim misinterpretations. Racism, in their view, is only a problem of reception, not of emission. Proof of racism always falls on the victim (unless, again, the perpetrator remains anonymous). But like the boy who yelled wolf too many times, the person who consistently complains will not be believed by the institution. Thus, the institutions only perceive as victims those people who do not complain (the silenced victims). Racism goes around in circles, concealing its face, forcing its victims into silence and its victimizers into hiding. Racism functions best as an unrealized idea, never seen face to face. People will acknowledge racism only if it remains hidden, only if it points no finger at any particular person, only if it gives no identities or personalities. Only under those circumstances will people actually call it racism. If racism shows a face, it shows the face of your ethnically insensitive-colleague or your ignorant politician (to wit, Ross Perot's addressing an African-American group as "you people").

The denial of racism explains the usage of masks to both cover and uncover discriminatory practices. Current critical theory would label the mask as the blind spot of racist discourse since it reminds viewers of their own hiding. The Ku Klux Klan intimidates because the person who hides behind the mask exposes the hidden code of racism. Etymology, in classical theater, ties the mask to both person and personality. The mask reminds us of our own performance. Contemporary border writers like Guillermo Gómez Peña and Emily Hicks, in their politically performative acts, have attempted to cross the Mexico-U.S. border wearing Mexican wrestlers' masks. The mask figures prominently in Gómez Peña's *Warrior for Gringostroika* not just on the cover but in several of the pieces as well ("Documented/ Indocumentado," "Border Brujo," "Family Portrait," "El Warrior for Gringostroika"). These performances, usually reported in the newspapers, ironically unmask socially prejudicial practices. The mask puts to the test stereotypical evaluations of what constitutes an "American" since immigration officials cannot tell whether the person has blond or black hair, white or brown skin. Thus the mask again works to expose the blind spot of this normative discourse, so socially accepted in immigration practices. The mask tests both the "fixity" of what Homi Bhabha calls the ideological construction of otherness and the permissible usage of the stereotype. The mask exposes the plurality of the United States, while denying particular singularities. "Superbarrio" ("the masked defender of the poor, and real life Super-Hero"), the Mexican priest who has also worn a wrestler's costume to disclose the abuse of Mexico City landlords when displacing tenants, also exposes the underbelly of the exclusionary practices. Latino actors, protesting their exclusion from the film of Isabel Allende's *The House of the Spirits,* called for a boycott. They were to demonstrate at the premiere wearing Mexican wrestlers' hoods, according to the newspapers. The mask thus becomes a symbol of justice under conditions of oppression, whether it be worn by comic-book super heroes (the Lone Ranger, Zorro) or Zapatista rebels in the jungles of Chiapas. The ski mask worn by Subcommander Marcos, "has become," according to the March 18, 1994, issue of the *New York*

Times, "the symbol of the Mexican Rebellion" (sect. A, 3). The mask proclaims that the ideal precedes the person itself. When Gómez Peña's "Warrior" undresses, his torso is scribbled with the words "Please don't discover me!" Obviously the words, in the year of the quincentennial, refer to the so-called discovery of America. Additionally though, the word *discover* in Spanish means both "to uncover" and "to turn in." Thus the sentence states the plea of the undocumented worker who asks to not be turned in to the Immigration and Naturalization Service. In these instances, the mask becomes a prop in the institutional quest for justice. The mask enhances, rather than negates, the Self. It reminds us that we were always already hidden.

The exposure of the Self explains the cultural anxiety behind the mask of the Ku Klux Klan. When the public observes KKK performances in film (such as *Places in the Heart*) or in a Madonna video, the KKK masks become the material object onto which the public projects its contempt of racism. This receptacle of projection safely covers the identity of the people. This immaterial racism has no face, just an ugly body which people have learned to condemn. Material racism, however, the one that statistics, proper names, and budgets can prove, becomes mislabeled; it goes by the name of quotas, misunderstandings, or financial straits. Did not the Reagan and Bush administrations try to change the burden of proof in discrimination laws from discriminatory effect to discriminatory intent? Attorneys find intent difficulty to prove because very few people admit, even to themselves, that they exercise prejudice.

THE WAITING GAME

The waiting game is another academic strategy. When incidents of ethnic bias occur, administrators always point to a mythical future in which the problems will take care of themselves. One person will soon retire, the financial future will improve, or a chair's tenure will soon end. The vicious venting of anger by those students affected by institutional policies usually surprises the universities, which do not realize that the frustration has been building for a long time. As Carlos Fuentes once wrote, when individuals do not see themselves represented in their institutions, they will revolt (to wit, the revolt of the Zapatista National Liberation Army in the Lacandon jungle of Chiapas).

Violence erupted at the UCLA campus when Chicano students purportedly went on a rampage, causing $50,000 in damages, after a protest demanding the establishment of a Chicano studies department. Chancellor Charles E. Young's announcement that he would not elevate the Chicano Studies Program to department status caused the demonstration. On May 13, 1993, ironically, a *Los Angeles Times* editorial advised Chancellor Young to reassess his decision, though itself falling into the waiting-game trap (sect. B, 10):

> It is clear that this nation's Mexican-American culture is complex enough and unique enough to merit serious academic study. Clear too is that no university is more appropriate for such study than UCLA. On that much both sides can agree. Given the terrible financial pressures the entire UC system is suffering, it is understandable that launching an academic department might not be advisable *now*. But *eventually* a full department is the preferable option—and not just because it presumably would elevate the status of Chicano studies [my emphasis].

To a reader of the social text, clearly those violent eruptions do work. The *Los Angeles Times* would not have come out in favor of a Chicano studies department were it not for the violence supposedly perpetrated by the demonstrators. People who advocate waiting do not realize that non-dominant groups have always been asked to wait. The waiting game, the card played by the status quo, is never, as producers of social texts would have people believe, an attempt at compromise.

THE HUNGER GAME

At UC Irvine, Asian American students have been demanding an Asian American studies program promised to them in 1991. They finally went on a hunger strike with the motto "We are hungry for Asian American Studies." Hunger strikes become a metaphor for the hunger within. One of the most read Chicano texts bears the title *Hunger of Memory*. César

Chávez, the leader of the United Farm Workers, used hunger strikes effectively to bring publicity to his cause. He did so much damage to his body that news reports blamed his death on the cumulative effects of food deprivation. A hunger strike personalizes a debate. Suddenly "society" does not harm an unspecified minority group, now a particular administrator does harm to a particular individual. The cultural group projects its own struggles onto the strikers. At UCLA, the hunger strikers elicited the sympathy of the maintenance crews (a majority of them Latinos working in the kitchen, on the landscaping, on the grounds picking up the garbage). Rumors were already circulating that they too would strike to show sympathy with the students.

The hunger strike (the result of the waiting game) makes visible the institutional void. The desire or need for food transforms into a craving for the culture the striker cannot institutionally have. In highlighting their status as victims the hunger strikers appropriate the symbol of need in order to characterize the struggle. The whole public, which at one point or another has become entangled in bureaucracy, will sympathize with the striker, the underdog, the person who finally shows the courage to stand up to a system, even if it means bringing it to a halt. The UCLA hunger strikers transformed their need for food into a hunger for the cultural memory which the institution refused to provide. And not because the food itself was not available (the institution already had the professors, the classrooms, the classes, the budget). The strike also highlights the inability to compromise. The UCLA chancellor often complained that he felt as though the strikers held a gun to his head.

THE HISTORICAL GAME

It is surprising to see how universities ignore their own history. When universities face protests or hunger strikes, they react to what they perceive as one incident when in reality institutional gossip has already done much to ferment the clash that inevitably comes. With or without basis, the minority community functions with the help of an informal network not represented in the official campus newsletters. This informal network circulates news of Latino activism on campuses around the nation on the Internet—in the same way that ballads conveyed counter discourses and counter histories.

Universities also do not realize that every single time they advertise a position for a U.S. Latino/a, the professional community finds out whom they finally hire. Thus the usual university spin-doctoring of the CVs to redefine the people hired hardly ever goes unnoticed. Not hiring specialists on domestic Latino issues, though at first seemingly a wise economic move, backfires in the long run. The universities will not fool the academic communities that those hires are supposed to represent.

THE FUTURE GAME

Carlos Fuentes once wrote that Mexico is the only country that honors its martyrs. Given the history of university exclusion of U.S. Latinos, the rapidly changing demographics, as well as the ambivalence of U.S. Latinos towards education, the university needs to reappraise its practices. The Mexican and Chicano/a cultural text is full of examples of exclusion, from the victimization of Malinche, Moctezuma, and Cuauhtémoc to the more recent assassination of Luis Donaldo Colosio. The Chicano text provides the Romantic legends of the Texan and Californian bandits Gregorio Cortez, Joaquín Murieta, and Tiburcio Vázquez—presently the subject of a play by Luis Valdéz. The Chicano perception that most of the Mexican migration occurred as a consequence of the Mexican Revolution, the mythification of César Chávez and his struggle in the United Farm Workers, the present sympathy with the rebellion in Chiapas, all these examples provide ample evidence of victimized heroes. The educational institution that does not foster the inclusion of U.S. Latinos therefore plays right into the U.S. Latino perception of itself as victim and into its fears/desires towards education's role in the formation and destruction of Latino cultural identity.

The U.S. Latino ambivalence towards education explains why the topic forms such a staple of analysis in Chicano artistic and literary discourse. The film *Stand and Deliver*, which made Jaime Escalante famous, explores the issue of inclusion (or exclusion) of Chicanos in universities. Education supplies the only hint of hope in *American Me*, the deterministic film directed by Edward James Olmos. María Josefina López's *Simply María* staged by the Teatro Campesino questions the role of education in the formation of cultural identity. Education plays a similar role in the infamous *Hunger of Memory*; Rodríguez perceives education as the original sin that triggered his exile from the community. Valdéz, the founder of the Teatro Campesino, made some of his educated characters—like Domingo in *The Shrunken Head of Pancho Villa*—objects of his scorn. The new activism on campuses obviously played so well because Latinos see education as a way out of poverty. But education also exposes the fabric of the U.S. Latino cultural text. Education appears as a medicine and an illness that can both save and kill the culture. Ironically, the Latino cultural text simply plays with both roots of the word *education: ducere* (to conduct) and *educere* (to take out). By providing a way out of the barrio, it also furnishes the tools of detachment from the community. And herein lies the ambivalence towards education, the Latino source of both desires and fears. Unfortunately universities have traditionally played into this ambivalence in their inability to understand the dynamics and metaphors of representation within their own institutions. Time and again the cultural academic text continues to provide a receptacle for the projection of everybody's fears: Latinos' fear of "losing" their identity, the dominant culture's fear that its "standards" will be diminished by their ambivalent Other. As long as the institution denies access, then Latinos will appropriately reject the educational institution.

When I read that, in the near future, "minority" students will make up the majority of the student population, I cannot help but notice that these demographics are a reality at UC Irvine, which calls itself the most multicultural campus in the United States. Nonetheless, even though the minority population makes up about 60 percent of the students, it makes up 12 percent of the faculty. If UC Irvine shows the way ahead, the future does not bode well. The UC Irvine statistics signal the fact that, unless changed, dedemocratization will survive and expose itself in the corridors of academia.

NOTES

1. I periodically receive calls from UCSB fund drives asking me to contribute to the endowment. On one of those occasions, the person on the phone told me that given my concern about Chicano/a issues, I should contribute to the institution since the current California fiscal crisis would first affect minority programs.

WORKS CITED

Acuña, Rudy. *Occupied America: A History of Chicanos.* New York: Harper & Row, 1988.

Bhabha, Homi. "The Other Question: The Stereotype and Colonial Discourse." *Screen* 24, 6 (Nov.-Dec. 1983): 18–36.

Castañeda, Jorge. "Mexico and California: The Paradox of Tolerance and Dedemocratization." In *The California-Mexico Connection.* A. F. Lowentahl and K. Burgess, eds. Stanford, Calif.: Stanford University Press, 1993.

Gómez Peña, Guillermo. *Warrior for Gringostroika.* St. Paul, Minn.: Graywolf Press, 1993.

López, María Josefina. *Simply María* (Fragment). In *Irvine Chicano Literary Prize 1988–1989/1989–1990.* Irvine, Calif.: Chicano Literary Contest, 1991.

Martínez, Demetria. "Troublemaker." In *Three Times a Woman.* Alicia Gaspar de Alba, María Herrera Sobek, and Demetria Martínez, eds. Tempe, Ariz.: Bilingual Press, 1989.

Mignolo, Walter. "Canons a(nd) Cross-Cultural Boundaries (Or, Whose Canon Are We Talking About)?" *Poetics Today* 12, 1 (Spring 1991): 1–28.

Morales, Alejandro. *The Brick People.* Houston, Tex.: Arte Público Press, 1988.

93106 (a newspaper for the faculty and staff of UCSB) 4, 2 (Oct. 6, 1993).

"Ode to the New California." *Harper's* 287, 1722 (Nov. 1993): 21.

Rajan, Roby. "Value/Anti-Value." Working Paper.

Rodríguez, Richard. *Hunger of Memory: The Education of Richard Rodríguez.* Boston: Godine, 1982.

Rosaldo, Renato. "Politics, Patriarchs, and Laughter." In *Nature and Context of Minority Discourse.* Abdul JanMohamad, ed. New York: Oxford University Press, 1990.

Smith, Barbara Herrnstein. *Contingencies of Value: Alternative Perspectives for Critical Theory.* Cambridge, Mass.: Harvard University Press, 1988.

Valdéz, Luis. *The Shrunken Head of Pancho Villa.* In *Necessary Theatre.* Jorge Huerta, ed. Houston, Tex.: Arte Público Press, 1989.

Ritchie Valens Is Dead

E PLURIBUS UNUM

Patricia Penn Hilden

State of California. Proposition 187. General Election, November 8, 1994. Section 53069.65:

> Wherever the state or a city or a county, or any other legally authorized local government entity with jurisdictional boundaries reports the presence of a person who is suspected of being present in the United States in violation of federal immigration laws to the Attorney General of California, that report shall be transmitted to the United States Immigration and Naturalization Service. The Attorney General shall be responsible for maintaining on-going and accurate records of such reports, and shall provide any additional information that may be requested by any other government entity.

1970:

> Newspaper reporter to Native American elder: "Do Indians think the United States should get out of Vietnam?"
> Elder: "We think the United States should get out of North America."

219

WE ARE *ALL* ILLEGAL ALIENS

Debts

Three quarters of the me born in Los Angeles in 1944 is illegal, anyway. Sometime in the seventeenth century ancestors arrived, from England, from Holland. They carried no documents, no permits to land on shores occupied for millennia by other ancestors. These adventurers sought much: wealth, land, a new way of life.

Though they would not speak of these things until much later, and then not about themselves but only about those they, with an arrogant dismissal of history, labeled "aliens," these forebears of mine from Europe inhabited an underground economy: on others' land, they lived precariously, stealing what they needed, killing, capturing, and selling into slavery those whom they were rapidly displacing. They carried foreign diseases. They spoke strange tongues (and refused to learn the languages of this place). They brought a knowledge of merciless, technologically sophisticated war making.[1] Their strange religion prescribed huge families, and they obeyed. When they couldn't feed all their children, or treat all their illnesses, they depended upon the kindness and generosity of those *indígenas* they encountered.

As time went on these aliens formed gangs, forcing the narrowest conformity among members. Nonconformists were exiled as heretics, hanged as witches, pressed to death beneath the heavy rocks of collective disapprobation (thus beginning a long tradition of majority social tyranny in North America). Gang leaders, autocratic, vain, and utterly hypocritical, justified their pillage of people and land in the baroque language of seventeenth-century Christianity. They protected their stolen territory with arms. They appropriated more and more resources. Driven by avarice, they soon discovered where the real money lay and organized an increasingly lucrative slave trade, seizing and selling Natives. Some kept captive girls and women to satisfy their lusts, and the first "mixed bloods" (the first "tragic mulattos") were born.

(Natives resisted: Edward Castillo reports that the rape of Native women trapped in mission slavery was so common that the people took collective action and "every white child born among them for a long period was secretly strangled and buried.")[2]

At first, most Natives followed ancient tradition and welcomed the new arrivals, overlooking their curious habits, their murderous intentions, their deviousness, their odd-sounding languages, the awful smell of their food, and their unwashed, pale, hairy bodies. Bemused, they tolerated Europeans' inept and aggressive attempts to live against the land by unceremoniously tearing down forests, damming rivers, slaughtering animals, ripping and moving the earth.

In the early days, only a handful of prescient tribal people resisted. They warned that these Europeans were not like others, not simply people to be welcomed into their world as custom demanded. One elder warned that these predators in human form, "as numerous as the leaves upon the trees," would "eventually crowd [you] from [your] fair possessions."[3] But few listened. Time passed. Whole nations vanished before guns and disease, before the lies, the inhumanity, the unbridled—and, to most Natives, incomprehensible—greed.

Walt Disney's version neatly captures the pervasiveness of the historical lie. His Pocahontas improbably—but oh, how the overculture wants to believe its master narratives!—falls madly in love with the English hero of a plundering expedition, a bland and blond John Smith. (As England disappears behind billowing sails, Smith roars, "For riches and freedom!" "Yes!" cry his shipmates, " for riches and freedom!") A cunning raccoon, a clever hummingbird, and a wise old (Grandmother) tree join with a cartoon Pocahontas to smooth the conquest. Though the rest of Disney's Powhatans aren't so sanguine (two of them—but none of the English—soon lie dead), the efforts of perky animals and talking trees, together with those of Disney's Indian Barbie doll, the raven-tressed, sexually precocious Pocahontas (ready to sacrifice her people for love), soon win out. The pillage begins. . . . [4]

The people took note. They tried to assess these "foreigners," so frantically ruining life on this earth, overrunning the land, draining resources, and, when they weren't killing the local populace or each other (guns provided the sport of these cruel men), purposefully destroying the traditional values of those there before them. They were not good: not for the land, not for social relations, not for spiritual life. Nearly everyone began to fear them.

How to drive them out? How to keep more from coming? The people built borders, set warriors to watch, to capture and punish transgressors, to send them home. Many retreated behind nature's fences—vast stretches of desert, towering mountains, wide rivers. Still, the invaders came. "What if we starve them out?" someone suggested at last. "What if we refuse to help them when they're sick? Refuse to feed them when they're hungry? Refuse to teach them how to live in this land that mystifies them so?" One seventeenth-century Micmac elder even tried reason: "If France . . . is a little terrestrial paradise, art thou sensible to leave it?" he asked the invaders of his land. "Why venture thyself with such risk . . . to the storms and tempests of the sea in order to come to a strange and barbarous country which thou considerest the poorest and least fortunate of the world? . . . We scarcely take the trouble to go to France," he remarked, "because we fear . . . lest we find little satisfaction there, seeing . . . that those who are natives thereof leave it every year in order to enrich themselves on our shores." "I must open to thee my heart," he concluded gently; "there is no Indian who does not consider himself infinitely more happy and more powerful than the French."[5]

Too late. Still illegal, without any documents save the visible European origins of the pale colors they bore—of skin, eyes, hair—backed by superior weapons and the will to use them ruthlessly against people, animals, land, they kept on coming. They overran the continents, spreading death everywhere until they were millions and Natives were few. A strange, restless avarice drove them on. They took. They possessed.

The East filled: my illegal forebears moved West, from land "bought" from an earlier (French) conquest onto land seized in the war with Mexico when Aztlán became "New" Mexico, West Texas, Arizona, (Alta) California. Now "ours" (personal pronouns swarmed with ambiguities), the West began to fill with Anglos. Then at mid-nineteenth century, catastrophe: material desire, driven by the discovery of gold, exploded all over California. Where once Native populations had offered rape victims, slave labor, and (on paper) converts for the wicked mission padres, or later, cheap labor for Mexican landowners who replaced Spanish Church fathers, now their very existence began to threaten those who had seized the land from Mexico. The Anglos, "Americans," intended to own all of

California, not least those thousands of acres of the land that contained, or might contain, gold.[6]

That a genuine Indian threat lurked mostly in greed-maddened Anglo minds meant little. Neither their traditional gentleness nor the scarcity of those tribal people whose land they yearned after slowed the spread of a violence even more terrible than that already familiar to Native people across the continent. Anglos viewed their courtesy and politeness with dismissive scorn. "Yankees," David Banks Rogers boasted, "fresh from contact with the natives of the plains who were prone to fight to the death in defense of their rights, treated with contempt the quiet, unresentful slaves of the Spaniards, in derision dubbing them 'diggers,' in common with all other coastal tribes. . . . Woe to the hapless native who, under the influence of liquor, attempted the terrorism that had been the dread of the 'paisano.' If he tried his violence upon one of the newly-arrived Anglo-Saxon lords, the chances were very slight of his ever again appearing before an accredited judge for sentence."[7] How slight? For California's remaining tribal people (a population of 310,000 Natives in California when the Spanish arrived plummeted to only 150,000 in 1848), the Gold Rush meant near-certain death.[8]

The 1850s were hideous. Whites—"Americans" or "Yankees"—killed, raped, mutilated, and sold Natives with utter, utter impunity. Only a few among the Anglo-Saxon lords objected. In 1861, after a decade of unbridled gold greed, an editor at the Marysville *Appeal* recorded the appalling facts: "From these mountain tribes," he explained, "white settlers draw their supplies of kidnapped children, [who are] educated as servants, and women for purposes of labor and lust."[9] As for tribal people who resisted, or who happened to get in the way of white vengeance (no one was very particular about identifying the victims, a red skin was a red skin, after all), merciless slaughter awaited. One goldminer, Edwin Franklin Morse, confided the gory details of one typical event to his diary. Two Grass Valley brothers, Samuel and George Holt, "were in the habit," he wrote, "of enticing the Indian women and girls into their [saw]mill and insulting them." (Remember: in this era, "insult" meant physical assaults, including rape, and thus this tale tells us that the play of sexual power relations, present from the first moments of "contact" between male Europeans and female Natives, continued unabated.) "When the bucks learned of this they rose in their wrath and, attacking the mill one night, killed one of the Holts and severely wounded the other with their arrows, and burned down the mill."[10] Soldiers—stationed here and throughout the West to protect settlers from Indians—responded immediately, "and, joined by some of the miners from Grass Valley, went down and killed several Indians in retaliation." Morse, bearing the European patriarchy that transformed relations between tribal women and men, expressed sympathy for those most offended in such events: "This always seemed most uncalled for to me, as the Indians were perfectly justified in resenting the insult to their women."[11]

But these same Anglos tried to "civilize" the Natives. When, soon after his arrival in Mexican California in 1839, John Sutter discovered a need for cheap labor to build and serve the colony of Anglo settlers he brought to Sacramento, he quickly "gain[ed] ascendancy over the tribes by persevering, by kindness and the exercise of skill and well-timed authority."[12] He even "supplied [poor] Mexicans and Indians with clothing, hats, and every thing necessary to humanize and civilize them," though to little avail. Most Indians, complained one Euro-American contemporary, persisted in their barbarism, dancing "a dance for the dead in which they are horribly disfigured with mud and tar and paints." The poor Mexicans in their turn, all vaqueros in the stereotype of those days, were initially not quite so despised. Unlike California's Indians, they were horsemen, cowboys, real *men*, the envy of recently arrived Eastern "greenhorns." They could work cattle better than anyone, better, even, than Anglos. Lest this pose an ideological challenge, however, Anglos soon offered an explanation: Mexicans' ranching skills were not acquired, but were, instead, a gift of nature. One goldminer explained that cattle ranching was "the life, and sport of the Mexican, who is almost born upon a horse [and] can accomplish daring feats upon his back." He "is absolutely good for nothing anywhere else," this writer was quick to add.[13]

For a brief moment around the turn of the century, some Mexicans and some Indians even achieved heroic roles in the spectacles of popular culture when "real Mexicans," together with representatives of a completely vanquished people carrying "pure blood," were featured players in Wild West

entertainments, roping, riding, warring, and hunting in endless reenact-
ments of the Western frontier myths. The key to acceptability had two sides.
First, Anglos had to believe that you were no threat (the contented citizens
of another country or members of a vanishing—or assimilating—race). Sec-
ond, you had to live somewhere else. Thus indigenous "Mexicans" and
"half-breed" Indians continued to threaten Anglo hegemony, and in these
popular entertainments they joined "white renegades" to portray villains.

(Not many years of this century passed before indigenous people of any color disappeared both from California and from the white imagination. The 1900 census counted only about 20,000 tribal people remaining.[14] To attract Easterners, the "new West's" boosters published a magazine reflecting this new reality. *Out West: A Magazine of the Old Pacific and the New* (its motto? "The Nation Back of Us. The World in Front") illustrated the myth beckoning more Anglo settlers: "The Genius of the West" showed (white) peopled covered wagons appearing over the rim of a broad mesa, empty of inhabitants. Below and in the foreground lay a broad, shining, equally empty valley. In the sky, however, skirted by roiling white clouds, rose a naked Anglo woman, pointing west with her raised left arm.)[15]

Endless public outcries, then as well as now, attest: out of sight was the only way nonwhites stayed out of mind. Thus "Home on the Range," beloved of presidents and schoolteachers since its appearance at the beginning of this century, included forgivingly agentless declarations of possession and dispossession: "Oh *give* me a home where the buffalo roam, / Where the deer and the antelope play, / Where seldom *is heard* a discouraging word / And the skies are not cloudy all day. . . . Where the air is so pure, the zephyrs so free, / The breezes so balmy and light, / That I would not *exchange* my home on the range / For all the cities so bright." The cheery tune ends with an even more ominous passivity: "The red man *was pressed* from this part of the West, / He's likely no more to return / To the banks of the Red River where seldom if ever / Their flickering campfires burn."

Well, the Indians were gone, vanished, or safely locked away on reservations. And soon, even the most grudging admiration of Mexican vaqueros, even of those "safely" foreign-born, dissolved in the face of fears that the Anglo-Saxon world was being overrun: by non-Anglo-Saxon southern and eastern Europeans in the East, by the descendants of Africans in the South, and by Mexicans and Asians in the West. And when cattle ranching yielded its economic dominance—to gold mining, farming, commerce (and, in the higher reaches of the Sierra Nevada, sheep ranching, which called for the skills of Basque herders, not Mexican cowboys), nonwhite cowboys (black, as well as brown and red) became obsolete. The threat that they and their descendants might choose to settle in white cities intensified. Unable to force most of them (or those of Chinese or African heritage) onto arid North American reservations, Anglos passed the Chinese Exclusion Acts and began to exile Mexicans "home"—to the nation now south of "our" California. And this meant a bigger and better border.

All was not well. Though most Indians stayed on their reservations, though most Chinese and Japanese stayed in their urban ghettos or in isolated, invisible rural communities, and though African Americans remained but a tiny minority of urban populations (they, too, invisible, locked into race-defined ghettos), Mexicans kept coming, across the Rio Grande, across to New Mexico, to Arizona, to California, to Aztlán, called by agriculture, by industry, and—eventually—by war.[16]

(So a Republican Congressman, frenzied in his xenophobia, declares in 1995: "I don't want to see the sons of Hispanics burning the flag that white men's sons fought and died for in World War Two and Vietnam." Was he color blind or is he an idiot? Did he really not know that Latinos—and African and Native Americans—fought in both wars, dying in vastly disproportionate numbers in Vietnam?)[17]

Here, in our West, brown (and red, Mexicans are Indios, too) immigrants just kept on coming. More borders. More guards, these deliberately the cruelest they could find to confront the frighteningly permeable line that ran east to west along the southern reaches of Angloland, this place they had begun to believe belonged to them by birthright. The "Texas Rangers" reigned supreme, their utter ruthlessness celebrated, justified by the nation's premier historians. Here is Walter Prescott Webb. Listen: "The Mexican has a cruel streak, which, in turn, must be dealt with cruelly."[18] (A 1942 Los Angeles County sheriff reported on the barrio violence that resulted from the arrival of the first thousands of braceros: Anglo-Saxons, he noted, preferred to use their fists in fights, while "the

Mexican" wanted knives.[19] "His desire is to kill, or at least to let blood. It is," he insisted, "an inborn characteristic.")[20]

Those Mexicans who ignored their Anglo guards, who braved their cruelty to cross into their ancestral lands (still often at the behest of California's rich Anglo settlers, unable to work the fields, clean the houses, tend the gardens, care for the children) were o.k. as long as they were content to use up their youths doing work no one else wanted at wages no one else would accept. But then they began to settle. Whole families. Anglos murmured, began to stir in their Brentwood, their Westwood, their Beverly Hills mansions. Listen: "First we got rid of the Indians and now this!" Listen: "They are taking our resources, overrunning our land. They won't learn our language. They have too many children. They don't eat our food. They smell funny. Their music is foreign. Their religion is not our religion.. They have brown skin, hair, eyes. They are destroying our traditional values" Listen: "They are *undocumented aliens*."

They sought variations on the solutions of their ancestors. I wrote to A:

Home again in L.A. after 30 years. Not my neighborhood, of course, this one for the rich, this Gringoland for sure. But, homesick after years in alien Manhattan, I strolled this morning, all unknowing, through the shiny streets of vast lawns and tall trees and sweet flowers—"bougainvillea, hibiscus," I practiced names recalled from childhood, "star jasmine, honeysuckle"—that climb the hills around the UCLA campus. The houses we remember seeing from a distance, from our childhood across town. In that tradition of historical forgetting, of the entire transformation of a genocidal past into a romantic nostalgia, most houses here are built to look like California Missions, with red tile roofs and arched doorways. To our eyes trained by childhood poverty and to mine trained more recently by years of New York crowding these are vast dwellings, made still larger by the whitewashed walls looming between passersby and the privacy within.

Stunned by so much color, so much, yes, beauty, I did not at first see the markers. But after a time I began to note. Each house bore a tiny blue sign anchored firmly in the sea of grass visible from the street:

"White People's Stuff Protection Agency"

Below this message, sized to disguise the truth of the sign's purpose:

"Armed Response"

ARMED RESPONSE!? I read it out loud, shocked as I went on walking, sadly less unknowing, up and down the hills, still smelling, feeling, but no longer *thinking*, "home."

So who provides the guns this time? No Texas Rangers here—too gross, too, well, vulgar. So who? I began to watch as I walked. Then I saw the first of what became dozens of cars, each marked with the logo of the WPS Protection Agency. Driving the cars were. . . . not Mexicans, not Indians. . . . African Americans—mercenaries, black-skinned people (men) hired to keep the brown/red-skinned people from stealing what they cleaned, moved, watered, tended, pruned, dusted, washed, polished for the people who evidently did nothing at all. They cannot imagine, these empty, greed-driven gabachos, that those who work for them do not long to own the appurtenances that spell American wealth, that constitute their identity as surely as it formed an identity for their ancestors. "White people," Robert Thomas once said, "confuse consumption with experience."[21] Too bad.

" WE HAVE BORNE EVERYTHING PATIENTLY FOR THIS LONG TIME "

JOSEPH BRANT, MOHAWK LEADER[22]

> The atrocities we've committed against each other
> haven't been on a grand scale. (As [Richard] Hofstadter
> noted, there is nothing in our history to compare with
> the slaughter of some 10,000 French Huguenots on St.
> Bartholomew's Night in 1572, or the massacre of more
> than 100,000 Indonesian Communists in 1965, let alone
> the official horrors of Stalin, Hitler or Pol Pot.)

SEAN WILENTZ[23]

In 1500, the population of Native North America numbered between 12.5 and 18 million people. "In 1890, [when] the federal government declared the period of conquest . . . officially over, . . . only 248,253 identifiable Indians remained alive within its borders, with another 122,585 residing north of the border, in Canada. . . . The census conducted in 1900 revealed only 237,196 Indians in the U.S., barely 101,000 in Canada."[24]

Proposition 187

Section 1: Findings and Declarations

Listen:

The People of California find and declare as follows:

That they have suffered and are suffering economic hardship caused by the presence of illegal aliens in this state.

That they have suffered and are suffering personal injury and damage caused by the criminal conduct of illegal aliens in this state.

That they have a right to the protection of the government from any person or persons entering this country unlawfully.

Therefore the People of California declare their intention to provide for cooperation between their agencies of state and local government with the federal government, and to establish a system of required notification by and between such agencies to prevent illegal aliens in the United States from receiving benefits or public services in the state of California.

Section 113

Listen:

Any person who manufactures, distributes, or sells false documents to conceal the true citizenship or resident alien status of another person is guilty of a felony, and shall be punished by imprisonment in the state prison for five years or by a fine of seventy-five thousand dollars.

Section 114

Listen:

Any person who uses false documents to conceal his or her true citizenship or resident alien status is guilty of a felony, and shall be punished by imprisonment in the state prison for five years or by a fine of twenty-five thousand dollars."

A Short History of Hate

1517: Jaguar priests of the Yucatán Mayas: "The offenses of the white people are all alike. . . . Gradually we discover that the Christians are great liars. Little by little we realize that they are cheats."[25]

The legacies of European genocide in the Americas are many and bitter. Two spread through everything, twisting all our lives here in the West. One we have seen. This is the continuous barrage of fear-driven efforts to keep California white—to keep, in other words, every material advantage gained by warfare and pillage in the grasping hands of the Anglo "us." The other is mixed blood.

The first produced oddities both serious and ridiculous. And its essentials were never consistent. Both Mexicans and Indians played good, played bad, played "indigenous," played "foreigner." No attitude was consistent, no official policy firm. But by the close of the nineteenth century, Californians knew at least one thing clearly. There, people of several ethnic origins lived too close to keep an endemic Anglo fear—perhaps of their own history—at bay. Together these people of color bore the brunt of Euro-America's hatred. Public policies were fear-driven, inconsistent, and random, aimed now at one group, now at another. But always directed by Anglos, those self-styled ("real") Americans.

Listen: In 1871, Chinese men living in that part of Los Angeles known as Chinatown were massacred.[26] A few years later, purportedly terrified of the "yellow peril," the U.S. Congress passed the Chinese Exclusion Acts, and even the wives and children of those men imported to work the railways and mining camps of the West were forbidden to enter the country. So scary were the "yellow devils" that the California legislature in its turn decided that while black and Indian children could begin to attend public schools, those "Chinese" children who were already in the state would be taught in segregated schools.[27]

But this exclusive focus on Chinese and Chinese Americans was short-lived. Whiteness requires constant vigilance, and there were other threats to the racial purity of Anglo California. In 1916, for example, the good Anglo folks of the Sherman School District in East Hollywood petitioned to have "Mexican" children excluded from their schools, on the grounds that they carried communicable diseases (an ironic recognition of how quickly

European diseases became "theirs"). Alas for these worried parents, however, the school board's physicians soon reported that the "Mexican" kids carried no illness not familiar in every Anglo school population. This didn't reassure parents since they were less concerned about disease than about racial mixing. But it was some time before this school board hit upon a satisfactory solution. Five years passed before they figured out how to segregate "Mexican" children from their "American" peers. Claiming that they were being helpful, they set up special "ungraded" classes for all the nonwhite children, defined as "non-English speakers."[28]

Ironically, these segregated classrooms were born in an era of frenzied "Americanization" efforts in the Los Angeles schools, aimed at assimilating those "foreign" children and making them into imitations of the Euro-American ideal. Central Junior High had its fairly anodyne "junior citizenship program" for both white and nonwhite working-class families. School children and their parents, led by Euro-American teachers (there were no others), were taken all over the city and invited to observe (and presumably to learn to desire) the appurtenances of white, middle-class "American" life. Exuding racial stereotypes, one participating teacher noted that "Mexicans, Polish, and Russians enjoyed rehearsals of the Philharmonic," while "Chinese, Korean, and Japanese students received the most pleasure from a visit to the different departments of the Hall of Records."[29]

Other such programs were more pernicious. Los Angeles public schools also aimed to humiliate "foreigners" into assimilating. School "christening days" assigned "Orientals" "given names the teachers could pronounce."[30] "IQ tests"—examining cultural knowledge held tightly in Anglo hands—became segregationist school boards' next weapon; classes began to be assigned not only on the basis of language, but also by "intelligence quotients."[31]

When schooling failed to re-form children of color into white images, policing took over. Then, as now, the Los Angeles police were unsubtle racists. During a bloody suppression of a Wobbly strike on the San Pedro docks, reporters discovered (purportedly to their liberal horror) that many of *their* policemen, including the chief, Louis Oaks, were active members of the Ku Klux Klan.[32] For those would-be cops who hated "foreigners" but couldn't find employment among the white bedsheet-hidden police of Los Angeles, that hate-filled decade created a second possibility, the Border Patrol.

This new police force was ready when another crisis, the Depression, struck. It was there when Anglos decided—again: they never tire of this sport—that they were in economic danger because of "Mexicans." Legal or no, Mexican-born or not, these "foreigners" were quickly "repatriated" to Mexico. (Not surprisingly, then—as now—particular victims of this race-driven exportation were those on public assistance.)

Listen: Governor Pete Wilson's mythical "Californians," are those who "have always answered adversity with bold thoughts, . . . always dared to dream." With a straight face and a stunning tolerance for eighth-grade social studies-textbook clichés, the governor celebrated his Californians who "followed a dream," pioneers who went "west in wagon trains across a desolate prairie and over frozen mountains. . . . These early settlers risked their lives crossing the mighty Sierra, till one day they crossed a ridge to find themselves gazing down from the heights upon a golden valley that held the promise of California."[33]

With unusual candor the governor admitted that "most of us are not the lineal descendents [sic] of those pioneers. We [!] came later. We came by ship from Asia and by station wagon from Ohio.[34] We came during the Great Depression from the Dust Bowl in pick-ups piled high with our possessions."[35] (He neglects to mention that those "we's," those "Okies" and "Arkies," were met by gun-toting Anglos, all too ready to shoot if the newer "we's" protested the nighttime burning of their Hoovervilles, their migrant camps.)

And the Dust Bowl refugees were not the same "we's" who came a little later to serve Anglo farmers who found themselves suddenly short of labor. Those "we's" were braceros, Mexicans imported to plant, weed, tend, and harvest California's crops in the absence of sufficient earlier "we's," the "poor white trash," pickers of John Steinbeck's grapes of wrath, who, only a few years before, had replaced the Mexicans "repatriated" south of the border. But however essential to feeding the Anglos of California, to sustaining the vast profits of what was even then a sea of agri-businessmen, these braceros, like their predecessors before them, soon posed a problem. Unlike the Okies and Arkies, braceros were visible; they spoke a "foreign" language, they had dark skin, (they worked hard and without complaining), they were *different*.

Once again, the Los Angeles County schools leapt into the breach, commissioning studies, then holding special workshops for Anglo teachers forced to confront brown-skinned, Spanish-speaking children in their classrooms. One commission report informed the teachers (with characteristic muddle), "Several investigations pertaining to the adjustment of Mexican and Spanish-speaking pupils in the various school systems disclose facts similar to those which follow: On the average they are retarded and over age for the grade, the retardation ranging from 50% to 86% of the enrollment." Still, there was hope. This stunning "retardation" was not due to race. "There are no significant inherent racial differences in mental endowment."[36] So what to do?

We—my sister and brother and I—know exactly what was done. We were children in those schools, children in heavily "Mexican" neighborhoods, first in downtown Los Angeles, then in the north San Fernando Valley (in a brand-new housing tract planted atop a dry desert wash just south of Roscoe Boulevard). In elementary school we learned about being Americans, Mexican- style, as we danced "La Jesusita," "La Cucaracha," the "Mexican Hat Dance." We sang songs: "Come break the piñata, Come scatter the toys," "For we are humble pilgrims, Jesús, María, y José." WE SPOKE SPANISH, caló, the soft language of our suburban barrio. BUT we were not Mexicans. We were even half-white. We were "smart kids," not sufficiently least to spend our days in Spanish-speaking classrooms. So, when we finished sixth grade, they put my sister and me on buses and drove us far across town, to an Anglo school where we learned the language of "civilization," French. Soon, the Spanish we all knew from our street play was gone, buried beneath the pluperfect, buried inside the throat-stripping r's of a new language, a better language, a *white* language. When Ritchie Valens was killed in the terrible plane crash that devastated our neighborhood in 1959, we two could still dance the *pachuco*, but we could barely remember the words of his signature song, "La Bamba," at our school's memorial assembly. Ritchie Valens—who crossed over, but only after Valenzuela was Anglo-ized—was dead.

And we came by jet-liner last year, last month, and last week.

Pete Wilson

Well, the American dream all right, though "we" no longer skulk across borders in the night; "we" are white; "we" are not Mexican or Salvadoran or Guatemalan families dodging searchlight-waving helicopters or the traffic rushing along the six-lane, eight-lane freeways we must cross, "free"ways posted with signs "PROHIBIDO."[37] Nor are we black-skinned Haitians, running from murder, from anarchy, from fear, paddling, sailing, swimming desperately, desperately toward Florida. "We" have plane tickets; "we" are white.

But still "we" are dissatisfied. Still the dream eludes "us." Pete Wilson tells us why. Listen:

> Ours is a generation that cannot take for granted the good life, the historically generous bounty of California unless we are prepared to make dramatic change.

Change?

> The People agree. . . . They ask "Why should federal law reward illegal immigrants for violating the law and punish California taxpayers and needy legal residents?"
>
> Pete Wilson

Here it is: Proposition 187 in a paranoid nutshell. American politics, driven by greed. We have heard it before. We shall hear it again, and again, and again.

What to do?

Well we can become like the "thems" who own the place now. . . . We can assimilate (or at least perform respectability). . . . Or, we can kill all our children who "look" white.

But that's me.

MIXED BLOODS

CHARGES

> Their relationships with other human beings are just a tactic, not a need. They are pilgrims in the world. Their search is directed either by utopia or nostalgia. Their present is always imperfect, made of change and doubt. The subject is always alien, exiled.[38]

(Partial) Payments

> I remember one later shame-filled day when I was living
> with my mother in Butte, Montana. A number of white
> classmates relentlessly made fun of my last name, and
> that filled me with shame and guilt. I believed that be-
> ing an Indian was no good and countered them by say-
> ing that although I did have Indian blood, a full 1/4 of
> my blood was French; therefore I did have some value. I
> said that often and even believed it. It was shameful.
>
> GEORGE P. HORSECAPTURE[39]

Twentieth-century Californians have depended upon two kinds of borders to keep "their" state Anglo. One is physical, symbolized by the
barbed wire of the nineteenth-century West (collected now by aficiona-
dos of a past romanticized, cleansed by myth of its blood). The other is
less visible; terror and self-hatred fence "alien" minds, converting people
with brown and red skins to whiteness. For mixed bloods, for George
Horsecapture and all of the rest of us, the process has been devastatingly
simple: our "white" blood forms the core of respectability, of an authenticity created to define insiders, dreamers of the American Dream.

The techniques developed to instill such identification in those not
purely white were first practiced on all Indians, mixed or "pure." As the
Board of Indian Commissioners explained in 1875:

> It is the aim of the Government of the United States to reclaim the Indian
> from his rude, wild, and savage state by the kindly influence of just deal-
> ing; by an undeviating observance of good faith; by a firm, but kind and
> paternal rule over him; by protecting him from wrongs and aggressions;
> and by educating him and his children in letters, arts, manners, and reli-
> gion. . . . In this way lead them up to citizenship and absorb them as we
> are absorbing men of all other races and lands and climes, into this
> Christian nation.[40]

Of course authentic whiteness could never be achieved, not even among
those whose mixed genes provided all the requisite visible characteris-
tics. ("Blue eyes are like money," Alice Walker famously observed; "they
buy your way in."[41] But not all the way in.)

Always in exile from themselves, then, these "alien" children. The cross-blood Indians among them discovered that some treaties had exiled them; some had kept them in. The earlier treaties, those of the Sauk and Fox (1830), the Poncas (1858), the Kansas (1859), the Omahas (1865), and the Blackfoots (1865—unratified), provided for their children whose blood was not whole. But many later ones (affected by the blood policies of the federal government) did not. As a result of this muddled history, Russell Thornton writes, "The status of these mixed bloods has often been problematic: sometimes they have been considered American Indian, sometimes not. . . . Generally, mixed-bloods who accepted tribal ways of life were welcomed, whereas those who preferred non-Indian ways were not."[42]

Whatever the efforts and policies of various Native nations, however, the numbers of mixed bloods increased steadily. In 1830, 46 percent of American Indians were "full-blood," 42 percent mixed blood, and 11 percent unspecified. By 1980, the majority of those identifying themselves as American Indians were mixed blood, while some "6–7 million [other] Americans had some degree of American Indian ancestry."[43]

Sherman Alexie:

1.

I cut myself into sixteen equal pieces
keep thirteen and feed the other three
to the dogs . . .

2.

It is done by blood, reservation mathematics, fractions:
father (full-blood) + mother ($\frac{5}{8}$)—son ($\frac{13}{16}$) . . . [44]

So what does this mean?

Payments (subset: Desire)

Frantz Fanon: "I marry white culture, white beauty, white whiteness."[45]

Sherman Alexie: "There is nothing as white as the white girl an Indian boy loves."[46]

Wendy Rose:

Step softly.
She is not of this world
And no one rides to the rescue.[47]

So we drown.

Suburban tides run clear before Fanon's confession,
Scrubbing the red.
Luna to Moon. Lunada.

Pulling the water
Pouring the
Washing the
Color. Gone.

Lacunae:
"White Women are nothing without their mirrors," Frances's grand-
mother tells us, gently . . .
I Hold Up a Red Mirror:

A pale statue of Ohio, Iowa, Kansas
(Names remember mine her ancestors slaughtered.)
She fits her colorless moon lines around your brown body,
Mud yellow hair, disarranged by the lust her holding flaunts,
Hangs firm, bronzed not by the exigencies of her mythic inheritance
But by white Europe's aversion to that clean that startled dirty
    Columbus . . .

("They were strange men," tribal people recall, "smelly and sweaty, igno-
rant of the delights of a frequent bath, hungry for gold and precious stones.")

No Medusa, then: No power. No passion.

And you, ése?
What can she (re)make of you?
Your hair—vanishing more surely than any Indian—worn long, tied back,
Defiant,
One silver earring marking culture.
You know, mi carnal. *You know.*

Seeing me
You circle, turn your back to my dismay. Amor de lejos, amor de
    pendejos.
You take Miss Middle America's beige, Burberry-shrouded arm
Hold your mirror before her pale face
And walk away.

Mi Mixed Blood Vida Loca
    Más vale que haiga un tonto y no dos.

R shows up at the American Film Institute's Award ceremony for the
famous Indian filmmaker shunning us, toting *his* prize: a woman whiter
than white, albino nearly. However trendy in Soho these days (and *au
courant* with black), to us it is the look of near-death and frightening.

> *Skin color matters, we know. My father used to criticize a self-conscious fif-*
> *teen-year-old over and over and over: "You are so pale. You look sick.*
> *What's the matter?" Near naming my mixed blood's adherence to the Euro-*
> *pean side. . . . For him, my blue eyes, paying my way into the overculture*
> *(like Wendy Rose's cousin, the "green-eyed boy / everyone loves"), shut me*
> *out of his world.*[48]

Payments (subset: "Real Authentick Indians"?)

That famous filmmaker, meeting all of our talking circle, reacts to blue-
eyed Shari and me. Summoned to swell the nearly all-white crowd with
some *indígenas*, a group of us went together. There, we joined a line heading into the auditorium. The filmmaker was standing outside the door,
nodding graciously, willingly receiving accolades from his dozens of admirers circling around. Without speaking, he watched those who passed
carefully. Dean, tall, black-haired, black-eyed, was first of our group. At
the sight of him, the filmmaker grinned happily and leaned over the
heads of several admirers to grab his hand. Then Carol, also dark but
much shorter. He had to reach across several people to grasp Carol's
hand. He shook it joyfully, enthusiastically, still smiling. But Shari and I
were next. The smile disappeared. He took in our blue eyes, nothing

more. His face went cold and still. His eyes moved rapidly past us, aimed at a spot just above our not-quite-black hair, came to rest. Smiling again, he recognized our next friend, Chris, black of hair and eye, red of skin.

Who *were* we to Mr. Princeton Indian? Mr. Rich New England Indian?

Are we, Shari and I, both almost pompon girl pretty, both blue of eye and light of skin, the same objects of desire as white women? Not blonde, of course. And (as A. wrote once, trying to explain our connections), blonde or brown or black, we share souls, we know race rage, we share, as Dean says, "blood." Does this complicate the straightforward assumption of our Lady Whiteness? Or does it make us safer for those men who understand the peculiarity Fanon named so long ago? "There IS nothing as white as the white girl an Indian boy loves."

New Charges (subset: Racism)

So, I say to a potential landlord, I am Indian. His face closes. He mutters mostly to himself. "Parties, alcohol, rent due. . . . " His wife freezes with embarrassment, chats mindlessly to cover what I realize only slowly. His Navajo jewelry, I see now, is about loving dead Indians, vanished—but quaint—people. It's about anthropology. It's about book learning and Hiawatha. And, of course, as Tim points out, it's about owning the material cultures of the conquest . . . the victor's spoils.

(subset: Tragic Mulatto)

Week after week I call A. from New York, asking advice. Always it is the same. A professor, a colleague, has telephoned. The requests are varied, endless. Could you: (1) Come to a party? There will be some Native Americans there, and you always make everyone so comfortable. (2) Help me understand why X isn't doing the work for my class? Her term paper doesn't explore all the readings assigned, so I don't think she's even done the reading; I think for her own good I'm going to have to fail her. (3) Explain why Y is having trouble with the financial aid office? We've offered all the help any student should need, but she still seems to have problems. (4) Bring "your group" to an event we're having on Friday? We want a Native American presence. (5) Meet an aboriginal filmmaker who is visiting New York for a semester? I know you'll all have a lot in common.

So I sit in rooms, hang on telephones, write, explain, tell, explain—all the time, though, swallowing a reaction not unlike F.'s, who pulls away when those Anglo women pet him and pet him. I am angry. I am horrified that I must do this. But what is the choice? It is, A. tells me over and over, the condition of *la frontera,* life on the border, mulatto life.

So, keenly aware that this act patronizes a good friend, betrays a sister, I explain (though with tongue firmly planted in cheek, fingers crossed behind my back) a nontraditional term paper to an anthropology professor. It is, I tell him, not the failure he perceives but rather a deeply confiding, seriously honoring work by someone who doesn't tell the things in the paper easily. My professor colleague is moved, is effusively grateful. My comrade gets an A in the course. (But she knows what the white professor does not. She tells me one day as we walk along the street, that X doesn't like her very much, that he avoids her as much as possible and won't even look in her eyes. "He may be an anthropologist," she says, smiling, "but he sure doesn't know anything about Indians.")

And after Shari and I sort out financial-aid problems, translating for the white woman in charge, for the black woman at the bursar's office, and then back into "Indian" for another friend (though this part is mainly whiteman jokes and not really an explanation), I carefully remember to telephone thanks to the first woman. More questions—about tribal traditions, about differences she perceives between this friend and another Native she knows. More exclamations: "Oh it's so interesting! I'm just realizing that all you people have different cultures. I just learned all about Sioux people last week from J.F., and now I see I'll have to go to the library to get some books out about Navajos in order to understand X. . . . "

"And," she adds, gathering Shari and me into the same mental fold, "you two will probably want to come to the Indian event we are planning to hold in March. I'll be sure you're on the mailing list."

But, I think with despair, how could I not be on the mailing list? *Someone* is going to have to translate. . . .

Payments (subset: Gifts)

Frances Peters. "Given" to our talking circle by an anthro professor, Frances is my *carnalita,* instant friend. She recognizes our New York University dilemmas straightaway. Even if she hadn't been one of us from the first, she would quickly have learned to see them as we do. First, the directors of the institute of which she is a six-month fellow made sure that she is terribly cold. Arranging her apartment, they have given her—right off the plane from Sydney's summer, from the red desert clan—one blanket! When she arrives at my door upstairs, I hand over several more, seeing shadows of the lost person I was fifteen years before, landing from Berkeley's summer in England, freezing. And in both places, not just the weather chills. Here what shrinks indigenous skins is the extraordinary closeness of the physical and emotional space in which New Yorkers seem to thrive. "They get right up in my face to talk," Frances tells me, surprised. "Do Indians find this as awful as we aboriginal people do? Do you need lots of space?" "Yes," I tell her, "yes! And touching? They keep touching. This drives us *loco.* And you?" "Oh yeah," she says in broad Australian English. "They've been touching me all the time. We don't touch at all, even families. And they do it in public all the time! Just the same as the way they always talk about themselves . . . stuff we'd never say, even to our closest friends and families. We'd get laughed out of town if we said some of these things!"

And then, despite that fact that it was she who assumed our indigenousness would quickly bind us all together, the anthro is distressed because Frances so quickly and easily joined this family of aliens. After all, it is her acquisitiveness, the anthro's desire to collect exotica that has brought Frances thither, and to us. So again she telephones me, insistent, wanting to know "What do you have in common?" I am briefly dumbstruck, so she begins to speculate about a bond she can never understand. "She *is* very intelligent, of course," she reminds herself. ("For an abo . . . " I add in my mind).

I know the answers, but this time I don't supply information for the thirsty anthro. It is none of her business. But it is, in fact, because Frances doesn't look around the table at all the people and say, "Are you all real

Indians? Am I spending time with real Indians?" She doesn't ask, "What do Indians think about . . . ? How does an Indian man feel about . . . ? What do Indian women think is most. . . . ?" She isn't exceptionally thrilled that she can add us to her collection of exotic encounters. She doesn't try to add herself to us by recounting some story that features something she associates with "Indians."

She's a woman of color, too, and knows the male desire that shuns her kind, our kind, firsthand. Painful it is, too. And we women talk about it among ourselves. We talk about the power relations that shape the guys' strange desires to own the other, to keep a trophy, to taunt the white guys by holding one of "their" women. Frances tells us that Fanon's truth describes Australia as it describes our world. There, too, Barbie dolls mean perfection.

Oh.

Payments (Listen)

Anglo professor writes on Indian student's thesis draft: "Read all my comments, go away and pray and meditate until you know what it is you want to say."

Anthropologist wants to know: "So, before there were chairs, how did you people sit down?"[49]

A Euro-American woman friend, an artist, meets Frances. She immediately starts collecting her, recounting a dream, set in Australia, a dream about paintings coming up out of the ground. Fixing her eyes intently on Frances's face she tells her how she's always felt a kinship with that continent . . . a sense that she knows something about aborigines in her artist's blood.

I writhe.

Then finally she concludes: "I need to try to trace my Chippewa ancestors. . . . No one ever mentioned them when I was growing up, so. . . . "

Aboriginal in a former life? Chippewa—though she never knew in fifty years—in this?

Why do people do this? A twentieth-century form of the historical violence, of the fencing, of the building of borders. . . .

She did it with A. when he visited New York, when she discovered that they had both attended the same Southern California elementary school. Burbling then about how "the Chicanos" at the elementary school they both attended were "never around" as far as she could recall, and, funny, she'd been a hall monitor and class president so. . . . She claimed to be charmed to meet A. because, she told him over and over, in all the years of grammar schooling she had never, ever known any of "you." As with Frances, she was "collecting," at once seeking common ground with something romantic about indigenousness, and erecting a wall, establishing a self different from the exotic other. Though here again, as in her encounter with Frances, she was revealing a deep, endemic racism to us, *she* imagined she was bonding.

Frances got it right off. A., usually more perceptive, was initially deaf . . . though he was in high form and talking and talking as though he felt close to everyone there. Later, he wept.

Payments (subset: Resistance)

1882. Frank Hamilton Cushing, "on a collecting trip for the Smithsonian Institution's Bureau of Ethnology, reported from the Hopi village of Oraibi that he had encountered implacable resistance from the village elders. Despite his threats and cajolings, Cushing had been unable to persuade the people of Oraibi to part with their belongings for deposit in 'Father Washington's' museum of glass boxes in Washington. 'They beg for war,' he wrote, 'and say: "When the Caciques of the Americans sit on our decapitated heads, then they can dress our bodies in their clothes, feed our bodies with their victuals; then, too, they can have our things to take with them to the houses of their fathers."' Having concluded that 'we can make no collection here, save by force,' Cushing hastily retreated from the Third Mesa village on Christmas morning."[50]

Final Charges

January 31, 1995, 1 A.M. In a San Fernando Valley neighborhood, near my childhood home, beneath a Hollywood Freeway overpass, a white man called William Masters pulled out a nine-millimeter pistol and killed eighteen-year old César Arce. With more shots, this thirty-five-year-old vigilante wounded Arce's friend, David Hillo. Why? The two young men were spray painting graffiti on the concrete bridge.

Masters claimed he shot the younger men in "self-defense." His victim, Arce, "armed with a screwdriver," was a "murderer" who "this time . . . died." Masters quickly became a hero to North Valley Anglos. Women were particularly charmed. "Diane" telephoned a radio talk show to assure her world that "I don't care if he's Looney Toons or what, but we need more guys like him around." Sandi Webb (what do you want to bet she dots her i's with little happy faces and wears salmon pink polyester pants suits?) made public a letter she wrote on behalf of the City Council, of which she is a member: "Kudos to William Masters for his vigilant anti-graffiti efforts and for his foresight in carrying a gun for self-protection. . . . If Sun Valley refuses to honor Masters as a crime-fighting hero, then I invite him to relocate to our town. I think he will find Simi Valley to be a much more compatible place to live."[51] (Well, he would. Simi Valley, once a childhood refuge of horned toads, cacti, tumbleweeds, manzanita, and shady live oaks, has become a center of paramilitary terror, another place where crosses, imported from the South along with the people, are burned in the dark nights by sheet-covered haters.)

"The police said . . . he had acted justifiably in self-defense. They set him free after holding him for what he said was six hours. 'In this case . . . this was not a difficult decision, . . . ' said Robert L. Cohen, the Deputy District Attorney. . . . `It's clear that what he did came under the law. Would a reasonable person in a like or similar case have reacted in the same way? And I think the answer is yes.'"

"Still," the New York Times reported, "the incident is not closed. The city attorney's office is considering filing misdemeanor charges against Mr. Masters for carrying an unlicensed gun. It would not be the first such case against him. In 1985 he was arrested in Texas for carrying two metal martial arts clubs and fought the case for four years until a state appeals court let stand a $1 fine levied against him."

As for Arce's companion, the survivor of this vigilante "justice," "Mr. Garcetti's [the district attorney's] office is considering bringing charges of attempted robbery against him. If it does, Hillo could face a murder charge, since under California law a person who takes part in a crime that leads to a killing, even of his accomplice, can be charged with murder."[52]

WILL BE

EXHIBITED

FOR ONE DAY ONLY!

AT THE STOCKTON HOUSE!

This day, Aug. 19, from 9 a.m. until 6 p.m.

THE HEAD

of the renowned Bandit!

JOAQUIN!

—AND THE—

HAND OF THE THREE FINGERED JACK!

THE NOTORIOUS ROBBER AND MURDERER

This poster advertised the exhibition, in Stockton, California, August 19, 1853, of Joaquin Murieta's "remains."

End

Thus the story, like a bad dream, left us stranded suddenly in the island of forgetfulness, prisoners. Not only that, but the genes that guard our culture, the essence of our history, have been left chained up, clogging the arteries that carry the impetus of the blood that animates the voice and soul of our people like rivers. Neither dignity nor education for the slaves, the masters said, only ignominy, prejudice, and death. . . .

RETURN BEYOND THE CROSSROADS. Break the silence of the centuries with the agony of our screams. You will see the fields in bloom where you planted your children and trees that have drunk the sap of the ages, petrified trees without songbirds and without owls, there where the voices of those who have succumbed dwell. Destiny is history, and history is the road stretched out before the footsteps that have not existed. Who has made you believe that you are lambs and beasts of burden?

Tiger knights, eagle knights, fight for the destiny of your children! Know, those who have been immolated, for in this region you will be the dawn and you will also be the river. [53]

◆ ——————— ◆

Oh my California! Oh my people. Ritchie Valens keeps on dying. *E Pluribus Unum.*

NOTES

The ideas in this essay owe a lot to repeated conversations with Timothy J. Reiss, though of course the conclusions are not necessarily his. In addition, Arturo Aldama engaged with the text so completely that his voice is heard throughout. Rainier Spencer, Shari Huhndorf, and William S. Penn also read the essay and offered many helpful suggestions, and I am grateful.

1. Jennings and others have expressed surprise at the absence of technologically sophisticated weapons or tools amongst the indigenous peoples of the Americas. Although they had knowledge of wheels, for example, they restricted their use to children's toys, just as the ancient Greeks used their knowledge of steam engines only to power children's toys. Francis Jennings, *The Founders of America* (New York, Norton, 1993): 44.

2. Edward D. Castillo, "The Impact of Euro-American Exploration and Settlement," in Robert Heizer, ed., *California: Handbook of North American Indians,* vol. 8 (Washington, D.C., Smithsonian Institution Press, 1978): 104.

3. Josiah Quinney, "July 4 Speech, 1854," quoted in Colin Calloway, *The World Turned Upside Down: Indian Voices from Early America* (New York, St. Martin's Press, Bedford Books, 1994): 40.

4. Is it necessary to say that Disney's version bears little, if any, resemblance to history? Perhaps so: Russell Means, the voice of Powhatan, has, after all, declared that this cartoon of singing rodents and talking plants "is the most authentic film ever made about Native America." Perhaps so when a bankrupt Wayne Newton suddenly "comes out" as an Indian, declaring himself a "direct descendant of Pocahontas," and, prompted by Disney, stands ready to disinter his ancestor's remains, bringing them home from their uneasy rest in England. Means's comment was made during a reading at Cody's Books, Berkeley, Calif., January 20, 1996. Newton's claims come from an unidentified newspaper clipping sent to me by a graduate student. For an analysis of Pocahontas's curious historical fortunes, see Jennifer Gray Reddish, "Pocahontas," *Tribal College,* vol. 6, no. 4 (Spring 1995): 22–33.

5. Chrestien LeClerq, "A Micmac Responds to the French, ca.1677," quoted in Calloway, *World Turned Upside Down,* pp. 51–52.

6. Although the ideas and evidence for what follows come from several months of reading in the archives of the Bancroft Library at the University of California, Berkeley, I have more recently discovered that many of my choices of themes, quotes, and incidents concerning the history of Mexicans, Chicanos, vaqueros, and Texas Rangers were also choices made by my colleague José David Saldívar in his wonderful book *The Dialectics of Our America: Genealogy, Cultural Critique, and Literary History* (Durham, N.C., Duke University Press, 1991). Thus, although I wrote this before reading his book, I should note that these similarities, though enormously pleasing, are coincidental.

7. David Banks Rogers, *Prehistoric Man of the Santa Barbara Coast* (Santa Barbara, Calif., Santa Barbara Museum of Natural History, 1929): 22.Owens notes that the Cherokee novelist John Rollin Ridge "embraced the 'digger' stereotype in 1854" in his *Life and Adventures of Joaquin Murieta, the Celebrated California Bandit.* Louis Owens, *Other Destinies: Understanding the American Indian Novel* (Norman, University of Oklahoma Press, 1992): 39.

8. Figures are from Albert Hurtado, *Indian Survival on the California Frontier* (New Haven, Conn., Yale University Press, 1988): 22. By 1860, when the new state held 379,994 inhabitants (a dream population for today's whining counter-affirmative-action-eers, it was 70 percent male and 60 percent white male), Indians, together with "coloreds"—who may have been Mexicans and those of Mexican origins as well as those of African

descent—and "Asians" (in the language of the census), formed but a small fraction of California's people.

9.   Quoted by Castillo, "The Impact of Euro-American Exploration and Settlement," p. 109. ·

10. *Bucks* was, and remains, a common pejorative for young Indian men.

11. "The Story of a Gold Miner: Reminiscences of Edwin Franklin Morse," in *Quarterly of the California Historical Society*, vol. 6, no. 3 (September 1927): 234–35. The women's feeling were not recorded. In nineteenth-century Euro-American eyes, females were possessions of men—like gold, like land. It is interesting—and horrible—to note that today's "paramilitaries," the armed, war-playing loonies, live primarily in areas where their vigilante forebears once flourished, killing, raping, and stealing from Natives and "Mexicans" with impunity and even—as in the case of the killers and beheaders of Joaquin Murieta in the 1850s—rewarded (in that case by a grateful state legislature). See *Klanwatch Intelligence Support*, no. 78 (June 1995): 7.

12. Such was, needless to say, the language by which those in power justified the use of brute force against their victims.

     The Sutter settlement was permitted by the Mexican governor, Juan Alvarado, who hoped that the presence of Anglo settlers would discourage the constant Indian raids against rich Mexican landowners. Too, as Hurtado points out, Alvarado hoped to stem the ambitions of his uncle, Mariano Guadalupe Vallejo, then commander of the northern frontier. Vallejo was in large part responsible for Native restiveness, as he had long been capturing Natives from *rancherias* and sending them to work for Mexican rancheros. In Hurtado's words, "Thus, Vallejo kept Indian society in turmoil and built a loyal following among rancheros who needed Indian labor." *Indian Survival*, p. 48.

13. "Jones' Pantoscope of California," *Quarterly of the California Historical Society* (1927): 240–41, 242. This reputation for horsemanship accompanied vaqueros through the decades, though clearly defined Mexican nationals were preferred for the dozens of Wild West shows that toured the United States and the world at the turn of the century. In the 1940s and 1950s, schools in Chicano neighborhoods, such as ours in the north San Fernando Valley, frequently invited a movie vaquero, Monte Montana, who regaled us with his roping skills. All of us, "honoring" those of Mexican descent among us, thus learned to do rope tricks with a lasso. One of the results of this curious effort at multiculturalism *avant la lettre* (as well as the bleak and nasty history of the Texas Rangers, as Arturo Aldama has pointed out) is that most of my Chicano friends from those days loathe and despise anything that has to do with "cowboys."

14. The figure is from Hurtado, *Indian Survival*, p. 195.

15. *Out West* was edited by a mugwump immigrant from the East, Charles F. Lummis, Indian collector, Los Angeles *Times* journalist, director of that city's Southwest Museum. See vol. 26, January- June 1902, for Dixon's unpaged picture.

16. Native Americans stayed on reservations, that is, until they, too, were needed, either to fight U.S. wars—in Europe, in Korea, in Vietnam—or to make up a reserve army of cheap and malleable labor in U.S. urban centers. Then they found themselves recruited for "relocation" to city sweatshops.

    An example of an isolated rural community is the little Chinese town of Locke, which lies along the Sacramento River delta; it remained a thriving community when I first visited it in the early 1970s. Then the only language heard in its streets was Chinese. Tourists have since discovered Locke, though it is still a predominantly Chinese community.

    In a wash of more hypocrisy than I have seen in a long time, California growers are once again pleading for the importation of Mexicans, "urging Congress to pass a new temporary guest worker program," according to a *San Francisco Chronicle* article. "Virtually all major grower organizations in California are backing a program that will allow them to bring workers legally from Mexico and elsewhere to temporarily work in the fields." Everyone remembers the so-called bracero program, which recruited Mexicans to labor at starvation wages and in awesomely horrible conditions (documented in Edward R. Murrow's *Harvest of Shame*, so critical of Americans' exploitation of agricultural workers that it was quickly banned from U.S. Information Agency libraries all over the world). That program brought some two million Mexican workers to California between 1942 and 1964, many of whom stayed to raise families despite the harsh conditions of their lives. (Charley Trujillo's *Dogs of Illusion* tells some of the story of these people, thousands of whose children were drafted for the front lines in Vietnam.) Of course hypocrisy has no limits. "The program that is being discussed has about as much similarity with the 'bracero' programs as the Kitty Hawk has to the space shuttle," said Russell Williams, president of Agricultural Producers, Inc., in Valencia. "As a practical matter, farmers will be responsible to see that workers are properly housed." But that is not what happened before, as all of us who were there remember vividly. Why should it happen this time? And what about those who stay? Only another draftee-needing war will discover their numbers. Louis Freedberg, "Growers Push for 'Guest' Field Hands," *San Francisco Chronicle*, June 30, 1995, pp. 1, A23.

17. This statement was reported as part of the debate about the Constitutional amendment to prohibit flag burning passed by the House of Representatives. *San Francisco Chronicle*, June 29, 1995, p. 1. Charley Trujillo's

Soldados and *Dogs of Illusion* (San Jose, Calif., Chusma House, 1990 and 1994, respectively) tell the stories of some of the Chicanos and Native Americans who fought in Vietnam.

18. Quoted in Joseph P. Sánchez, "Hispanic American Heritage," in Herman J. Viola and Carolyn Margolis, eds., *Seeds of Change* (Washington, D.C., Smithsonian Institution Press, 1991): 177.

19. The singular Mexican, in contrast to plural Anglo-Saxons, represents not a group of individuals but rather a stereotype.

20. Quoted in Philip Durham, *Down These Mean Streets a Man Must Go: Raymond Chandler's Knight* (Chapel Hill, University of North Carolina Press, 1963): 44, 59.

21. Quoted in Stan Steiner, *The New Indians* (New York, Dell, 1968): 154.

22. Joseph Brant, speaking to a council in an Onondaga village on Buffalo Creek, April 21, 1794; quoted in W. C. Vanderwerth, *Indian Oratory: Famous Speeches by Noted Indian Chieftains* (Norman, University of Oklahoma Press, 1971): 50.

23. Sean Wilentz, "Bombs Bursting in Air, Still," *New York Times Magazine* (June 25, 1995): 40–41. With an utter absence of irony—suitable to accompany the blithe indifference with which he airbrushes the genocide that lies at the heart of the nation stolen by his immigrant ancestors—Wilentz fails to note the fact that the United States was very directly responsible for at least one of the heinous 'other peoples' wickednesses' he cites, that in Indonesia. But this Princeton history professor here wants only to do two things: remind a historically ignorant populace that violence is nothing new in the United States and soothe every European American with the assurance that "we" never do or have done things that are as bad as what "they" do or have done.

24. Lenore Stiffarm with Phil Lane, Jr., "The Demography of Native North America: A Question of American Indian Survival," in M. Annette Jaimes, ed., *The State of Native America: Genocide, Colonization, and Resistance* (Boston, South End Press, 1992): 36–37. As these authors demonstrate, there is much dispute about all the early figures. It serves the myth to believe that the Americas were mostly uninhabited when Europeans arrived. But recent demographic studies show a much larger population than anthropologists and myth makers had previously described. Such figures also underscore the problem most non-Latinos encounter when they think of Indians. For most writers, including Native scholars, "Indians" live north of the U.S. border with Mexico.

25. "Introduction," in Rene Jara and Nicholas Spadaccini, eds., *Amerindian Images and the Legacy of Columbus* (Minneapolis, University of Minnesota Press, 1992): 82.

26. See Judith Rosenberg Raftery, *Land of Fair Promise: Politics and Reform in Los Angeles Schools, 1885–1941* (Stanford, Calif., Stanford University Press, 1992): 7. This book, while full of useful—and terrifying—information about the history of race hatred in California, is written entirely from the point of view of an Anglo. There is not one word by or from anyone of another race.

27. In this California, the category of Chinese included American Indians, at least for the purposes of exclusion from public schools.

28. Rosenberg Raftery, *Land of Fair Promise*, p. 112. See also Arturo Aldama's essay in this book for a more contemporary description of these classes.

29. Ibid., p. 94.

30. Ibid., p. 94. Such renaming was by then a familiar colonialist tactic. Native American children were given "white" first names to go with their translated Indian surnames on the first day they entered boarding school. Biblical names were common. Thus a child whose translated last name was "Standing Shield" was dubbed "Mary Standing Shield" and so on. Ngugi wa Thiong'o tells of a similar practice at his boarding school in British Kenya. There he was assigned the name "James," which the school officials added to Ngugi, making a nonsense of Kikuyu naming practices but a strong statement of power. (Personal communication to author.)

31. What an irony that now that Euro-Americans have lost control of intellectual production, allowing large numbers of nonwhites to gain "IQ." test ascendancy, they are among those dependent upon racially determined quotas to keep their children in the classes and schools initially set aside for "whites only"!

32. Rosenberg Raftery, *Land of Fair Promise*, p. 103.

33. These and subsequent quotations come from Governor Pete Wilson's Second Inaugural Address, "California: Forging America's Future," January 7, 1995. Desolate? Frozen? Why did whites want them badly enough to kill thousands who loved those lands?

34. The reference to Asians is Wilson's cynical recognition of the Asian-American community's newfound economic prosperity and thus respectability.

35. The Great Depression was, of course, one of the many eras of xenophobic hatred in California, when the "we" of Wilson's discourse were busily throwing poor Mexicans, and those of Mexican heritage, out of the state. "Pick-ups" has a nice, friendly, Chevy ring to it. But these migrants from the Midwest, these who had been sharecroppers and tenant farmers, didn't drive shiny new trucks. As Dorothea Lange's unforgettable

photographs show, as John Steinbeck's prose tells, they came in ancient, broken-down cars and trucks—and anything else that moved.

36. Marie M. Hughes and Reuben R. Palm, eds., *Proceedings: Los Angeles County Schools Workshop in Education of Mexican and Spanish-Speaking Pupils* (Los Angeles, Office of the County Superintendent of Schools, 1942): 12.

37. This example, like much else in this essay, comes from Alfred Arteaga. He has used a picture of such a sign on the cover of his edited collection *An Other Tongue* (Durham, N.C., Duke University Press, 1994).

38. "Introduction," in Jara and Spadaccini, *Amerindian Images and the Legacy of Columbus*, 86.

39. George P. Horsecapture, "An American Indian Perspective," in Viola and Margolis, *Seeds of Change*, p. 203.

40. Fisk et al., *Seventh Annual Report of the Board of Indian Commissioners for the Year 1875* (Washington, D.C., 1875): 6.

41. Alice Walker, reading at Emory University, March 1990.

42. Russell Thornton, *We Shall Live Again: The 1870 and 1890 Ghost Dance Movements as Demographic Revitalization* (New York, Cambridge University Press, 1986): 41–42.

43. Ibid., p. 42.

44. Sherman Alexie, "3/16," in *The Business of Fancydancing* (Brooklyn, N.Y., Hanging Loose Press, 1992): 16. This "feeding to the dogs" of a white self is symptomatic of the currently trendy and rather simple-minded attempt to establish the author's essentialist Indian purity.

45. Frantz Fanon, *Black Skin, White Masks*, trans. Charles Lam Markmann (New York, Grove, Weidenfeld, 1967): 63.

46. Sherman Alexie, "Distances," in *The Business of Fancydancing*, p. 18.

47. Wendy Rose, "Forty, Trembling" in *Bone Dance: New and Selected Poems, 1965–1993* (Tucson, University of Arizona Press, 1994): 99.

48. Rose's poem "Dear Grandfather Webb from England" is in *Going to War with All My Relations* (Flagstaff, Ariz., Entrada Books, 1993): 47.

49. I owe this unforgettable formulation to Dean Curtis Bear Claw.

50. Curtis M. Hinsley, *The Smithsonian and the American Indian: Making Moral Anthropology in Victorian America* (Washington, D.C., Smithsonian Institution Press, 1981): 11.

51. Seth Mydans, "A Shooter as Vigilante, and Avenging Angel," *New York Times*, February 12, 1995, p. 20.

52. Ibid.

53. Miguel Méndez, *Pilgrims in Aztlán*, translated from the Spanish by David William Foster (Tempe, Ariz., Bilingual Press/Editorial Bilingue, 1992): 178.

Notes on Contributors

ERIKA AIGNER-VAROZ, born of a Mexican mother and a German father, is a first-generation American from El Paso, Texas. She holds degrees from the University of Texas at El Paso and Ohio State University, and currently attends the University of New Mexico, where she is specializing in Native American literature and language/rhetorical theory.

ARTURO ALDAMA was born in Mexico City and moved to California as a child, first to San Francisco and then to Sacramento. He received his Ph.D. from the University of California, Berkeley, in ethnic studies, writing a dissertation on the politics of identity and representation for Mexican immigrants, Chicanos/as, and Native Americans in different narrative genres, ethnography, autobiography, and novels. He is currently an assistant professor at Arizona State University.

KIMBERLY BLAESER is an associate professor of English at the University of Wisconsin—Milwaukee. Of Anishnaabe and German ancestry, from the White Earth Reservation, she has published *Trailing You* (poems), which won the 1993 Diane Decorah First Book Award from the Native Writer's Circle of the Americas, and *Gerald Vizenor: Writing in the Oral Tradition* (a critical study).

253

DIANE DUBOSE BRUNNER is an associate professor of English at Michigan State University. Her work combines critical theory, cultural studies, and critical pedagogy. She has published widely on narrative representations of identity, and her books include *Inquiry and Reflection: Framing Narrative Practice in Education* and *Between the Masks: Resisting the Politics of Essentialism,* which combines the study of identity with performative inquiry.

PATRICIA PENN HILDEN took her doctorate in history at King's College, Cambridge. Her books include *Working Women and Socialist Politics in France, 1880–1914; Women, Work, and Politics: Belgium 1830–1914;* and *When Nickels Were Indians: An Urban Mixed-Blood Story.* Currently, she is a professor of Ethnic Studies at the University of California at Berkeley.

SHARI HUHNDORFearned her Ph.D. in comparative literature at New York University, with a dissertation titled "Simulated Indians: Native American Images in American Literature and Film from the 19th Century to the Present." Currently, she is an assistant professor at the University of Oregon.

CAROL KALAFATIC is an artist, activist, and writer whose work has appeared in *News from Indian Country, Akwesasne Notes, The Circle,* and regional magazines. She contributed to a University of Toronto anthology on Canadian cinema and co-authored *Fry Bread and Wild West Shows: The "New" National Museum of the American Indian.* She works for the International Indian Treaty Council.

WILLIAM S. PENN is professor of English at Michigan State University, where he teaches comparative multicultural literature, Native American literature, and creative writing (fiction and narrative essay). His books include *The Absence of Angels* (novel), *All My Sins Are Relatives* (narrative essays), *The Telling of the World: Native American Stories and Art* (edited). His new novel is *Killing Time with Strangers,* and he is working on a new collection of essays, *Feathering Custer.* He is a winner of the North American Indian Prose Award from the University of Nebraska Press and a Critics' Choice Award for the Most Acclaimed Books of 1995–96.

INEZ PETERSEN is from the Northwest; her mother's people are from Taholah, a village at the mouth of the Quinault River; her father is a full-blood Dane from generations of loggers. She earned her M.A. in creative writing from the University of New Mexico at Albuquerque. Widely published in literary journals, she has recently received residencies at the MacDowell Colony and the Villa Montalvo.

ALFONSO RODRIGUEZ is professor and chair of the Department of Hispanic Studies at the University of Northern Colorado. He is a cofounder and has served as editor of *Confluencia: Revista Hispánica de Cultura y Literatura*. His essays, articles, and creative writing have appeared in different European, American, and Latin American journals. His books include *La estructura mítica del Popol Vuh* (The mythical structure of Popol Vuh), *Salmos para migrantes* (Psalms for migrant workers), and *Levantando la palabra* (Proclaiming the word), his second collection of poetry. He is also author of *La otra frontera* (The other border), a book of short stories, and he has just completed his third collection of poetry, *Polvo en la luz* (Dust in the light).

ROLANDO ROMERO is a professor of ethnic studies at the University of Illinois- Champaign-Urbana. His essays on poststructuralism, border theory, and hybridity have appeared in many journals such as *Siglo 20/20th Century*, *Borderlines, Gestos, Revista de Estudios Hispanicos, Revista Iberoamericana,* and *La Palabra y el Hombre*.

RAINIER SPENCER is an assistant professor in the Department of Anthropology and Ethnic Studies at the University of Nevada, Las Vegas. He is currently working on publishing his dissertation, "Pandora's Box: "Theorizing Multiracial Identity Politics in the United States," as a book.

CRAIG WOMACK teaches in the Native American Studies Department at the University of Lethbridge (Canada). Of Creek/Cherokee descent, he grew up in Martinez, California. His creative work has appeared in a number of anthologies and journals including *Earth Song, Sky Spirit,* and *Christopher Street,* and his critical work has appeared in journals such as the *American Indian Quarterly* and *American Literature*.

Compositor:	BookMasters, Inc.
Text:	Palatino
Display:	Snell Roundhand/Bauer Bodoni
Printer and Binder:	BookCrafters